What People Are Saying About

Love and Suffering

It is so refreshing to have Zach's spiritual guide as a framework for understanding the unifying nature of love, the growth properties of suffering, and the healing nature of both. This book provides context and inspirational hope to some of life's biggest, deepest, and hardest questions. I am so grateful to have it — for myself as a healer, and for all humans.
Jackie Wielick, LMFT, owner of Therapy by Jackie and coauthor of *Help for High Conflict Couples*

In his book, Zach Beach offers comfort through compassionate answers to some of our most difficult questions we ask about life. He masterfully blends his personal experiences and knowledge, with ancient literature in a way that makes even the most complex spiritual figures and concepts feel approachable. Anyone who is seeking spiritually, or finds themselves supporting or counseling anyone who is, will truly gain so much from this outstanding book.
Dr. Amelia Kelley, PhD, MS, LCMHC, ATR, CYT, coauthor of *Surviving Suicidal Ideation: From Therapy to Spirituality and the Lived Experience*

With a seeker's heart and the mind of a poet, Zach illuminates the mysteries of love for a new generation. I am particularly thrilled to see teachings from the mystical traditions of east and west included here to offer depth and inspire practitioners. In an age of increasing confusion and psychological fragmentation, Zach is a trusted guide.
Dr. David M. Odorisio, PhD, core faculty, Pacifica Graduate Institute, Santa Barbara, CA

This is a book about suffering that exudes joy and compassion, offering us wisdom from many traditions. In this book Zach Beach is doing for the 2020s what Alan Watts did for the 1960s, giving us insights from Buddhism in a form Westerners can appreciate. And we need it now more than ever! Read it and you'll benefit not only yourself, but those you love as well.
Dr. Bruce Chalmer, PhD, author of *Betrayal and Forgiveness: How to Navigate the Turmoil and Learn to Trust Again*

Zach Beach's 'Love and Suffering' is a beautifully crafted meditation on the interplay between life's challenges and our capacity for love. This book will inspire you to embrace suffering as a means to open your heart and enrich your life.
Darren Main, author of *Yoga and the Path of the Urban Mystic*

If more spiritual leaders focused on helping us understand both sides of the coin—love AND suffering—we wouldn't be a society that needs MORE to the point of misery and dissatisfaction. Zach Beach is the perfect guide for this concept, and his essence, lightness, and wisdom transcend each page.
Heather Bartos, MD, Women's Health and Sexuality Expert

This book is an excellent guide for anyone on the path of personal and spiritual transformation. It is the perfect blend of personal and spiritual transformation. Guaranteed to leave readers with inspiration, growth, and healing.
Jennine Estes Powell, MFT, coauthor of *Help for High Conflict Couples* and founder of Estes Therapy

Love and Suffering

A Spiritual Guide for Helpers,
Healers, and Humans

Previous Books by Zach Beach

Pebbles — 979-8805381172

108 Savasana Poems:
Blissful Words From the Heart of Yoga — 978-1092978712

The 7 Lessons of Love:
Heart Wisdom for Troubling Times — 978-1983940705

Drinking Roses on Sunday:
10,000 Words to Open the Heart — 978-1497489141

Love and Suffering

A Spiritual Guide for Helpers,
Healers, and Humans

Zach Beach

BOOKS

London, UK
Washington, DC, USA

CollectiveInk

First published by O-Books, 2025
O-Books is an imprint of Collective Ink Ltd.,
Unit 11, Shepperton House, 89 Shepperton Road, London, N1 3DF
office@collectiveinkbooks.com
www.collectiveinkbooks.com
www.o-books.com

For distributor details and how to order please visit the 'Ordering' section on our website.

Text copyright: Zachary Beach, 2024

ISBN: 978 1 80341 928 2
978 1 80341 945 9 (ebook)
Library of Congress Control Number: 2024944611

All rights reserved. Except for brief quotations in critical articles or reviews, no part of this book may be reproduced in any manner without prior written permission from the publishers.

The rights of Zachary Beach as authors have been asserted in accordance with the Copyright, Designs and Patents Act 1988.

A CIP catalogue record for this book is available from the British Library.

Design: Lapiz Digital Services

UK: Printed and bound by CPI Group (UK) Ltd, Croydon, CR0 4YY
Printed in North America by CPI GPS partners

The authors of this book do not dispense medical advice or prescribe the use of any technique as a form of treatment for physical, emotional, or medical problems without the advice of a physician, either directly or indirectly. The intent of the authors is only to offer information of a general nature to help you in your quest for emotional and spiritual well-being. In the event you use any of the information in this book for yourself, which is your constitutional right, the authors and the publisher assume no responsibility for your actions.

We operate a distinctive and ethical publishing philosophy in all areas of our business, from our global network of authors to production and worldwide distribution.

Contents

Introduction ix

Chapter 1. The Suffering of the Buddha 1
Chapter 2. The Love of the Buddha 37
Chapter 3. The Suffering of Christ 61
Chapter 4. The Love of God 95
Chapter 5. The Suffering of Humanity 131
Chapter 6. The Suffering in Love 167
Chapter 7. The Love of Humanity 202
Chapter 8. The Love and Suffering of the World 228

Afterword 257
About the Author 260
References 261

May these words
be the water

that penetrates
the dark—fertile soil

of your heart
to awaken

the many
sleeping seeds

of love within.

Introduction

If you're reading this, you're human. And if you're human, there are three truths to your existence:

- You are suffering
- You do not want to suffer
- You want love

As a human being wanting love and not wanting to suffer, this is the book for you.

To love and to be loved is the deepest human need. As a result, you are most likely either looking for love, trying to keep the love you have, or trying to prevent your love from leaving. You think if you were to make all the right decisions, you could experience all of the love and none of the suffering.

Well, I have some bad news: love leads to suffering and suffering leads to love. But I have some good news too. Recognizing this and welcoming both into your life puts you on a path to wholeness, fullness, and transformation. They are like two wings that can take us to heaven; with only one, we end up going around in circles. Let love and suffering have a wedding in your heart, and they will give birth to joy.

The Story of Miao Shan

Once upon a time, there was a beautiful princess by the name of Miao Shan. In her early years, Miao Shan felt called to a deeply spiritual life. When she came of age, her father, the king, ordered that she get married, but Miao Shan refused. To punish his insolent daughter, who had up until then lived a life of luxury, the king banished Miao Shan to do hard labor in the basement with the cooks and cleaners.

But Miao Shan, with her budding compassionate heart, soon learned she enjoyed cooking and cleaning alongside the workers and loved bringing food to the hungry people of the castle. Furious, the king banished Miao Shan to the stables to sleep on hay with the animals and clean up their waste. But Miao Shan loved spending time with the animals and found joy in keeping their pens clean. With a growing love for all sentient beings, she lovingly attended to all the creatures, large and small, while singing the mantra, *lokah samasta sukhino bhavantu*.

Even more angry, the king then sent her to the local infirmary, which was full of sick patients with open wounds and ungodly smells. Rather than shy away in disgust, Miao Shan loved getting close to the patients, tending to their wounds and cleaning their bedpans. She got so close to the patients she began to understand what they needed to get better, and at night would go and get medicinal herbs to heal them. As she picked flowers, she sang *om mani padme hum*, finding the indivisible wisdom at the heart of each flower to help her patients move from dis-ease to ease.

Seeing the patients getting better under her care, the enraged king then sent Miao Shan to hospice care where the patients were definitely going to die. Here Miao Shan knew what she had to do: offer healing prayers, a warm presence, and kind attention to shepherd these beautiful souls into the next life. She sang at their bedside, *om gate gate parasamgate gate gate bodhi svaha* to encourage their spirits to go beyond, far beyond this earthly realm to the next, and saw herself as a raft for their journey.

The king then realized nothing would be sufficient punishment for Miao Shan, so he sentenced her to death. When the executioner raised his axe to kill Miao Shan, the light of her heart briefly blinded him, causing him to miss her neck, hit the ground, and shatter the axe blade and handle. The king then ordered the executioner to death for failing to do the job. Miao Shan, out of compassion for the executioner, stood up and said,

"But he did do the job," before falling on the ground and dying. The executioner couldn't believe what he saw and fell to his knees in tears in the realization that Miao Shan had sacrificed her life for him.

Having left her body, the spirit of Miao Shan was banished to hell, where she realized this was the perfect place to help those who are most in pain. With an open and compassionate heart, she taught the souls there how to free themselves from suffering, live with pure intention, and practice forgiving themselves and others. She sang, *aditya hridayam punyam sarva shatru vina shanam*, "all evil vanishes for the one who keeps the sun in their heart," and over time, hell became a brighter and brighter place, eventually resembling heaven.

Satan became so worried he'd be punished for doing such a bad job at maintaining hell, that he banished this benevolent spirit to an island off the coast of China. There, this spirit was reincarnated into a new body to serenade the ocean with prayers of compassion, healing and love. She became a beacon of light encouraging all of us to handle the waves of life, the ups and downs, the joys and sorrows, with peace and equanimity. This reincarnated spirit became known as *Kuan Yin*, the goddess of mercy and physical embodiment of compassion; the Bodhisattva "who hears the cries of the world." Soon everyone in the land was singing her mantra, *namo kuan shi yin pusa*.

Keeping Our Heart Open

I was thinking about Miao Shan's journey one night as I was leaving San Francisco airport. Earlier that day, I had waited in line for four hours just to be told my flight had been cancelled. I was supposed to fly to Dallas en route to Peru to lead an immersive yoga course, but the airport was its own kind of hell.

Everything was in total disarray. It was the height of a new wave of COVID-19, and three people were working at the desk for international destinations. Unfortunately, with over 150 countries in the world and continually changing rules and regulations around COVID-19, it was confusing for everyone involved. People would get to the front of the line to learn that they had gotten an antigen test but needed a PCR Test, or they had a test 72 hours ago when it needed to be within 48 hours. Some found their passport expiring in five months when they needed a minimum of six. Others were supposed to have proof of onward travel, while many had not filled out the public health form or had forgotten to download the government tracking app.

As people tried to communicate with each other behind two layers of masks and a wall of plexiglass, you could see the anger and frustration building. It was one of those scenes where strangers, knowing that misery loves company, start commiserating with each other. "Ugh, can you believe this?" a person said to no one specific, looking around while rolling their eyes. Someone was yelling at an attendant; another person was crying on the phone talking to relatives saying that there was no way they would make their flight. Tensions were high, attitudes were sour, and after getting up so early to be surrounded by fluorescent lighting in a poorly air-conditioned space, everyone was grumpy and disheveled. Excited travelers would arrive at the airport and become crestfallen to find the long line snaking multiple corners, staring in disbelief at how things could have ever gotten so bad.

As I took a taxi to my sister's house somewhat close to the airport, I noticed my own annoyance, frustration, and anger. I then thought of Kuan Yin and asked myself, what would it be like to keep my heart open, even in hell? How might I too be a beacon of light and compassion in a turbulent and uncertain world?

The next day I returned with the intention to love. I remembered the simple truth: *what we see in the world is a reflection of ourselves. We don't see the world as it is, we see the world as we are.*

While we may think we perceive reality objectively, our mind is limited and perspective narrow. Most of the time that limited view focuses on what is wrong rather than what is right. As the saying goes, "When a pickpocket sees a saint, they only see the saint's pockets." We can, with the power of our intention, shift our awareness to see the world in a new way.

This time around, as I waited in line, I noticed the father entertaining his child with funny faces. I saw the loving couple resting their heads on one another, giving each other solace, and listening to music with headphones in each ear. I looked at the flight attendants struggling and felt an overwhelming sense of love and compassion for them, knowing they were just trying their best and with enough time we would all get to our destinations. Rather than resisting the moment, separating from it to judge and complain, I tapped into the loving nature of my own heart. I felt light, caring, and almost floated to the front of the line, a smile hidden behind my mask. I realized yes, it is possible to keep our hearts open in even the most trying of circumstances.

This Book and Me

I know the hell of waiting in line at the airport is nothing like the hell of death, war, famine, violence, or chronic illness. But I have found a story that is the same throughout the big and small challenges in our lives, from intense emotional pain to minor inconveniences. That story is the theme of this book, the main thesis of which is:

> The two greatest gurus in life are love and suffering. When we combine our cultivation of love with an awareness of suffering, we create compassion, which is the medicine this world needs, now more than ever. If you are looking for meaning, joy, purpose, direction, spiritual awakening, or God in your life, look no further

than finding the courage to love this world with a wide open heart even amid intense suffering.

If you want to know suffering, know love. If you want to know love, know suffering. They are like two points on a circle, go enough in one direction and you will find the other, and by joining them together, we become complete.

Suffering, rather than being something to avoid and shy away from, is one of our greatest teachers. Love, rather than a cliche or temporary feeling for another person, will always be the greatest source of happiness and the deepest human need. Love and suffering are our great gurus because they will teach us more about life than any book, teacher, or experience. Getting in touch with love and suffering will bring us closer to God, the Universe, and even our own true nature. All the great saints, from Jesus to Buddha, Lao Tzu to Patanjali, have discovered this profound teaching and sought to spread it across the world. If we can keep our hearts open, even in hell, it will be a path of reward beyond measure.

For over a decade, I have been leading classes, workshops, and trainings on love, connection, intimacy, and compassion. Sometimes what I teach is called *Mindful Self-Compassion* or *Eight Steps to Limitless Self-Love*, other times it's called *yoga, tantra,* or *tonglen*. I love coaching couples and individuals on how to deepen their love and relationships. I have traveled to and taught from 40 countries to learn from anyone who might guide me along on this spiritual journey of awakening to truth. Across degrees, certifications, intensives, trainings, workshops, conferences, altered states, and so much more, every lesson I learn points back to these two fundamental human experiences: love and suffering.

This book will be a journey through how love and suffering shape our lives, and how getting in touch with them is a path of personal and spiritual transformation. This book is particularly useful for anyone working in professions that involve love and suffering, such as healthcare professionals who have dedicated themselves to alleviating the suffering of others and find it challenging to cope with the suffering and burnout within themselves. It is also useful for therapists who are seeking to alleviate their client's suffering without getting overwhelmed by it.

We will look at a variety of disciplines, from the grounded empiricism of neuroscience and psychology to far-out regions of religion, philosophy, and spirituality. We can look anywhere we want, actually, because at the essence of all human experience lie the great gurus of love and suffering and the truth of what it means to live with a heart fully wide open.

Chapter 1

The Suffering of the Buddha

Only when I finally learned to let even the deepest pain be okay, and hold it with kindness, did it begin to release. Jack Kornfield

It was day four of the silent retreat and I was miserable. I was on Koh Samui, an island close to the southern tip of Thailand, at a Thai Forest Theravada meditation center. Theravada is one of the three main branches of Buddhism and hails itself as the most traditional, strictly adhering to the Buddha's teachings. Monastics of the tradition follow an austere life, forgoing most material possessions and comforts in place of disciplined spiritual practice. The Forest tradition places its monasteries deep into the woods, far from bustling metropolitan cities.

Well, as I learned, in Thailand there aren't forests, rather there are jungles. And these jungles provide a home to more creepy crawlies than any other landscape on Earth. The constant rain was bringing out every animal and insect imaginable, including snakes, frogs, scorpions, and spiders. Mosquitos were breeding in the many standing puddles of water, so it was hard to walk a few steps without feeling five of them sucking the blood from my ankles, bringing to mind all the tropical diseases they might be injecting.

Before I got there, I was eager to "get away from it all" to this retreat but did not realize how much material comfort I would be forgoing. We had locked up all of our electronic devices, journals, and books, so I had nothing to entertain myself. My room wasn't so much a room as a subdivided cubicle in a dark basement underneath the meditation space. My bed was a wooden platform with a thin straw mat and wooden pillow. I hadn't even realized wooden pillows existed until I was provided one in my "room."

Despite the heat and humidity, there was no fan, let alone air conditioning. There was also no shelving, no chair, no desk, and no lighting of any kind, but I did have a mosquito net. Everything was dark, dingy, and dirty. The bathrooms had three sinks and four toilets shared amongst forty men (the women and men were kept in separate dormitories), all open air and inviting every insect imaginable to lay their eggs and spin their webs in every crack and crevice. Since we were silent, I had no one to complain to (or scream at) and mentally referred to using the bathroom as *Zen and the Art of Not Touching Anything*.

Each night I was hot, sweaty, and sleep deprived, and my back was really starting to hurt from the bed. Every morning we woke up at 4 a.m. to meditate in a mosquito-infested hall. In the afternoon, I would attempt to wash my smelly clothes in dirty buckets and hope the wind wouldn't blow the drying clothes into the mud, which it often did. I had had enough. I signed up for an interview with the teacher that day and told him this meditation center was terrible. I said adamantly, "I am done, and I am leaving!"

The teacher, an older monk who had been practicing for decades, listened patiently as I expressed my frustrations. Once I finished, he looked at me with a gleam in his eye. He then started to grin, the kind of smirking, sly, cheeky grin where you know they are up to something.

Then he said to me, "I see, always running away from your problems, eh?"

I was appalled at the question. "MY problems?" I thought. "What do you mean, my problems? These are clearly YOUR problems, your stinky meditation hall and your failure to put up screens anywhere that might be useful. What do you mean, *my* problems? I'm not running away from my problems!"

Our meeting ended and I got to sit down and watch all my self-righteous thoughts. As I continued to sit I had to ask myself: *am I always running away from my problems*? Is that the key? To stop running, and finally face that which troubles me the most; to feel exactly what I don't want to feel?

The Buddha's Approach to Suffering

If we want to begin any discussion around suffering, including what it is and what we may want to do about it, the Buddha is a great place to start.

When you first learn about Buddhism, the deluge of information can be quite overwhelming. There is a lot to learn, like the three poisons, the four noble truths, the six realms, the eightfold path, the ten non-virtuous and ten virtuous actions, the twelve branches of dependent origination, the fifty-nine Lojong slogans, the—you get the point. A vast ocean of philosophical concepts and spiritual guidelines, with countless texts and commentaries.

This is to be expected, any comprehensive religion with millions of followers is going to have a lot to learn about it. Buddhism has also been around for almost 2500 years, so it has had many centuries and millions of followers to develop new theories and understanding.

Fortunately, we can distill down to the essence of Buddhism with the Buddha's very own words. "Know this, O Monks: Now, as formerly, I teach only of suffering, and the elimination of suffering." The Buddha did not spend much time talking about the afterlife, the existence or absence of God, how the universe was created, and so on. He actually only taught two things, suffering and the end of suffering. That's it. Full stop.

I have studied and practiced at Buddhist monasteries in Nepal, India, Malaysia, Thailand, Vietnam, and across the United States. No matter where I go, the lessons are the same: with enough study and practice, we can free ourselves from suffering. The highest goal is to free our mind and rescue us from suffering. This idea was repeated again and again no matter what talk or teaching I explored.

Because the Buddha taught only suffering, he is not considered to be a God or deity of any sort. Rather, he is often described as a *physician*. He diagnosed the human condition, identified its cause, and spent his life teaching the cure.

Many scholars argue that Buddhism isn't a religion at all, as it doesn't require you to believe in anything. It is more of a philosophy, a psychology based on logic and reasoning, a simple line of thinking where one is encouraged to *ehipassako* or *see for oneself*. Practitioners are encouraged not to take anybody else's word for it, no guru or teacher or leader, but to examine the truths for themselves and see if they apply to their own life. The Buddha encouraged his disciples to question everyone, including himself, and see their own truth, what is the true source of suffering, and how can it be alleviated?

To learn more about what the Buddha meant by suffering and what drew him to his conclusions and teachings, we can look into the life of this great sage.

The Prince Who Awakened

The story of the man who became the Buddha is well known. Born a prince by the name of Siddhartha Gautama, he spent the first 27 years of his life in luxury inside the palace walls. One day, dreaming of life outside the palace and wanting to see more of the world, Siddhartha asked for a tour of the town. The king and queen, worried about the innocence of their little prince, organized a parade route through only the most beautiful streets of town and placed only the best, most beautiful townspeople along the route.

However, during this parade, Siddhartha sensed he wasn't experiencing the realness of life, so he secretly snuck out of his chariot and went down an alleyway, where he met three people who would change his life forever: a sick person, an old person, and a dead person. These conditions shocked the young prince. A sudden realization went over him: every single human being will suffer from sickness and death, and if they live long enough, old age. This meant he too would experience this suffering, and no amount of wealth would protect him from it. There is no avoiding the reality of suffering.

Upon such a realization, Siddhartha left his palace, wife, and son, to embark on the path of freeing himself from suffering. He became a practicing ascetic, renouncing the material pleasures of life. Fasting, controlling his breath, sleeping on the hard ground, and sitting on one leg in the middle of the day staring at the sun, Siddhartha thought perhaps the opposite of indulgence would free him from suffering. However, the path of complete renunciation did not work out either, as fully embracing suffering seemed just as bad as running from it.

One night Siddhartha sat down underneath the Bodhi tree and meditated. During that night, as the legend goes, he "awoke" to the truth of suffering, which in turn showed him the true nature of reality. Siddhartha's awakening liberated him from *maya*, this world of illusion, and from *samsara*, this everlasting cycle of birth and death. Becoming "awakened," Siddhartha was then referred to as the Buddha, which simply means *awakened one*, and points to the realization that we all have Buddha nature, the capacity to become awakened ourselves.

The Buddha's realization freed him from the trials and tribulations of this world, and he spent the rest of his life giving the teachings of his realization: suffering, and the end of suffering. For many people, having to learn about suffering can be a huge turn-off. After all, it seems pessimistic to focus so much on suffering. But looking at suffering is only step one on a longer path that promises an end to one's suffering and the capacity to lead a joyful, relaxed, and peaceful life. What could be more optimistic than that?

Thus, the Buddha was a physician. Just as a doctor will diagnose what disease you have, its causes, whether there is a cure, and the treatment plan, so did the Buddha. Human life contains suffering, there is a cause to this suffering, that suffering can end, and there is a path to free oneself from that suffering. These became known as the Four Noble Truths: *suffering, cause, end, path*. Thousands of books and commentaries have been written on the profundity of this finding, because getting to the nature of suffering tells us more about ourselves and about life than anything else possibly could.

Dukkha

If we were to focus more on the Buddha's exact words, we can use Pali, the original language of the Buddha, to say that he taught "dukkha, and the end of dukkha." *Dukkha* is most often translated as *suffering*, but it can also be thought of as *chronic dissatisfaction* or *unease*. Just like Mick Jagger singing, "I can't get no satisfaction," the human experience is full of unhappiness. Life constantly goes in directions we do not want it to go. Time and time again, we are disappointed or let down.

While the first noble truth is sometimes translated as, "life is suffering," it would be more appropriate to just observe, "there is suffering in life" or that "any feelings of pleasure or happiness will not last forever." We can also foreshadow the next three noble truths by saying, "Life as we normally live it is suffering."

It is easy to think that suffering only refers to intense emotional pain like dying of cancer, losing a loved one, or getting Alzheimer's. But there's more to it than that. As soon as we wake up in the morning, we are suffering. Our alarm doesn't go off so we are late to work. There is an accident on the highway so traffic delays us even more. We spill coffee on our new pants and go into work to find our boss already yelling at us. Our computer program crashes, our lunch order is wrong, the air conditioner breaks and it's way too hot. In big and small ways, all day and every day, we suffer.

Even the good times contain a hint of suffering. When we are doing well, we fear it won't last. As expressed in the satirical headline, *Man Returns from Vacation With Renewed Hatred for Job*, our dual mind always compares the good to the bad. I remember staying at a fancy newly built resort in Costa Rica, where everything was perfect in every way. The beds were soft, the rooms spacious, the pool the perfect temperature. But I knew it wouldn't last. After staying for a month and getting accustomed to the luxury, all subsequent hotels seemed poor and lacking in comparison.

Suffering includes regret and nostalgia. The Zen master, Bashō (Hirshfield, 2024) wrote:

even in Kyoto,
hearing a cuckoo,
I long for Kyoto.

While experiencing something good, we think of how it was, how we would wish it to be, or how it's failing to live up to our expectations. In the back of our minds, there is a nagging, a recognition that nothing will last, and our attachment will make it worse. Another one (Hass, 1994) by the great master goes:

First day of spring—
I keep thinking about
the end of autumn.

Many things we think we want only give us more suffering. We wait excitedly for our kids to leave for college, only to find ourselves sad and alone in an empty nest. We can't wait to see the new movie, but when we finally watch it, it's garbage. Living in a world of expectations, we find ourselves in a world of disappointments.

Stressed Out

Suffering is fundamental to the human experience, and if we are to be free of it, we must first understand it. Nowadays, I might translate *dukkha* as *stress*. The average person in modern society operates from a place of stress practically 24/7. In our increasingly fast-paced, capitalistic, hustle-and-grind world most people feel that if they are not constantly moving then they are falling behind. We wake up already thinking of all the things we have to do and go to sleep thinking of everything we weren't able to finish.

Although we want to be happy, we are conditioned not to be. Our modern world thrives on dissatisfaction. Every advertisement, including those same meditation apps espousing ancient wisdom, expresses the same message, "You are suffering, so buy this thing to feel better." Imagine walking into a store with a big sign on the front saying, "You already have everything you need." A content populace is not very good for business. Every day we are pummeled with messages that happiness requires buying this product or watching this show, but it is never about sitting still and finding peace.

Millennia before we all wanted the newest phone and to see the newest hit movie, the Buddha observed that the human experience is moving from one state of dissatisfaction to the next. We are thirsty, so we get a glass of water. This stimulates our hunger, so we eat some food. We get indigestion from the food, so we take an antacid, which makes us tired, so we go to sleep. Then, we wake up with a headache, so we take another pill, which makes us drowsy, so we down a cup of coffee.

Suffering is an inextricable aspect of life, and we make doomed attempts to avoid it. There's a joke about a man who goes to his doctor. The doctor says, "I'm sorry, you have cancer." The man, shocked, exclaims, "Well, I want a second opinion." So, the doctor says, "Ok, you're ugly too." Most attempts to circumvent suffering just make it worse. This 2000-year-old teaching is just as relevant today.

Suffering, the Buddha taught, is *any time things are not what we wish them to be*. Whether our beloved parent is on their deathbed, or our new car just got a scratch, the common human experience is wishing things were different. It is always either too hot or too cold, too dry or too humid, the show we are watching is too boring or too confusing.

One metaphor to describe humanity's insatiable desire is that of the "hungry ghost." The hungry ghost is a humanoid-like figure with a very large belly but a very long and thin neck. The neck constricts the amount of food and drink that can pass into the belly, so the ghost never feels full. It goes on consuming and consuming but is never fully satisfied. We live in a world of hungry ghosts, as the richest amongst us accumulate multiple villas, supercars, and private jets, and still want more, often at the expense of the poorest. Thousands of years before everyone was running after the newest, biggest and best thing, the Buddha knew that nothing would quench our innermost desires. We are all slaves to our bellies.

The Buddhist psychologist, Mark Epstein, put it this way: "desires are endless. Indulging them keeps us in their grip and traps us in a never-ending cycle of brief satisfactions followed by the relentless pursuit of more" (Epstein, 2019). As long as there are people there will be desires, and as long as there are desires there will be suffering.

The Cause of Dukkha

Now that we understand what suffering is, we must find the courage to meet it head on in order to understand its true cause. We must muster up the courage not to run away from our problems, because if we try to avoid suffering, then we are resisting life and will fail to discover the truth.

Interestingly, when a small, microscopic virus has invaded our upper respiratory tract, we don't experience it that way. We don't notice the virus entering, nor feel it duplicate DNA in our cells and invade other parts of our body. Our experience is only the *symptoms* of it, which are often not the virus itself but our own immune system's reaction to it. We experience fatigue, runny nose, and sore throat. The *symptoms* are very different from the *cause*.

In the same way, our suffering is a *symptom*, not the disease. It is a *consequence*, and to eliminate the consequence, you have to know the cause. This was the Buddha's most important insight. It can be very easy to blame the external world for our problems. Especially if there are clear circumstances like war, famine, an oppressive government, or our house burning down, it could certainly seem like the cause of our suffering must be external.

But the Buddha said the cause of suffering is internal. The cause and solution to suffering is in our own minds. It is not what happens to us, but how we respond to what happens to us. The Buddha says if you look deeply into the nature of suffering and happiness, it will inevitably take you back to your mind. The Buddha was probably the world's first cognitive therapist because he identified that *it is not the situations in our life that cause our problems, it's how we think about the situations that causes the problems.*

The first two lines from the *Dhammapada* (Muller, 2014), a profound text of Buddhist slogans, goes:

All that we are is the result of what we have thought: it is founded on our thoughts, it is made up of our thoughts. If a person speaks or acts with an evil thought, pain follows them, as the wheel follows the foot of the ox that draws the carriage.

All that we are is the result of what we have thought: it is founded on our thoughts, it is made up of our thoughts. If a person speaks or acts with a pure thought, happiness follows them, like a shadow that never leaves them.

We are what we think, says the Buddha. This idea is so important that it's repeated twice.

One line of inquiry I love to ask my students begins with the question, "Where are your eyes?" To which the students reply, "In our heads." I then ask, "Where is your visual cortex?" and the students reply again, "In our heads." Then I ask, "Where am I?" and after a few moments of pondering, they must again conclude, "In our heads." Finally, the great reveal, "And where are your problems?" To which they must admit, "In our heads."

It doesn't take an enlightened being to recognize that our experience in life is largely in our own minds, the central processing unit of everything that happens to us in life. We have never had a single experience outside our own minds, which leads some Buddhist traditions to call themselves *no mind* or *all mind* schools. To think that the cause of our problems is anywhere other than ourselves is complete delusion.

Finding Freedom

Life is not a problem, it's how we cope with life that causes us problems. It's not about who we are, it's about how we relate to who we are. Suffering is a psychological issue. The Buddha diagnosed humanity with *CNST*: Chronic Non-Stop Thinking. The mind endlessly creates suffering as it regrets the past and creates anxieties about the future. Suffering arises from the desiring mind, one that clings to illusion. Because we always want things to be different, we don't see things as they are, we see them as we wish them to be. If we had no desires, we would not suffer, and would be in touch with reality as it is. Rain isn't falling on our wedding day to ruin our life; it is simply raining.

Our insatiable desires manifest in two fundamental ways: craving and aversion. Craving is wanting something; aversion is not wanting something. These are two sides of the same coin, since aversion is just craving for something not to happen. In their extreme forms, craving and aversion turn into greed and hatred: greed for the things in life we want, and hatred at anything and anybody standing in the way. Our internal suffering creates suffering for others in the world, as we constantly seek to meet our own desires at the cost of the well-being of others. Together these conflicts make up the three poisons: greed, hatred, and delusion, which cause a lot of suffering, both to ourselves and others.

Our limited beliefs and illusory notions keep us stuck. There is a story of a tiger born into the circus, who lived in a 10-foot by 10-foot cage for most of its life. When activists came together, bought the tiger, and put it in a beautiful field in a zoo, it paced back and forth in a 10 foot by 10 foot square until it died. This is the human condition: a mind that keeps us in bondage.

The End of Dukkha

Remember the four noble truths: suffering, cause, end, path. The bad news is that life contains suffering. The good news is that there is a cause: the endlessly desiring mind clutching to illusion. The better news is that there is an end, known as *nirodhah*. The best news is that there is a path to get there, known as the *marga*.

You might be tempted to think that the end of dukkha, or *nirodhah,* means going into the nature of the desiring mind and why we are never satisfied with what we have. But the Buddha did not expand on the cause of suffering too much, he said it was a useless mental exercise. He likened it to having an arrow in your leg. You can spend a lot of time thinking about who shot the arrow, why they shot it, the trajectory that made it hit you, what the arrow is made out of, and more. You could even wallow in self-pity and all the reasons you should not have been shot by the arrow and how unfair life is.

Or you could simply remove the arrow and tend to the wound, which is exactly what the Buddha says to do. We remove the arrow by tossing it away with everything else. "Nothing whatsoever should be grasped at or clung to," the Buddha taught.

There it is. Clear as day. All you need to do to free yourself from suffering is *let go*. Let go of everything. Every single thing. Let go of your thoughts, opinions, judgments, beliefs, and attachments. Let go of anything you might cling to as "I, me, or mine." We are here to take out all the garbage, there is no need to separate and analyze the candy wrappers from the banana peels. Just toss it all out. If you think you have nothing to let go of, let go of that too.

Unlike most religions where people cling to beliefs for a sense of stability and certainty, Buddhist practice tells us to let it all go, to be completely cleansed of all beliefs and ideas. All concepts are relative, and in the face of absolute truth, become total falsehoods. So release it all, toss it into the fire, and let it burn away. The more we let go, the happier and freer we will be. We even let go of the Buddha, hence the phrase, "If you see the Buddha on the road, kill him."

The more we identify with things, the more we will suffer. We are here to let go of our superiority complex, inferiority complex, and equality complex. "Nothing to cling to as I, me, or mine" was the Buddha's way of encouraging us to drop out of our selfishness and thinking the entire universe should go exactly the way that we want it to. This is why the Buddhists are such fans of *non-words*: nonjudgment, nonharming, nondoing, nondual, nonstriving. They seek to not cling to any extremes or concepts in life, to find the special middle way. We even let go of the idea of letting go.

The state of *Nirvana* is totally desireless and at peace with all that is. *Nirvana* literally means *extinguishment*; it is the total extinction of all notions, ideas, and concepts. It is not to be found in the afterlife but in the here and now by fully letting go and letting be. There is nothing lasting and true to hold on to, so we might as well let go of it all. Hence the phrase, "Relieve yourself from suffering the same way you go to the bathroom. Just let go!"

Freedom from suffering is available, but it requires us not just to leave our comfort zone, but to leave *all of our comfort zones*. We must let go of the illusions we cling to for safety and security, and instead cultivate a "heart that takes hold nowhere." Buddhist practice is like jumping out of an airplane, discovering you have no parachute, realizing there is no ground, and seeing the truth that no one jumped. We go from surrender to fear to relief to lasting peace. We remove the armor protecting our heart, and after some trepidation, we realize we never needed the armor in the first place. The heart is our only true home, our true refuge.

Another translation for dukkha is, "that which is hard to bear." So what's the solution? To stop bearing it! The way out of suffering is to cultivate another *non*-word: *nonattachment*. Simply put, if there is attachment, there is suffering. Rather than being attached to the way things are or how we wish them to be, we remain open to what comes. We must remain flexible; with rigidity comes suffering.

Letting Go and Letting Be

Letting go does not mean detaching ourselves from reality. Quite the contrary, it means letting go of our *aversion* to reality. Letting go means meeting this moment exactly as it is, not what we wish it to be. Most importantly, that requires us to let go of our *resistance* to what is.

There's a famous story of the master Hakuin which exemplifies these points. Hakuin lived in a village hermitage, close to a food shop run by a couple and their beautiful, young daughter. One day the parents discovered that their daughter was pregnant. Angry and distraught, they demanded to know the name of the father. At first, the girl would not confess but after much harassment, she named Hakuin. The furious parents confronted Hakuin, berating him in front of all of his students. He simply replied, "Is that so?" When the baby was born, the family gave it to Hakuin. By this time, he had lost his reputation and his disciples. But Hakuin was not disturbed. He took delight in caring for the infant child; he was able to obtain milk and other essentials from the villagers. A year later, the young mother of the child was troubled by great remorse. She confessed the truth to her parents—the real father was not Hakuin but rather a young man who worked at the local fish market. The mortified parents went to Hakuin, apologizing, asking his forgiveness for the wrong they did to him. They asked Hakuin to return the baby. Although he loved the child as his own, Hakuin gave him up without complaint. All he said was: "Is that so?" The lesson here is simple: the sage asks for nothing, refuses nothing, and is content with everything.

Suffering is a result of our *nonacceptance* to this moment. Aging is suffering because we are holding onto youth, sickness is suffering because we are holding onto health, and death is suffering because we are holding onto life. If we are suffering because we lost our job, we are still holding onto a job that no longer exists. If we are suffering because a person we love is dying, we are holding onto the idea that none of us will die and that we will live forever. Suffering through any loss is holding onto the idea that forms are meant to last. Depression is suffering because we are holding onto the idea that we're supposed to be happy all the time.

What We Resist

When we do bring our attention to whatever we normally avoid, an extraordinary transformation happens. The pain begins to loosen its hold on us. As we feel our back pain shift from painful pulsing to a radiating warmth to a heavy ball, we realize that everything is temporary, everything changes, and this too shall pass.

This is the fundamental reason we must let go: nothing lasts. If we rely on the world for happiness, we will be at the mercy of what happens or what doesn't happen. Shunryū Suzuki claimed he could sum up the Buddha's teachings in three words, "not always so." Life is impermanent; when trying to hold on, we get rope burns. We are constantly trying to find even ground while the rug is continually being pulled from underneath us. We forever build castles made of sand, only to suffer the grief of watching it all fall apart with the next unpredictable wave. We must learn to let go of our desire for control and for things to be a certain way.

When we do let go, we realize the ultimate paradox: by releasing any desire for things to be a certain way, they happen naturally on their own. Our resistance to a lot of pain in life is like when we brace ourselves against the cold. We shiver, complain, tighten up, and resist, but if we can relax and feel the cold, it will lessen its hold on us, as our body and mind become calm. When we stop protecting ourselves against life, we can finally get in touch with it.

This happens with our feelings. When we really take the time to feel our emotions, we realize it only takes a few minutes for them to move throughout our bodies. But try not to feel them, and they only get more powerful. *What we resist, persist,* but *what we can feel, we can heal.* Any psychologist will tell you the same: any attempts to suppress our emotions only make them stronger. Emotions are like storms that need to run their course; if we let things build up, they become hurricanes that destroy our life. Only by being present with our emotions, and holding them with love, will they fall away on their own time. Nonattachment doesn't mean not feeling, it means not getting stuck with the feeling. We embrace the emotion and then let it go.

We can also look at our thoughts and realize they are just thoughts. They come and they go, and we do not have to get so caught up in them. We don't have to believe everything we think, including the thoughts that make us suffer. The thoughts are *real*, but not *true*. We don't even have to think everything we think, we can notice the thought without entertaining it.

The End of Resistance

The Thai teacher, Ajahn Chah, said that there are two kinds of suffering. There's the kind you run away from, and the kind that you are willing to face (Chah, 2013). The first kind will follow you for the rest of your life, the second one is the only place you can find liberation and a wide-open heart. This is the most fundamental lesson we can learn about the connection between love and suffering. *We must meet suffering with a loving heart for it to transform our lives.* If there is no loving presence to meet our suffering, then we just suffer, and suffering stinks.

The more we welcome our suffering, the less it has a hold on us. Hence the equation:

Pain × Resistance = Suffering

When we stop resisting and turn resistance down to zero, suffering turns to zero too. Sadhguru says that while pain is physical, suffering is self-created, which is his take on the old adage, pain is inevitable, suffering is optional (Isha Foundation, 2016). We will all experience tremendous challenges in our lives, but those challenges only turn into suffering when we actively resist them. Even venturing into better memories of the past or drifting off into an imagined better future is a strategy to resist the reality of this moment.

Referred to as *the second arrow,* suffering is that additional layer we put on top of the pain that actively resists what is happening in the present moment. We rarely just experience pain. Instead, we resist by thinking of all the way things should be. We get sick and rather than recognize that getting sick is part of life, we say we shouldn't get sick. Because we exercise, eat well, recycle, and pray, we think nothing bad should ever come to us. In this case, our suffering is pointing us to exactly where we are holding on and what we need to let go of.

Sometimes that second arrow of resistance shows up as anger and hatred. Perhaps we stub our toe on the coffee table. We could relax around the pain and sit with it for a few minutes before it subsides, but we don't. Instead, we rage at our toe for being so sensitive and ourselves for being so careless. We send hatred to all the coffee tables that ever existed and vow revenge against the coffee table industry.

One of the greatest resistances we have is resistance to the pain itself. If we are able to fully experience it and see it for what it is, it will release its hold on us. Maybe our pain manifests as anxiety and fear. It can be easy to run from these emotions or numb them with drugs, food, or alcohol. But if we are instead able to see and embrace them, then we can learn from and grow beyond them. Suffering is not caused by how we feel, it is when we wage a war against what we are feeling.

Suffering is our greatest teacher because it points us to exactly where we are clinging. Resistance is a flag that asks us for more of our attention. Once we let go of that resistance, suddenly it doesn't seem so bad. Rather than a big monster we are trying to avoid, it's just a feeling. We can handle feelings. We then become wholehearted participants in life. We open ourselves to every moment, we remain present in the face of pain, and are able to keep our hearts open in hell.

What Are You Unwilling to Feel?

Suffering is a signpost pointing out exactly where we are stuck on the path to peace. It points out where we are resisting the most and where we need to let go. Suffering, to someone on the spiritual path, is a gift. Hence the saying by Zen master, Shunryū Suzuki, "To a Zen student, every weed is a treasure" (Shunryū Suzuki & Dixon, 2020). To an awakened being, all of life is grace, including suffering; all of life is a series of exercises for awakening, including suffering. Suffering puts us on the path of awakening. Challenges are opportunities. This is where a guru can be helpful, because true gurus are mirrors, reflecting back to a spiritual aspirant exactly where they are stuck. Usually a small and succinct phrase, like a Zen Koan, said at the right time can catalyze a person's spiritual awakening.

There is a story often told in meditation circles about a holy man with magic so powerful it could relieve the most severe suffering. After seekers of healing traveled through the wilderness to reach him, he would swear them to secrecy about what information was to pass between them next. Once they took the vow, the holy man asked a single question: "What are you unwilling to feel?"

The lesson here is that even the most unbearable emotions contain information; they are telling us something that needs to be looked at deeper. Unfortunately, in our immediate-satisfaction society, we rarely sit with discomfort for long. Any hint of thirst or hunger immediately gets satisfied. If boredom starts to rear its head, we whip out our phones. So this inquiry—What are you unwilling to feel?—is a beautiful one to ask about so many areas of our life. What are we avoiding and what would happen if we stopped avoiding it? What is happening right now, and can we let it be?

"What am I unwilling to feel?" is a wonderful mantra to bring into a physical yoga practice, when we move the body into intense stretches and poses. Rather than shying away from the discomfort of a deep hamstring stretch, we can go directly into it. We can also apply this same practice to the intense emotions and mental patterns that can come up during a meditation session. If we are feeling pain in our hip, rather than shying away from it or wishing it would disappear, we can bring our attention to it. The practice of nonattachment encourages us to shift from, "I am angry," to "I am feeling angry." Our task is to *feel* our feelings, not become them. A condition like depression isn't something to *get over*, it's something to *move through*.

When we stop running from anxiety, we can use that energy to channel it in ways that are more life-serving. Many people feel anxious and it gives them an uncomfortable energy they want to get rid of, but we can use that energy and transform it into something productive. Maybe we are anxious about climate change and use it to start a composting program in our neighborhood. Maybe we wake up too anxious to work so we go on a 30-minute jog, thereby burning away the anxiety and giving ourselves the benefit of exercise and being outdoors. It's like taking a small bit of poison to strengthen one's immunity; we can titrate the so-called negative experiences of our life to build strength and resilience. Remember: *what we resist persists, what we can feel we can heal.*

Awareness of Pain

We can even apply this approach to our traumas, as long as we take the time to process those extra challenging emotions to not re-traumatize ourselves. Simply put, the willingness to face and feel our traumas is key to healing from them. Otherwise, they will continue to control our lives and create more suffering. Notice the phrase isn't, "What are you unwilling to *think* about?" Our job is not to think, it is to feel. Metabolizing our traumas involves the body, where the actual trauma resides, so this involves actually feeling them, which means pausing and allowing even the painful stuff.

We don't just need to become aware of our past, we must make sense of it, literally by tuning into our senses. Maybe our parents got divorced, but how did we actually *feel* about it? What happened to us matters a lot less than how we interpret and make meaning from it. This is why the Buddha recommended mental training. Only by getting in touch with suffering, without being overwhelmed by it, can we begin to transform it. The Zen master, Gensha, was said to have become enlightened through pain when he stubbed his toe and thoroughly examined the question, "From where does this pain come?"

Our *awareness* is key, it's the secret sauce to transformation. Meditation is not some abstract navel-gazing, a 20-minute respite from a stressful day, or a cognitive exercise like a sudoku puzzle. Meditation is meeting our habits and conditioning head-on. It is a kind of contemplation, a method of turning our attention inward and looking deep into the nature of suffering and happiness.

As one practitioner from the retreat I mentioned earlier concluded, "This place will push all your buttons so that you end up without any buttons." I realized after my meeting with the head teacher that everything I wanted in that moment—air conditioning, a clean private bathroom, a pillow, someone to tell my hilarious jokes to—were all attachments that were causing suffering. It would take some time and a lot of effort to be able to let go of them.

Facing Our Problems Head-On

Another way to think of meditation is the practice of concentrating our attention in the heart. Not the physical one, but the eternal spiritual heart that has a ground of unconditional love. Simply put, you cannot learn the mysteries of your own psyche from a book, nor get in touch with a source of inner wisdom without any effort. You have to do the work. This is the practice, the path, the *marga*, or the fourth noble truth. Training our mind to meet this moment head-on, to be fully present with whatever comes. In order to free ourselves from suffering, we must get to know it very well. We learn to embrace suffering, live with it, and then transform it.

Any therapist knows the two most common psychological defenses are *denial* and *avoidance*. Mental health professionals have to gauge all the time what their client is ready to hear, if they can handle the truth or will instead deny reality. It is not easy to face our emotions; many people choose, often unconsciously, to avoid them altogether. We distract ourselves with our phones, numb ourselves with drugs, alcohol, or food, or ignore it altogether with psychological complexes, like suppression. Blame is a great way to absolve ourselves of taking responsibility, which would require us to actually face our mistakes and imperfections. For many people, overworking is a form of avoidance, distracting ourselves from our true work and telling ourselves we don't have the time to listen to what our heart is trying to say.

Once we do find the courage to face our emotions, we discover they are impermanent just like everything else. Emotions are "energy in motion," and in reality it only takes

60 to 90 seconds for an emotion to run its course through the body. Given a proper channel, emotions will flow right through us. The reason they stay longer is because we resist them. When we are suffering, we are caught in a negative feedback loop of thoughts feeding our feelings, and feelings feeding our thoughts. We have to short-circuit this loop by waking up out of it and remembering a larger love. As parents, we hold our children as they have tantrums, touching them, caressing them, all the while being hit or yelled at. An open heart treats our own emotions the same way: touching them, listening to them, even as they have their tantrums. It doesn't take long for their energy to run out and for the tantrum to pass, and for a natural peace to arise.

Therapists call the process of breaking out of negative feedback loops *anti-rumination strategies*, and the more we employ them, the happier we will be. Once we acknowledge, see, and hold the pain, it's set free.

Waking up From the Dream

Since suffering is an inevitable part of life, one of the things we can let go of is the idea that there is something wrong with us. During the painful times in our lives, it's easy to blame ourselves and think we must have done something wrong, or are doing something wrong. Perhaps someone close to us commits suicide and we agonize over whether there was something we could have done. Perhaps we are stressed at our job and think we made a mistake in accepting it over a different one. But suffering isn't wrong, it is life. The one life we all share.

Glennon Doyle put it this way, "If you are uncomfortable—in deep pain, angry, yearning, confused—you don't have a problem, you have a life... You will never change the fact that being human is hard, so you must change your idea that it was ever supposed to be easy" (Doyle, 2020). Once we stop seeing suffering as wrong, we can start using it to our advantage and grow from the difficult experience. We can see our problems as assets, they are what make us human.

Suffering is not our fault, but it is our responsibility. What the Buddha taught was fairly controversial at the time. Contrary to the current Brahmanical traditions that put only the priestly caste on the spiritual path, the Buddha taught that anyone, absolutely *anyone* can become enlightened as long as they are willing to undergo the necessary training. We all have the capacity to wake up from this dream, we all have a Buddha nature inside of us. You, your mother, and your annoying coworker, all have Buddha nature.

Zen master, Ryōkan (Mitchell, 1993) wrote the famous haiku:

The thief left it behind:
the moon
at my window.

The moon represents the light of our awakening, which bathes the world in its light, and our own Buddha nature, which can never be taken away from us.

The goal of the practice, if you can call it that, is not to become a Buddhist; it is to become a Buddha, to become awake. We get there by letting go because we are uncovering what we already are, not becoming something else. Hence the phrase, "gain is illusion, loss is enlightenment." By losing all that we are not, we discover everything we are. When your house has burned down, there is nothing to block your view of the moon.

There's a story of a farmer who goes to his guru and says he is depressed because he lost all of his cows. The guru replies "Great! Now you have no more cows to lose." The farmer is now ready. He's been forced to let go of what he holds most dear, and in such an existential crisis lies a fertile ground of awakening, to discover his true nature that goes beyond "farmer" and all limited identities. A Zen master is said to "steal the farmer's cow" or "snatch the beggar's bowl," to remove a person's deepest attachment to force the death of the ego-self.

To borrow a metaphor from the ancient texts, imagine yourself walking down a path in a field. Suddenly you see a snake right on the path, and you jump up, getting ready to run. Before you fully turn away, you take a closer look, only to discover it wasn't a snake at all, it was simply a coiled rope that looks like a snake. Once the mistaken idea was dispelled, your fear melted away. The snake is illusion, the rope is reality. This is what we say of suffering. Suffering is illusion, inner peace is truth.

The ego is an illusion too, we have forgotten who we truly are. You might call your true nature Buddha Nature, your higher self, divinity, the Divine Indwelling, awakened heart, loving awareness, Great Spirit, or something else entirely. You might even call it the kingdom of heaven. The point is there is a part of us that is more loving and accepting than anything we can possibly imagine.

No matter what pain we are in, there is a larger space inside of us that can hold the pain. We all have an open, clear, unobstructed energy inside of us, a shared essence of timeless, boundless love. Buddhist practices help tap into this essence to cultivate it and expand it. Far enough along on the path, there isn't a single situation on the planet where our heart would close. We get to the point where nothing is excluded, nothing is unworthy of our acceptance.

Breaking Through to Break Free

To paraphrase Shantideva, we can cover the whole world in leather so as not to be pricked by its thorns, or simply wear shoes (Shantideva, 2008). The shoes in this case are a disciplined mind, open heart, and relaxed body. The shoes are having our attention in this present moment and a loving intention in our hearts. This reflects one of the greatest insights of the Buddha:

we are not passive recipients of life's negativity, we can play an important role in how we respond to it. "Your worst enemy cannot hurt you as much as your own unguarded thoughts," the Buddha said, reflecting how often we talk to ourselves more critically than any friend would.

The Holocaust survivor, Viktor Frankl, famously wrote, "In between the stimulus and the response, there is a choice. Within that choice, there lies our freedom" (Frankl, 1946). Our task is to increase that space between stimulus and response so that we can respond from a place of love, compassion, kindness, and understanding rather than a place of reactivity, which often breeds anger and violence. A psychologist would call this widening our *window of tolerance*. This is the deepest transformation we can make in our lives; to stop being at the mercy of our unconscious beliefs and rigid storylines and instead come from a place of loving presence.

This is the process of awakening: noticing our patterns and breaking free of them. Just as when we wake up from a dream and are able to see it for what it is, to an awakened being the general human experience is unconscious. Most people have no space whatsoever between the stimulus and the response and are essentially in a trance. We don't realize how much of our life is spent running from pain and searching for pleasure, guided by urges of which we are barely cognizant.

Underneath all this running around is the assumption that, if we eventually get enough of what we want and avoid enough of what we do not want, we will be happy. But it never works. Our happiness is only ever known in relation to our sadness. We will never find peace stuck in the endless cycle of craving and aversion. Instead, we must feel the entire human experience—the good and the bad, the pleasurable and the painful. We ask ourselves "What am I unwilling to feel?" and head right into the necessary work we must do. The more uncomfortable it is, the deeper the healing process becomes.

In this way, our pain turns to medicine and our constant searching turns into a resting peace. Spiritual practice does not offer an end to our problems, but it does keep us from getting too caught up in them. We find a new kind of freedom, not one of not having any emotions, but a freedom from complicating them. Keeping our hearts open means being present with our emotions without needing to do something about it, whether it's expressing our anger in the form of violence or suppressing our sadness in the form of numbing. The Buddha didn't just say that *anyone* can discover their innate loving nature by accepting what is, he also said that anyone can do it at *any time*. Even times of incredible loss, illness, and suffering are fertile ground for awakening.

Seeing This Moment

There are a litany of teachings and slogans all designed to encourage a young practitioner to sit with discomfort, and to approach what one normally finds uncomfortable. When we experience a challenging emotion, *we tend and befriend it*. When we meet difficulty, *we invite it in for tea*. There is the mantra of intimacy, *this too, this too*, that meets our entire experience with a loving recognition. The meditation teacher, Tara Brach, teaches *radical acceptance*; the Buddhist nun, Pema Chödrön, tells her students they must cultivate a fearless heart, *go to the places that scare them*, and *welcome the unwelcome*. John Kabat Zinn calls it *full catastrophe living*, which includes meeting the "crisis and disaster, the unthinkable and the unacceptable" and "all the little things that go wrong and that add up."

Suffering must be digested, must be synthesized, and used for growth. Like using waste as fertilizer, we also can digest the proverbial compost in our life to nurture our growth. We cannot have growth without suffering, hence the famous phrase, *no mud, no lotus*. The lotus represents enlightenment and the mud represents suffering, The mantra speaks to how we can all rise from the mud of our anguish and reach a state of peace that is not beyond it but instead has fully integrated it. The raw material in our life can, and must be, used for a greater synthesis. We are organic beings, and so are our thoughts and emotions. Pain, sorrow, anger, fear, jealousy, despair, we can learn to make use of this "garbage" by transforming it into compost to nourish the flowers of compassion, joy, insight, and aliveness.

We get there by feeling. No one says that they *think* love or *think* they are alive. We *feel* love, we *feel* alive. To fully feel what we want, we must feel what we don't want. The only way out is through. Carrying pain alone results in shame and loneliness, trying to avoid pain creates anxiety and endless activity, and reacting to pain results in numbing and avoidance. We must see, hold, and assimilate it with an open heart and a loving presence.

Presence

When Siddhartha sat underneath the Bodhi tree one final night before attaining enlightenment, he was tempted by the great demon, Mara, back to the world of sensual pleasures. When that didn't work, Mara tried sending every demon of pain and suffering at the young prince. Each one was met with the open heart of compassion and turned to flowers that lay on the ground at his feet. Finally, rather than shun Mara away, he simply said, "Hello Mara, I see you." This is the practice of *bearing witness*, of noticing our suffering without trying to fix it or get rid of it.

The lesson of bearing witness shows that how we meet this moment is how we meet every moment. If we are to increase our capacity to be present, to be in the present moment, to *be here now,* and discover the *power of now*, then we have to learn to be with discomfort. A wise person is able to hold the extremes of life, paradoxically finding peace by embracing chaos. Just as the Buddha bore witness by saying "Hello Mara," we can say "Hello jealousy. Hello pain. Hello anger. I see you, and I will take care of you." We don't practice to eradicate negative emotions, we practice to take care of them.

Our capacity to be with suffering is the same as our capacity to be present. It is easy to be present when we are watching an exciting movie or gazing out at a beautiful landscape. But when our body is in pain or we are with someone who is sick and suffering, that is the challenge and the opportunity. We have to open our hearts to all of it, the entire human experience. This is why Zen master Dōgen said that "enlightenment is intimacy with all things" instead of "enlightenment is intimacy with that attractive person over there." Life is full of ten thousand joys and ten thousand sorrows; we have to learn to sit with it and be with it all. Strength does not mean being impervious to pain or not letting others affect us, it means being able to hold the pain and let it pass through us with love and compassion. The follow-up question to, "What are you unwilling to feel?" might just be, "Can you keep your heart open, even in hell?"

Presence implies awakeness, openness, and tenderness. That is the true measure of our practice: how unconditional is our loving presence in this moment?

The Choice

Another way to look at our response to suffering is to ask, *when life doesn't go my way, how do I respond?* This inquiry will tap directly into our unconscious reactions to the vagaries of the world. We must learn how to respond rather than react. We must cultivate *response-ability*.

Our response to life not going our way isn't always anger. For example, when you were a kid and your parents punished you by saying something like, "We are taking your phone away, and you are not allowed to go out this weekend," how would you typically respond? One teenager might be sad and run to their room sobbing, while others might be angry and yell back, while another might try to disregard their emotions altogether by muttering "I don't care." This will show up later in relationship conflict, as we either attack, withdraw, or numb, also known as fight, flight, freeze. If we don't look seriously at our own mental patterns, we will stay stuck in those same layers of reactivity.

Fortunately, the mind is pliable, the brain is plastic, and every challenge in life is an opportunity to rewire the mind in ways that serve us better. Seeing suffering as a guru means recognizing that when life doesn't go our way, it is actually the best time to heal and grow. This is why Ram Dass said that everything we encounter in life is grist for the mill and what I believe Mary Oliver was describing when she wrote, "Someone I loved once gave me a box full of darkness. It took me years to understand that this, too, was a gift" (Oliver, 2006). It's easy to be at peace in the world when everything is perfect, when the sun is shining and the weather is beautiful and we just hiked to the top of a mountain to bask in the glory of the world. But when the weather changes and we are soaking wet on the way down the mountain, that may be the most beautiful moment of all, because it provides an opportunity to ask, "When life doesn't go my way, how do I respond?"

Grist for the Mill

Carlos Castaneda observed, "The basic difference between an ordinary man and a warrior is that a warrior takes everything as a challenge while an ordinary man takes everything as a blessing or a curse" (Castaneda, 2016). This perspective exemplifies the duality of craving and aversion of which we're already familiar, and also points to the path of spiritual awakening that involves seeing every circumstance in life as an opportunity for healing and growth, which turns us into warriors. When you meet resistance, when life is tough, what do you do? You use it. Whatever is happening in our life, even right now, no matter how hard it may be, can serve the awakening of the heart and mind. But we also need the courage of the warrior to venture into the darkness. This path is not for the faint of heart.

Suffering forces us to let go in order for us to understand that letting go is true freedom. As part of our path of awakening, on the path to freedom, we have to welcome pain into our lives as just another experience. In the words of Kahlil Gibran: "Your pain is the breaking of the shell that encloses your understanding" (Gibran, 2018). On this path of transformation, we can use suffering and everything that is happening as just another vehicle for growth. Everything we encounter on the path becomes part of our path. Contrary to the popular belief that spirituality is just about "finding your bliss," a genuine spiritual path is not focused on attaining higher states but increasing our capacity to be with what is, the good and the bad, the positive and the negative, the joys and sorrows, the laughter and tears.

Suffering is like the meat and potatoes of spiritual practice; it is like gasoline to the engine of our spiritual life. That which stands in the way is the way. Ajahn Chah, said that if you can't practice in the city, you can't practice in the forest, and if you can't practice when you are sick, you can't practice when you are healthy. Everything is a practice, and we don't become free from suffering by avoiding it.

The next time you are on the way to work and suddenly find yourself in slow-moving traffic, that is the perfect time to observe your own thoughts and reactions to things. Do you tense up, get angry, and frustrated? Do you see the beginning signs of road rage, shouting expletives at the cars around you? Or do you get sad and wallow in your own self-pity, thinking "Why does it always happen to me?" In his book, *Peace is Every Step*, Thich Nhat Hanh recommends using brake lights in traffic as a reminder to simply sit and breathe, like the eyes of the Buddha blinking back at you.

We can use the times that life doesn't go our way as an opportunity to return to and deepen our spiritual practice. The next time the doctor cancels an appointment, our partner says something unintentionally hurtful, or our child's report card really stinks, we can drop out of the dream of reactivity and shift to responding in a way that serves our life and our love. We are human as a result of suffering, not despite it.

Drop Out of the Trance

From a spiritual perspective, humans are asleep. We are locked in a trance. We are deeply conditioned to think and respond in certain ways, largely guided by unconscious behaviors and mental patterns instilled in us by our parents, families, societies, and culture. We have knee-jerk reactions to hot-button political issues and countless triggers we are barely aware of. Nowadays, there is a lot of interest in self-driving cars, as if we aren't already going through our lives on autopilot. We already drive places without even knowing how we got there, already sleepwalking through our days, zombies on our phones, checked out at work. The spiritual path involves awakening from this slumber, seeing the dream for what it is, and becoming one with the feeling-sensing-living-breathing-heart inside.

Sometimes when our computer has a glitch or virus, we have to turn it off and reboot it in "safe mode." Safe mode only runs the essential programs for the computer to turn on and shuts everything else off. This is how most of us operate. To get through our days and put on a happy face for others, we shut down most of our functioning, most of our humanity, and simply run the *Make Breakfast* and *Drive to Work* programs. We don't feel, listen to our intuition, live from the heart, or even taste that breakfast we made or watch the sun rising over the hills. We stay in the "safe mode," or safe zone, that avoids vulnerability and puts up walls between us and the world.

Many people spend their entire lives trying not to suffer and regard any discomfort as bad news, which results in the endless pursuit of control. A separation is created between who we are and what is happening. We get cut off from our experience. After my interview with the monk, I realized that although I had arrived at the meditation center, I hadn't actually *arrived*. I was still separate. From the perspective of spiritual awakening, this strategy of endless control ignores the fundamental nature of reality, which is that everything changes, nothing lasts, and there is no way to protect ourselves from the world. Our task is to let go of our false protections and finally touch this magical and frustrating, mystical and agonizing, sad and joyous life.

Just as a person who is asleep isn't aware of the external world, we are said to be ignorant. Ignorant doesn't mean dumb or stupid, it just means we don't know. We don't know who we are or the true nature of reality. Rather than the old adage that ignorance is bliss, from a Buddhist perspective, *ignorance is suffering*. Because of our ignorance, *avidya*, we need insight, or *vipassana*, to be free from suffering. We can gain that insight by recognizing that everything that happens to us, including our deepest pain, is a vehicle for our awakening.

Every breath is an opportunity to come back home to the heart. People often put up a sign in their houses, "home is where the heart is." But where is your heart? Inside of you. So where is home? Also inside of you.

Everyone Has Buddha Nature

Sometimes when I teach that we all have the capacity to free ourselves from suffering and enlightenment is our true nature, students who are passionate about social justice will object. "As a white man, it is easy for you to say to be open to and accept suffering. You're not suffering under oppression," they say. This perspective is what I sometimes call "relative truth." Relatively, there are oppressors and oppressed, majority and minority, powerful and powerless, victim and perpetrator, war and peace. This is true and has been the case throughout all of human history. We can recognize this and seek to create a world of freedom, justice, and equality, which we will talk about in future chapters.

However, the Buddha was quite clear: we *all* have Buddha nature, and no matter our race, gender, caste, class, history, sexuality, experience of violence, or trauma, we can awaken no matter our life circumstances, no matter where we are on humanity's timeline. *Relatively*, there is difference, which can be honored and recognized, but *Absolutely*, we are awakening itself. Enlightenment is never more than a breath away, nothing more than our natural state of being. Your next step could set you free. "The gate is wide open and nothing blocks your way," taught the Zen Buddhist Mumon Yamada (Simpkins & Simpkins, 2020).

Every generation of humanity will have its own special suffering—for some it's polio, for others it's traffic. The Zen poet, Jane Hirshfield, says, "I have been given this existence, these years on this Earth, to accept what has come into my lifetime—wars, loves, trucks, betrayals, kindness. I must take them… You can't refuse it" (Hirshfield, 2021). The purpose of Buddhist practice is simple: a complete acceptance to all your present circumstances and an end to the seeking mind. Whatever is right here in front of us is our practice, whatever comes to our life is our life.

Rich or poor, we are all bound to this wheel of conditioned existence, this cycle of suffering. Whether you are bound to suffering with gold chains or iron chains, you are still bound. Drowning in ten feet of water is no better than drowning in a thousand feet of water. The richest and most well-off person that you know is still suffering. Desires are endless, the hungry ghost's belly only grows bigger as the throat gets smaller. Many of those who spend their whole life trying to get to the top to find the tiniest sliver of light only find more darkness, resulting in even greater disappointment and dissolution of hope. Those who work extra hard to accumulate as much wealth as possible lose out on social connection and meaningful experiences. They end up so poor, all they have is money.

One of the biggest regrets of the dying is wishing they worked less. Suicide rates are higher in more developed countries and much higher for men, who are supposedly the more privileged and well-off. Interestingly, suicide rates increase in springtime, as depressed people expect things to get better; but when they don't, they think it never will. Many of the world's richest people in the world's richest countries end up killing themselves. We are all broken in our own way.

There is a Russian expression: if you wake up feeling no pain, you know you're dead. Pain is an undeniable and inextricable part of life. Yet the Buddha offers a promise: even after multiple decades or lifetimes of pain, you can awaken right now with no suffering, feeling truly alive for perhaps the first time. You can be happy without imposing your will on the world. For the almost five decades that the Buddha taught, he never said "believe in me." Rather he said, believe in yourself.

Opening the Door to Love

If you were to go running three times a week, you would experience a lot of benefits in your life. Your heart will improve, you might lose weight, your mind will be stimulated, and you will be more relaxed just by going outside and getting some sun. Similarly, going deep into the nature of suffering also results in many ancillary benefits. Namely, you will become a more peaceful and loving individual. Despite all this emphasis on chronic dissatisfaction, many Buddhist practitioners are the most kind, generous, loving, and compassionate individuals you will ever meet.

What gives? Why does getting in touch with suffering also get us in touch with love? Because on the path of alleviating oneself of suffering, you will encounter a large obstacle on the way: you are not alone nor separate from others. Your suffering and the suffering of the world are forever interlinked. From there, a natural ethic arises, and a new and exciting path forward unfolds.

Chapter 2

The Love of the Buddha

Why are you unhappy? Because 99.9 percent of everything you think, and of everything you do, is for yourself—and there isn't one. Wei Wu Wei (Terence James Stannus Gray)

Half the harm that is done in this world is due to people who want to feel important. T. S. Eliot

I go around the world and the United States teaching love. I love love and all the way it manifests in this life and beyond. I believe that life is a classroom, love is the lesson, and every moment is an opportunity to learn.

When I go into interviews and tell people that I have devoted myself to love and believe that love is the reason we are here on this planet, I am inevitably asked, "What do you mean by love? What is love?"

When people hear the word "love" the first thing they think of is the ecstatic romantic love that happens between two individuals. The intense longing, the rampant desire, the butterflies in the stomach, the love that we sing about in our songs and talk about in our stories. Falling in love, what psychologists call *limerence*, is an important piece of the love puzzle. But it's just a piece, and we will cover it later when we get into the science of love. Because we also have brotherly love, friendship love, self-love, family love, altruistic love, and as many ways to love as there are people on this planet. If we want to cultivate any kind of love, it greatly helps to understand what it is at its most fundamental level.

Buddhist teachings provide one of the most straightforward, easy to understand, and robust models of love I have ever found, one that gives us a perfect roadmap for growing our love. Why is that so? For a practice that focuses on meeting suffering, why does this also deepen our understanding of love? If the Buddha taught suffering and the end of suffering, why did he also teach, "As the farmer channels water to their land, so the wise one directs kindness and compassion to their own heart and mind"?

Love and suffering are great gurus, and one will always lead to the other. The essence of Buddhism is understanding suffering, but experienced practitioners do not have a grim outlook on life. The Dalai Lama has an exuberant, joyful energy that simply exudes love. Read any book by great Dharma teachers and you will find countless guides to more compassion, kindness, and generosity. The French monk, Matthieu Ricard, gained the title of "world's happiest man" when researchers scanned his brain to find the parts of the brain associated with happiness to be ten times larger than normal.

Why does meeting this moment and all the suffering in it lead to more love?

It's All Connected

The answer lies in the connection between all things. Once we undergo intense mental training to face our own suffering and be alleviated from it, we soon discover there is nothing permanent and unchanging to our experience. Although we easily identify with our thoughts, emotions, beliefs, and opinions, upon closer examination, there is no fundamental, lasting essence to these aspects of our being. Along with *dukkha*, the Buddha also taught of *Anatta* in Pali or *Anatman* in Sanskrit, which is often translated as *non-self* or *egolessness*.

This is another teaching that can be easily misconstrued. The Buddha did not say that you, or the self, do not exist. He simply taught that what you think is you does not exist separately from other things. Any physicist or scientist will tell you the same. We exist in a web of relationships; tug on any strand of the web and we will undeniably be pulled. Everything, including you, is a result of causes and conditions. Everything depends on a network of infinite other things in order to exist. Everything is always changing and interacting with everything else.

The Buddha taught about suffering, yes, but imagine if you were put in charge of figuring out how a leaf works. To explain the leaf, you would have to explain how the sun gives it energy, how the rain falls, how water cycles work, and how the tree itself funnels nutrients to the leaf. Then you have to explain how the sun was formed and the Earth was positioned at the perfect distance from it. What is the "cause" of a leaf? The only real answer is the whole universe. Just as following the branch will take you to the root of the tree, following the path of suffering will take you to compassion.

There is no separate isolated self. This is not a spiritual idea but a simple physics lesson. You would not be here if not for planet Earth being at the right placement in front of the sun for the right temperature and atmospheric pressure. You drink water, breathe air, and eat food every day to sustain your life. You speak the language that was spoken to you. Millions of external conditions have come together to form, for one brief moment in time, what you call "I," and if any of those conditions were to change, "I" would be no more. At some point across space and time, everything is made by and made up of everything else, and what you call "I" will be part of a million other things.

The Realization of Interdependence

Seeing our connection doesn't just mean recognizing the web of relationships that ties it all together. It means understanding that we come into being together too. Buddhists refer to this understanding as *pratityasamutpada*, meaning co-arising, reciprocal causality, or dependent co-origination. *Pratityasamutpada* is the basic idea that you cannot have any one thing without a litany of other things, hence the phrases "This is, because that is," and "This is not, because that is not." It is impossible for just one thing to exist.

This is why our happiness is only known in relation to our sadness and we can't have one without the other, the two are interdependent. Unfortunately, or fortunately, depending on how you look at it, love and suffering are interdependent too.

Thich Nhat Hanh has a famous dialogue where he holds up a blank piece of paper. "Do you see the cloud in this piece of paper?" he would ask his audience. "Since this paper came from a tree, and you cannot have trees without a world that has rain and sunshine, and you cannot have rain without clouds, so there is a cloud in this piece of paper" (Thich Nhat Hanh, 1991). It's an incredibly profound teaching, and we can take this metaphorical cloud with us everywhere. We can see beautiful clouds in all the bright flowers and taste the clouds in the apples we eat. We can see the sun in our food, and when we consume the food, we can see the sunlight in ourselves and others. We can see the beauty of the world reflected in ourselves and others. We can look at a match and see a spark of light lying within it, just as we can see the love waiting to awaken in every child. We can see the redwood tree in the seed, we can see our ancestors in ourselves. Rather than 70% water, we are 70% cloud.

Within the flower, there is no inherent *flower-ness*, however there is the entire cosmos, just as there is infinity in a grain of sand. Within you there is no *you*, but there is everyone who shaped you. Within another person, there is everyone and everything that shaped them. Thich Nhat Hanh often summarizes this teaching as *interbeing*, "To be is to *inter-be*" he would say, "And we *inter-are*." He came to this realization that we are all connected when meditating in his temple in Vietnam during the war. He went on to become an incredible peace activist and spoke against the war alongside Dr. Martin Luther King.

Life is Meeting

In other words, letting go of an isolated sense of self is the beginning of opening up to connection and interdependence. Hence the Buddhist phrase, "That which is threatening to the ego is liberating to the heart." Our attempts to solidify and assert our separateness creates suffering for ourselves and others. The less we reaffirm our separateness, the more connected we become to others, and the more our hearts open to love and compassion for all beings, which are part of the same *being* that we are. The ego is our attempt to create an isolated and constant separate identity. But separation is the opposite of connection, and *relating* is the literal essence of *relationship*. The ego hates change, while the heart revels in it. The ego seeks to have what it loves, but the heart loves what it has.

This is not some pie in the sky notion, it is a recognition of the way things are. Everything in this universe is *relational*, nothing exists independently. The realization of our interdependence helps to fuel our love, because it removes the harsh blame and judgment we put on individuals. Interdependence takes a systemic view of the world and recognizes that our actions are not solely our own, but the result of all the causes and conditions that made us the person we are. A person growing up surrounded by crime, abuse, and violence will be more likely to end up committing a crime than someone raised in a safe and loving environment.

We all recognize "it takes a village to raise a child" but still blame that child for their own mistakes when they get older, rather than recognize the role of the village. We easily blame individuals, especially those in poverty or experiencing homelessness, on what are really societal failures. Criminologists, child psychologists, and Buddhists agree: all behavior makes sense in context.

Last chapter we learned that the Buddhist path is to awaken from ignorance, and that most people are asleep. Unfortunately, unconscious behavior creates a lot of pain. When you look at actions that create suffering in others, rarely are they done out of malice, but out of ignorance. We believe that we are separate and thus violence to someone else doesn't affect us. We are deceitful to others because we have deceived ourselves. Our interdependence means that everything is connected, including our own capacity to love and be loved. The more we awaken from this illusion of separateness and rest in an ocean of connected being, the more our love blossoms.

All Beings Everywhere

There is some debate in the spiritual world about what a person does once they become fully enlightened—fully free from the endless cycle of karma and reincarnation. Some say that once you awaken, you are fully finished with life, free from this world and your body. There are stories of famous saints entering full *samadhi* or *nirvana* and staying in the lotus position until they died, and their bodies decayed, their consciousnesses fully resting in bliss.

But enlightenment as a final escape is a minority perspective, as most spiritual practitioners have understood that our personal liberation is wrapped up in collective liberation. The Bhagavad Gita, which encourages the path of action, concludes that the soul can remain in service to the world after liberation. In yoga it is called the path of the *jivanmukta*, "liberation while living," and Ramana Maharshi is said to have been one. In Buddhism, this is the path of the *bodhisattva*.

Bodhisattvas are enlightened beings who have put off entering the paradise of *nirvana* in order to help others attain enlightenment and be free from their own suffering. They are committed to awakening in every circumstance that life has to offer. There have been numerous Bodhisattvas throughout history, venerated like Gods in entire temples devoted to them, like *Amitabha*, the Bodhisattva of limitless light, and *Kuan Yin*, the Goddess of compassion mentioned in the introduction.

Bodhisattvas are often referred to as defenders of the defenseless and lights to the blind. They are dedicated to the awakening of all beings, as evident in the Bodhisattva Prayer for Humanity:

> May I be a guard for those who need protection
> A guide for those on the path
> A boat, a raft, a bridge for those who wish to cross the flood
> May I be a lamp in the darkness
> A resting place for the weary
> A healing medicine for all who are sick
> A vase of plenty, a tree of miracles
> And for the boundless multitudes of living beings
> May I bring sustenance and awakening
> Enduring like the earth and sky
> Until all beings are freed from sorrow
> And all are awakened.

Note the second to last line: *until all beings are freed from sorrow*. One is not free until everyone is free. The Bodhisattva is not finished being a raft bringing sentient beings to the shore of freedom until the last blade of grass has been taken to the other side.

This brings us to the ultimate paradox. An awakened being is free from their own suffering, but still committed to alleviating it for all others. We become free of suffering through our own shift in awareness but take action in the world to alleviate the suffering of others. The suffering of others demands action.

Suffering is a call for help, it is a call for attention, which itself is a movement of love. Spiritual development and mental training do not end with facing our own suffering; we must also open up our hearts to the suffering of others too.

The fundamental lesson of the Bodhisattva is this: *a truly awakened heart has an innate and intense desire to alleviate suffering.* The path of the Bodhisattva naturally practices kind actions for others. It is not helping others out of pity, sympathy, or duty. It is a relationship between equals. We help others because we know they are us. Rather than being motivated by guilt or wanting to be seen as a kind person, altruism isn't self-sacrifice. Helping another person becomes like our left hand bandaging our right hand that is cut, there is no thanks necessary. It is just what we do.

To the Bodhisattva, nonviolence springs from an inner realization of spiritual unity amongst all sentient creatures. When we open our heart to the world, we open our heart to the sufferings of the world. We can no longer turn away and ignore it, because it is in us and part of us, just as we are in and part of the world.

The love of an awakened being lights up the whole world, like the sun giving its warmth without any expectation of return from the Earth. The Bodhisattva has cultivated what is known as *bodhicitta*, what some might call *vast universal altruism,* an awakened, boundless heart that encompasses the world, open to the griefs and joys of all beings. Just as alchemy changes any metal into gold, bodhicitta can transform any experience into a vehicle for awakening our compassion.

The Bodhisattva acts with goodwill but without attachment to the results of their actions, which are always out of our control. They are grounded in a peace and love that's not affected by the outcome of their efforts. The goal is to be like the sun, radiating warmth and light for everyone, emanating healing energy at all times.

Bhavana

While we don't all need to become Bodhisattvas, we can deepen our capacity for love and understanding. The Pali word for meditation is *bhavana*, which means to cultivate, develop, or grow. Practice is seen as tending the garden of the mind. We plant the seed of love in the heart and water it with our attention. We cultivate a fearless heart that loves everything it touches. We notice the weeds, like jealousy, envy, and ill-will, and rather than toss them in the trash, we pull them out and return them to the earth, to act as more compost to grow our love even more.

Spiritual wisdom is attained by cleansing the mind of all distractions and purging the heart from all hatred. Intentionally cultivating positive states of mind is a practice desperately missing in Western culture. Many people have daily habits like body hygiene and physical exercise, but few take time every day to cleanse the mind and exercise the heart.

In the last chapter we learned about the importance of letting go. In the practice of love, we call letting go *generosity*, which is infinitely richer than any clinging. The more love you give away, the more you'll get back. The Bodhisattva cultivates a nonattachment to the world, and themselves, so they can return to it with a fully open heart ready to face the most intense suffering. It is said the Bodhisattva "sits in the fire"; they can sit in the fire of pain because they have developed a positive relationship with it.

Because of the truth of *egolessness* or *non-self*, there is no such thing as an enlightened person. There is only enlightened activity. There is only loving with a wide-open heart in the midst of pain and suffering. There is only alleviating the suffering of others through kindness and compassion.

This is key for anyone learning the ancient wisdom teachings that say suffering is optional. No one—and I mean *no one*—wants to be told that their suffering is an illusion. You can't teach someone who doesn't want to be taught. Being free from suffering is a *personal* path, being with other people's suffering without trying to change them or fix them, that is the *relational* path. Suffering in ourselves is a call to wake up, suffering in others is a call to love them. Spirituality, fundamentally, is the art of listening. By ourselves, we listen to our inner wisdom. With others, we listen to them with an open, loving, and compassionate heart.

Just as the Buddha offered simple, elegant truths around suffering, so too we have a very straightforward approach to love and opening the heart. It involves cultivating what are known as the four *Brahma Viharas*, one of the best and most powerful understandings of love ever made.

The Essence of Love

In Buddhist psychology, love is quite simple: it is a genuine concern for another person's well-being. That's it. Love is wanting someone not to suffer, for them to be happy, and for their happiness to blossom. The qualities that love takes are summed up in the four *Brahma Viharas*, known as Divine Abodes, noble qualities, or immeasurables. It is said that a person who embodies these qualities becomes a noble person. Those qualities are called *metta, mudita, karuna,* and *upekkha,* often translated as loving-kindness, sympathetic joy, compassion, and equanimity.

If you want a person to be happy and not suffer or be in pain, that is love. We can apply this to family love, brotherly love, friendly love, and intimate love. This allows one to love freely and openly, without attachment or conditions. Most love is conditional, "I'll love you if you do these things for me and act this way," but the Buddhist kind of love does not need anything in return. It just loves—a love that is always offered, never imposed.

When your genuine concern for another person touches them, it transforms depending on how that person is doing in the moment. If they are feeling neutral, love turns into *loving-kindness*: the desire for this person to be happy. If the person is already happy and doing well in life, then that love turns into *sympathetic joy*—feeling joy for their joy. If a person is suffering, then our love turns into *compassion*, the desire for that person to be alleviated of their suffering. So, we have a few more equations to add to our love algorithm:

Love + Pain = Compassion

Love + Friendliness = Kindness

Love + Happiness = Joy

The fourth abode is the natural equanimity that arises once we truly get in touch with a sense of peace in our own hearts. These feelings of compassion, kindness, sympathetic joy, and equanimity are likened to the feelings a mother has for four children: one with a disability (compassion), one who is a child (loving-kindness), one in the flush of youth (sympathetic joy), and one who is busy with their own affairs (equanimity). We can also think of them as generosity, kindness, and wisdom, which are antidotes to the three poisons of greed, hatred, and delusion.

Each *Brahma Vihara* has its own meditations and its own mantras. For loving-kindness, we say things like "May all sentient beings have happiness and the causes of happiness" and "May all beings touch great and natural peace." For compassion we say, "May all sentient beings be free from suffering and the causes of suffering." And for sympathetic joy, we say, "May all sentient beings be inseparable from the happiness that is free from suffering." You can change the phrases in any way that suits your heart's desires, "May you be happy, free from suffering, and may your heart and mind awaken" or perhaps, "May you have all the jelly beans you want."

Removing the Obstacles

Buddhist training is elegantly designed to cultivate a genuine concern for others, for compassion to bloom like a flower. You would think that cultivating warm feelings of love would result in a beautiful meditative experience. While this does happen occasionally, more often than not challenges arise. Rather than experience those positive qualities themselves, we often feel quite the opposite. When we sit down to cultivate more positive qualities of mind and heart, we experience restful thoughts and resistance to love.

We sit on our meditation cushion to watch our breath but are unable to follow it for even a few seconds. We sit to be mindful and spend 20 minutes being totally aimless. We sit to find peace, only to discover our mind is completely all over the place. Our thoughts shift from the million things we've left to do on our to-do list, to that one time last month we were insulted by another person, to worries about getting cancer or the impacts of climate change, to the dust that needs sweeping and the dishes that need to be washed. This makes us frustrated and often angry, the exact opposite of what we think we "should" be experiencing.

Contrary to popular notions about what meditation is supposed to be, this is by design. It is, in fact, the point. Whether we like it or not, we cannot grow without experiencing some difficulty. Meditation isn't there to show us sunshine and rainbows, it's there to show us exactly where we are stuck.

This truth can come as quite a surprise for those who come to spiritual practice in order to avoid their own issues. Many young practitioners experience challenges in their work, family, or love lives, and seek to go on a "retreat" away from it all to meditate and find peace. They spend a lot of money to go to a nice fancy retreat center in paradise and as soon as they sit down to watch their thoughts, all the mind wants to think about is the challenges around work, family, and love.

Metta

I have experienced this firsthand. One of my favorite meditations to practice is *metta*, loving-kindness. *Metta* meditation is designed to cultivate feelings of kindness and goodwill toward others. You start by extending your loving-kindness to a loved one, a dear friend, or a pet. Then you think of a friend, then an acquaintance, then a stranger, and someone who rubs you the wrong way, before finally shifting your attention to an enemy or someone you have a strong resistance towards. The point is to begin by "greasing the wheels" of the heart by loving people in your life that are easy to love. Then you have to progress to incrementally more challenging people. The final step is to look at exactly what you are holding onto that prevents love from flourishing.

Metta is sometimes translated as *unstoppable friendliness* and is said to be where mindfulness meets the world with appreciation. Some call it a love affair with life. The practice of *metta* is designed to touch all sentient beings with the love of our own hearts. We can, at all times, hold the world in our heart. In Sanskrit, *maitri*, comes from the word for *friend*, and is closely connected to words like brotherhood and sisterhood.

When I first started to do *metta* meditations, I had an incredibly hard time. Actually, I remember tears falling from my eyes the first time I did it, as I realized all the people that I was withholding my love from. I realized I wasn't the unconditionally loving person I thought I was. I wanted to love others but felt constricted when I thought about those who had wronged me or those who perpetuate pain and suffering in the world. As I tried to extend love to all sentient beings, I felt blockages around people I disagreed with, bosses who have mistreated me, and injustice from governmental institutions.

I soon learned that my own difficulties were the point. We must be able to meet our obstacles head-on in order to free ourselves from them. As Rumi so famously put it, "Your task is not to seek for love, but to remove all the obstacles against it." To attain most things in life, we must first face what is getting in the way.

Another way to summarize the Buddha's teachings is this: Life contains innumerable difficulties. There is a way through. You will be rewarded for passing through.

Any difficulty is an opportunity to recognize our attachments, delusions, and self-centeredness, while growing into wisdom, compassion, and freedom. The difficulties themselves are referred to as *Dharma Gates*: entryways to truth. Passing through them, we are rewarded with the truth of love. In this way, all obstacles are offerings, all offerings are teachings, and all teachings point back to love.

Love Reveals Everything Unlike Itself

In Mindful Self Compassion Courses, we teach a simple truth: *love reveals everything unlike itself*. Our attempts to cultivate an open-hearted unconditional love will reveal all that is not love and all that is standing in the way. When we give ourselves unconditional love, we discover the conditions under which we were unloved. It is completely normal to sit for 30 minutes of a loving-kindness or compassion meditation and actually feel quite the opposite of loving-kindness or compassion. We are being shown exactly where we are the most stuck so that we can learn and grow from it.

All neuroses serve a function: to avoid suffering. If we feel the compulsion to lock a door five times, it is to avoid the anxiety of thieves coming in. If we are always attracted to emotionally unavailable people, then we don't have to deal with the pain of emotional intimacy. While many clients go to therapy to get rid of their neurotic tendencies, they have to first recognize that there's a reason the behaviors are there in the first place. Only by looking at ourselves honestly and compassionately will we be able to break free of the neurotic tendencies that perpetuate suffering.

The spiritual path is not feeling happiness, joy, and ecstasy all the time. It is cultivating the courage of a warrior with no fear of going into the darkest of places. Psychology has confirmed that the parts of us we try to avoid create internal distress. While often unconscious, this internal conflict turns into negative external behavior. To address the behavior, we must face the conflict. As Carl Jung observed, "One does not become enlightened by imagining figures of light, but by making the darkness conscious" (Jung, 1993).

Challenging emotions and the suffering that they cause come from the unseen, unfelt parts of ourselves. Only by being present to them and integrating our shadow, will we ever find healing and wholeness. Higher spiritual development always *includes* the lower stages, rather than going beyond them. Spirituality is *whole-istic*. By integrating the light and dark, the good and the bad, we eventually realize the distinction is illusory; as dead leaves become compost to nourish the birth of new ones, everything is part of the same process.

Our job is to investigate all the places in our being that are not love. There is no other way. In practicing patience, we get in touch with our impatience; in practicing generosity, we get in touch with our stinginess. In cultivating peace, we look at all the ways we wage war with ourselves and others. In other words, before you take your heart out for a spin, you better check under the hood first, especially if you have left it in storage for too long.

Imagine if you went to a doctor to remove a tumor, but the doctor only knew about how to exercise and eat right. They do not have any actual knowledge of tumors or how to remove them because in their mind, "it is best to avoid it." Well, they would not be a very good doctor now, would they? Unfortunately, that is exactly how many spiritual practitioners fall into the trap of spiritual bypassing, with an unconscious belief that spiritual practice can be used to avoid any mental or emotional suffering. But it doesn't work that way. What we resist, persists; that cancer will continue to grow if we do not address it. Running away from the problem increases the distance to the solution.

This is why suffering leads to love. We use the darkness to find the light. Those prone to spiritual bypassing try to avoid the necessary emotional darkness it takes to become the figure of light. Only by embracing all aspects of life within ourselves will we ever understand the wholeness of it all. As Lao Tzu put it, "If you want to become straight, let yourself be crooked. If you want to become full, let yourself be empty. If you want to be reborn, let yourself die. If you want to be given everything, give everything up" (Laozi & Mitchell, 2006). I might also add, *if you want to love, let yourself suffer.*

The Pain Is in the Medicine

Love asks us to look at what is not love. In our practice of love, we see everything that is standing in the way of love. Love reveals everything unlike itself, from patriarchy to racism to sexism to injustice to a system of capitalistic materialism that puts money and things over people and connection. Love asks us to recognize the deeply entrenched disconnection that runs rampant in the world and the true epidemic of loneliness. As Sadhguru put it, "Too many people are hungry not because there is a dearth of food. It is because there is a dearth of love and care in human hearts" (Isha Foundation, 2019).

I like to teach that the four "P"s of meditation are: Place, Posture, Practice, and the most important one: *Problems*. While many think that meditation is a relaxation technique or a way to clear the mind, in reality it is meeting our problems head on. We meet our neurotic games and hidden fears, our hatred and regrets. The problems are grist for the mill, fertilizer for our awakening, a tunnel taking us to the light. The point of the practice is not to be comfortable; it is to be present with what is. We are not being present if we are using the moment to get somewhere, attain something, or avoid discomfort.

No path will match the potential for growth as the path of unconditional love and goodwill for all beings, including yourself. Your path of self-love will bring up all the grief, loneliness, longing, anger, fear, and self-doubt that gets in the way. You will see all the ways you have been treated in the past, both personally and culturally, get in the way of loving and accepting yourself just as you are.

This is something that comes up a lot in self-compassion trainings. Participants come to practice the beautiful experience that is self-compassion, only to find themselves feeling bad. The light is finally shining on the darkness, and it's normal to not want to face it. But we must. The alcohol is finally disinfecting the wound and there will be some pain as a result. There is a term for why we often have to feel worse before we can feel better: *backdraft*. The phenomenon of backdraft happens when firefighters come to a burning house and finally open a window. The environment, previously devoid of all oxygen, gets a sudden burst of influx from the outside, making the fire seem much larger. This is a necessary first step in putting the fire out.

The Tibetan word for meditation is *Gom*, meaning "familiarization." We are becoming familiar with all of our mental patterns and conditioning, and also becoming familiar with the nature of the emotions that we try to ignore. Experienced meditators are like surgeons to their own minds, recognizing there will be pain that arises from the incisions. This pain is necessary for us to remove the feelings of hatred, greed, jealousy, and ill will that prevent love from flourishing.

Mudita

In loving-kindness, we are encouraged to cultivate a positive feeling of goodwill for all beings. The practice of *mudita*, or sympathetic joy, asks us to take it one step further by rejoicing in the happiness of others. *Mudita* is joy in someone else's joy.

If *metta* is a solid foundation for friendships, *mudita* is crucial in intimate relationships. Relationship psychologists have found that while being there for your partner during the hard times is important, an even greater measure of relationship satisfaction is how often partners rejoice in each other's good fortune and happiness. If you come home from work excited over your new promotion and ready to share it with your partner, only to find them blowing you off in favor of watching their favorite TV show, that will not bring you deeper into connection. Instead, if they say, "Wow! That's amazing! Let's go celebrate!" you know you have a keeper. Because love is connection, we will be and feel more connected to another if our happiness is vested in theirs.

Happiness researcher, Barbara Fredrickson, defines love as a kind of *positivity resonance*. In psychology speak, "a type of interpersonal connection characterized by shared positivity, mutual care and concern, and behavioral and biological synchrony" (Major, *et al.*, 2018). In other words, *mudita*: a shared positive emotion, a smile that is returned, and a motivation to support and celebrate each other together. The more positive emotions you share, the more loving connection you will feel.

Mudita is contrary to what we are often taught and believe about the world—that it is a dog-eat-dog world, a zero-sum game, that someone getting more means someone else will get less. When our coworker gets that promotion or a friend wins the lottery, we have a hard time feeling happy that they are happy. The Brahma Viharas are antidotes, and *mudita* is the antidote to the envy and jealousy we feel when someone has or gets what we want.

Karuna

The third Brahma Vihara is *karuna*, most often translated as compassion. If sympathetic joy puts us face-to-face with our own envy, jealousy, and insecurity, compassion puts us face-to-face with that one thing we try to avoid the most: suffering. Even the word compassion comes from the Latin *compati*, which means *to suffer with*. Compassion means embracing the suffering of others.

One simple example of compassion is that feeling you get when you see someone step on a nail. There is an internal "oof" we feel, that stems from an innate love and care we have for others. In other words, it is a felt sense, and to experience it, we must be open to it. Once we recognize that everyone suffers, the first noble truth, we can then extend our compassion to everyone too. The poor and the rich, the worse off and the well off, are all deserving of compassion. Even evildoers are suffering and deserve our compassion.

Unfortunately, we cannot embrace the suffering of others if we have not embraced the suffering within ourselves. Compassion is impossible if we cannot learn to bear our own sufferings and difficulties, if our old habits of denying and running away continue to have their way with us. Naomi Shihab Nye opened up her famous poem *Kindness* with "Before you know what kindness really is, you must lose things" (Academy of American Poets, 1995). This points to a key lesson of suffering and why we shouldn't turn away from it: suffering is a gateway to compassion. Our own suffering can turn into something beautiful if we are able to face it with mindfulness and an open heart to give ourselves the love that we want and deserve.

The Buddhist approach tells us plainly and clearly that peace, kindness, humility, and gentleness naturally arise when we openly approach life with compassion for others and ourselves. When we are able to touch those moments of suffering, when life doesn't go our way, it has the capacity to awaken a heart of love. Hence the Tibetan prayer, "Grant that I might have enough suffering to awaken in me the deepest possible compassion and wisdom."

The anger, judgment and hatred we receive from others can be used to awaken the heart of compassion. The Bhagavad Gita says "If you want to see the brave, look at those who can forgive. If you want to see the heroic, look at those who can love in return for hatred." Compassion is not weakness, it requires strength. We live in a hard world; it takes courage to stay soft.

Tonglen

Cultivating a loving heart is more than just utilizing simple mantras; there are also profound visualization exercises one can practice. One such practice is known as *tonglen*, a Tibetan word meaning "giving and taking." This profound meditation practice meets the suffering of the world with the light of compassion, by visualizing taking in the pain of others with every inhale and sending out whatever will benefit them on the exhale.

Legend goes that the creator of tonglen was an Indian Buddhist master named Atisha. He knew that difficulty always led to greater wisdom and compassion, and was worried about journeying to Tibet because he heard the people there were very nice. So, on his journey to bringing tonglen to Tibet he brought an immature, mean-tempered, and ornery Bengali tea boy to keep him spiritually awake. Fortunately, as the Tibetans like to joke, there was no absence of difficult people in Tibet.

Tonglen didn't kick off until a few centuries later, when the Master Geshe Chekhawa was deeply inspired by the practice of taking in pain for oneself and giving out all pleasure to everyone else. His first students were lepers, who miraculously cured themselves through the practice. Seeing the power of loving wide open, Geshe Chekhawa spread the practice across Tibet.

One way to practice tonglen is to imagine inhaling heaviness and exhaling lightness. That might involve visualizing inhaling heavy, warm, stale air and exhaling light cool air. Then you imagine suffering, perhaps the suffering of yourself, someone who is dying, or all the suffering of the world. You imagine that suffering turning into a big giant cloud of polluted black smoke, that comes closer and closer. Eventually, it touches the heart but as soon as it does, it turns into light. Like the Buddha turning Mara's demons into flowers that lay at his feet, *tonglen* demonstrates that any dark suffering in our life turns into light when met with an open heart of compassion.

Tonglen practice often starts with getting in touch with the heart's deepest desire to free all beings from suffering. This means "greasing the gears" of compassion by remembering a specific and personal experience of witnessing suffering and being unable to help. Chögyam Trungpa said he would remember having seen a puppy being stoned to death when he was a child (Halifax, 2005). That would tap him into the desire to do anything to relieve the dog of its suffering and tap into the compassion of an open heart. Other participants might use a time they held their parent on their deathbed or dealt with a child who is sick. We too can use past events in our life where we witnessed suffering and wanted to help as fuel for a more loving life.

A Meaningful Life

This brings us to another key insight into how compassion and suffering work. How we relate to suffering depends on who is suffering. If the suffering is our own, it is a signpost to where we are stuck. If the suffering is in another person, it is a gateway to compassion and a call to action. From an Eastern cosmological perspective, you were incarnated into a body to free yourself of suffering and be a compassionate presence to others. The freedom we seek on the spiritual path is freedom from suffering, the actions we seek are those that help others.

We can use the principle that everyone wants to be happy as the foundation of a kind of secular ethics. If we all want to be happy and none of us want to be in pain, then "good" things are those that make others happy and alleviate suffering. Bad actions are those that increase pain and suffering in the world.

Good actions don't exist in isolation, they inspire others to do good actions too. As the Buddha himself put it, "The fragrance of flowers drifts with the wind as sandalwood, jasmine or lavender. But the fragrance of good actions goes further than the wind, encompasses the world, and even goes to the heavens." Our task is to plant seeds to trees we may not live long enough to climb, to drop pebbles of love into the lake of time even if we don't see the ripples on the opposite shore.

If you are looking for a meaningful life or are trying to figure out what the purpose of life is, the answer is quite simple: seek to alleviate suffering. Seek to improve the lives of others just a little bit. Verse 3.25 of the Bhagavad Gita reads, "The wise should act without attachment, intending to maintain the welfare of the world." The Buddha taught that selflessness and care for others is the best path forward for any human to take. In this way, recognizing suffering is a call to action, a stick that pokes us to get off our butts and actually do something. Rather than wallowing with the question "Why am I suffering so much?" or "Why is there suffering in the world?" we can ask ourselves, "What action is this suffering asking me to take?" In this way, suffering is a gift that awakens our love and gives meaning to our lives.

What About the Good Life?

In the previous chapter, you might have disagreed that there is suffering in your life. Indeed, life can be pretty good sometimes. Especially in the beautiful country of Thailand—the land of smiles—where you can stuff your belly full of delicious pad Thai and mango sticky rice, get a luxurious 90-minute Thai massage, and drink straight out of fresh coconuts in the infinity pool overlooking the sun setting over the ocean. Indeed, it would seem crazy to confine yourself to a 6-foot by 6-foot room with no fan in order to meet every difficulty the mind can conjure. I often don't feel like life is suffering until I go on retreat and attend the lecture that says life is suffering.

We are the most comfortable of any generation before us, but can we say we are the most loving? Are we the happiest? The most at peace? Some people are worried about subsequent generations losing the ability to write in cursive or do long division. In my experience, generations are losing the ability to rest. Despite all our material comforts, most of us can't relax. We can't even sit down and enjoy ten minutes of breathing and being alive. We lay down on the couch only to think of a million things we have to do; we go on vacation and need a vacation from that vacation.

With dozens of painkillers at our disposal, our society has done a good job at lessening pain, but with the rise of depression and anxiety, done little to stop suffering. Our bodies are full of food, but the heart is empty of love and the soul is empty of meaning. Our spiritual development has lagged far behind our material development. Despite great scientific and technological advances, we still don't know who we are or what the point of it all is. The internet is full of answers, yet we have not resolved life's fundamental questions. Inevitably, on the path of material comfort, a nagging, existential dread starts to poke the back of your mind. "Is this it?" "Is this a meaningful life?" Whatever material comfort we may surround ourselves with, we often aren't even present for it. We are cut off, separate, constantly lost in our own thoughts.

The path of presence, of love, compassion, and understanding, the path of selfless service, the path of living with a clear mind and open heart, this is the one most fulfilling. We are constantly running from one thing to the next because we don't realize the peace, joy, and love that is available right here, right now.

Such a relief it will be when we learn the truth: what we are chasing after isn't running.

The Buddha Wasn't the Only One Who Taught About Suffering

In almost all Buddhist regions around the globe, the Buddha is often portrayed as a serene and supreme being. Most statues place the Buddha in a calm and regal lotus position, with hands in delicate mudras and sitting on a bed of flowers. In art, he is often seen with a halo around his head, a peaceful expression on his face, surrounded by gentle monks on a sunny day. In sculpture, his head is often represented as having a thousand lotus flowers each with a thousand lotus petals, representing the bliss of enlightenment. For a religion focused on suffering, the Buddha is almost always portrayed as supremely serene, totally at peace, and exuding love. In some traditions, there are strict rules as to how the Buddha can be portrayed, including a polished appearance without the appearance of bones.

But the Buddha did not have a monopoly on suffering. If we want a deity that suffers right along with us, there is another spiritual system we can turn to. This one has put a suffering figure front and center, often bleeding, emaciated, and indeed, crucified. The divine symbol for this belief system is an instrument of torture. In stark contrast to the serene bliss of how the Buddha is often portrayed, it is the Christian faith that has expressed the suffering of man in all of its gruesome imagery.

Indeed, there is much more to learn about what suffering is and how we might bring it into our lives. For that we can look at the man who is said to have taken on all of humanity's suffering—past, present, and future. Jesus of Nazareth, Christ the Anointed One.

Chapter 3

The Suffering of Christ

If you cannot refuse to stay down,
lift your heart toward heaven,
and like a hungry beggar,
ask that it be filled...
It is in the middle of misery
that so much becomes clear.
The one who says nothing good
came of this,
is not yet listening.
Clarissa Pinkola Estés, *A Prayer*

When I begin any deep philosophical discussion with my students, I like to start with the idea that all philosophy and, indeed, almost all religious and spiritual traditions are rooted in a fundamental *unease* about the human condition. We are rarely satisfied with the way things are, regardless of religious context. We find ourselves unhappy with life, work, and relationships, and wonder if there is anything more to it all. Feeling lost and alone in an infinitely expanding universe, we continually look for greater meaning and purpose behind it all.

We look at a dog merrily bathing in the sun without a care in the world, and think, "Why can't I be like that?" We sit on the dimly lit subway, look around at the expressionless faces, and wonder, "Is any of this worth it? What's the point of it all?" Looking at history, it seems depression and its disillusionment have existed for as long as humans have had the capacity for self-reflection.

Life seems to have evolved a consciousness so well, it finds itself unhappy with life. If God had a "Complaint Form," we'd fill the whole thing out with gusto and add a 200-page addendum. On Page 1, "Childhood Cancer" and on page 127, "Really? Mosquitos?"

The beginning of any genuine spiritual inquiry is the same as any scientific one. Both seek the truth. What is real? How was the universe created? How did this all come to be? What happens after the universe ends? Like a child continually asking *why*, our questions eventually enter into a more metaphysical territory. Why does the universe exist? Why is there something rather than nothing? Who or what is God? Is humanity alone in the universe?

Any comprehensive system of religion or philosophy will attempt to answer these questions, and, in seeking to understand the universe, also strive to understand our role in it. We seek to know what it means to be a good person and how we should live our lives. On the path of understanding the universe and humanity as a whole, eventually we have to ask about the presence of another fundamental problem with the world: **Why is there so much suffering?**

Even in today's modern age, where human beings have developed a wide array of material comforts and technological wonders, there is still suffering. There is pain all around us and inside of us. There is genocide, war, violence, sickness, poverty, and slavery. So, if we are to envision an all-knowing, all-capable God, we have to ask ourselves some questions. What is God's role in the face of enormous suffering? Is He/She/It unable to prevent suffering? Or just unwilling?

Unable or Unwilling?

Atheists often use the presence of suffering as kind of a "gotcha" question for theists. "Well, if your God is so powerful and loving, then why do children die of cancer?" Atheists ask this question of believers because they would probably ask that exact question to God if they were to actually meet this entity in the afterlife. Did He/She/It/They fall asleep during the Holocaust?

In the presence of a just God, it is difficult to explain why bad things happen to good people and good things happen to bad people. What are we to make of the death, disease, violence, and hatred that we see in the world? Wouldn't a loving and protective God want to alleviate it?

Rather than a gotcha question, it is a question many religious people struggle with too. Some people of faith are unable to reconcile this question themselves and may even leave the Church for that very reason. Prophets ponder the question too. In the Book of Jeremiah from the Old Testament, Jeremiah (12:1) asked directly, "Why does the way of the wicked succeed?" The sixth century BCE prophet, Habakkuk (1:13) also pleaded with God, "Why do You remain silent when the wicked devours one more righteous than he?"

This is actually an incredible inquiry because in order to resolve it, we have to look deeply at the nature of suffering and why it exists. Fortunately, suffering is still a great guru, and perhaps even more so in the presence or permission of God. Resolving suffering is key to the human experience and resolving that suffering in the face of a supposedly loving and omnipotent entity is one of the most rewarding investigations there is.

Suffering Is a Consequence of Freedom

Let us cover a few simple explanations for why God might allow suffering in our lives. One of the most basic explanations for the presence of evil in the world is that it is an unfortunate consequence of free will. Suffering is a natural result of us being in control of our destiny. God wants us to do good and gives us the freedom to do good, but that also means the freedom to do bad. God even provided an infallible guide (the Bible, Torah, or Quran) to lead us on how to behave. However, like parents trying not to be too controlling over their children, we are left to learn from our own mistakes. God *could* fix the world, but it would be like fixing the lamp that the kids just knocked over and broke. If God fixed the world, humans would just break it again.

In other words, the suffering we experience in life is a consequence of duality. God wants us to seek the true, beautiful, and good, which requires the option of error, ugliness, and evil. This world is a multiple choice test and there are wrong answers. In a world of demons there will be angels; a world of suffering gives us a world of hope. As Saint Thomas Aquinas put it, "just as the silent pause gives sweetness to the chant, so it is suffering, and so it is evil, which makes possible the recognition of virtue." Putting us in alignment with the divine will guide us to goodness, while evil deeds will bear bitter fruits.

This perspective takes an altogether different view of faith. While many people misunderstand faith as a blind belief in religious doctrine, faith can be thought of as a recognition of the natural way of spiritual life. Faith involves honoring what William James called an "unseen order" that we must harmoniously adjust ourselves to. God is G.O.D.: A Good Orderly Direction. While belief clings, faith lets go. Faith trusts. Faith is an inward sense of this truth.

A tenet of modern science seems to be that everything has happened by accident. With enough physical matter, energy, and time, statistically at least one planet will form, produce intelligence, and sing opera. But faith is a vote for something more, for a fundamental benevolence and purpose to the world. Faith says there is a reason there is *something* rather than *nothing*, and *someone* rather than *no one*. It is the pressure we feel from spirit that urges us to do better, a recognition that there is a positive direction to creation. Doing right takes us to the good, doing wrong puts us on a path of suffering. This is the most important lesson of Alcoholics Anonymous: there is a higher order, and that higher order has your best interests in mind.

From this perspective, God is as much *The Great Allower* as He is *The Great Creator*, teaching us that love means patience and forgiveness. In God's infinite love, we are given the most precious gift of all: freedom. This is a lesson we can all take into our own love lives. Love is freedom. Learning to love is learning to be free. Love is not controlling, demanding, or commanding; it is where we accept another person for exactly who they are. It is when we bless our children, *may you be who you are, and may you be blessed in all that you are.*

We cannot love someone and try to change them at the same time; that means we are only loving part of them. We must love someone so that they feel free, free to be themselves, and free to act in their own interest. Hence the phrase, "If you love someone, set them free; if they don't come back, it wasn't meant to be." We can't force anyone to love us, nor convince our partner not to leave us by telling them, "But you *must* love me!" True love is given freely, not out of duty. If freedom is a flower, love is the nectar; they grow and flow together.

Suffering Contains Lessons

Free will might explain why humans commit incredible acts of violence against each other and create untold suffering despite the presence of an omniscient and omnipotent God, but it doesn't quite predict tragedies like natural disasters or being born with a terrible terminal illness. So, another reason God might send suffering our way is to teach us a lesson. As Pádraig Ó Tuama writes in his poem, *The Facts of Life*, "you will learn most from the situations you did not choose" (Ó Tuama, 2020). Pain is a guru; without it, we wouldn't learn a thing.

One time I was on a tour of the beautiful cathedrals in the colonial town of Antigua, Guatemala. Our guide was telling us that the cathedral we were in had to be rebuilt multiple times by the Spanish because earthquakes kept destroying it. I asked him, "If an earthquake destroyed the church you were building, don't you think that's God telling you that you shouldn't be building it?" Thinking he would offer a cliche like, "God works in mysterious ways," instead he surprisingly replied, "Absolutely! It was absolutely a lesson." He theorized the earthquakes were punishment for the violence and slavery that the Spanish had done to the Mayan population. If the Spanish had actually befriended the Mayans, who were indigenous to the land and knew a lot about it from centuries of living there, they would have explained to them that earthquakes happen all the time and given guidance on how to build structures the right way and where the best place to build them would be. Instead, they treated the Mayans very poorly, and God destroyed the cathedrals to wake them up to this truth. God gives tragedies in order to perfect humanity.

The secret to getting through difficulties is to accept them. Then we can shift from asking "Why is there suffering?" to "What is this suffering trying to teach me?" Suffering is a teacher, a great guru. "Welcome this pain, for you will learn from it," wrote the ancient Roman poet, Ovid.

Suffering Changes Us, for Good

Those are two possibilities: suffering is a consequence of free will, and suffering teaches us lessons. But another even more compelling reason is that God allows suffering because it catalyzes, or sometimes even forces, an inner transformation within us.

I often joke that one of the most lamentable aspects of the human experience is that we are not plants. Plants have what seems like a pleasurable growing process: they get to sit out in the sun, absorb the wonderful light, take in the gentle rain, soak up delicious nutrients from the earth, and bloom into a wide array of colors and textures. Human beings, however, aren't built that way. Human beings grow through *stress*. Hence the term *growing pains*. Stress is essential to healthy development; it represents a demand on the system that asks it to get stronger. Physically, emotionally, and mentally, we have to challenge ourselves if we are to actually grow. Simply put, we won't change without being challenged.

On a physical level, that means stretching muscles to make them more flexible or lifting weights to make them stronger. On a mental/emotional level, truly challenging experiences ask us to grow to meet them. We exercise our bodies and also can exercise our minds through learning new things and solving difficult puzzles. Try to teach a young child math and you will see the suffering they go through to understand new subjects. The mind must be stretched too. Without the friction of suffering, without a single challenge, our brains and bodies turn to mush. After just a few weeks in space, astronauts will have dramatically lower bone density, because they didn't have the stress of gravity on their bodies to keep things strong.

There are many religious scholars and theologians who do not see the sacred texts as an infallible guide, because that would mean we weren't given a chance to figure things out for ourselves. It would be like our grandfather leaving us a hundred million dollars, we would never learn how to succeed on our own. Parents know they have to let their children fall, fail, and make mistakes so that they learn from them.

Opportunities

We can be thankful for any painful or challenging experience in our lives because it forces us to grow. God gives us difficulties to make us strong, problems to make us wise, and suffering to make us compassionate. We won't get what we want, but we will get what we need. The most challenging times in our life are the ones with the greatest potential for learning, growth, and transformation, and even the worst things that happen to us can be a doorway to transcendence. Everything God sends us is meant to wake up something within.

For many people, the times in their lives that contained the most suffering were the times that were most transformational. The cancer diagnosis became a wake-up call. The divorce catalyzed an entirely new and much more meaningful life path. The loss of a loved one or pet served as a reminder of the preciousness of life. While we shouldn't wish these experiences onto anyone, years later they are seen as a necessary forcing function for the work and healing that needed to be done. Every human being will go through numerous cycles of loss and renewal, and unfortunately, we often won't experience the renewal without the loss. Behind the suffering, there is grace.

Our failures in life are gifts. We know this. All the gurus say it: The light comes in at the cracks; the invisible shift happens at the broken places; the ground is where we find gold. Why is this so? One way is when people come to the path known as the "wounded healer," where a deeply painful or traumatic experience turns into a source of empathy, compassion, and understanding. Often those who have gone through a "dark night of the soul" end up leading others out of the same. Former drug addicts help others become free of their addiction. Sexual assault survivors become therapists and help others recover from trauma. Former convicts create boy's groups and men's groups to keep people out of the criminal justice system. Parents whose kids become victims of gun violence create organizations for non-violent resolutions.

It becomes a lot easier to empathize with and understand someone's experience when you have gone through it yourself. The more in touch we are with the suffering of any experience, the better able we are to help others who have gone through the same. Once you know the way through the dark, you can help the next person find their way through their dark. Often, there's no other way. Only once you have saved yourself from drowning and put yourself on firm ground, can you then lift up the next person.

Calling On Something Deeper

Knowing that suffering teaches us lessons and helps us grow is all well and good, but perhaps not enough. God could have easily structured the human experience to grow without needing suffering. Another explanation for why there is suffering in this world is so that we finally discover something beyond this world that helps us bear it. God allows suffering to happen so that He can show his power.

Many people finally turn to God in the face of immense suffering. Many people on their deathbeds or those going through some intense experience, always skeptical of the presence of God, finally turn to prayer to discover a strength within themselves to help them survive the tragedy. In *When Bad Things Happen to Good People*, Rabbi Harold Kusner explains, "When we reach the limits of our own strength and courage, something unexpected happens. We find reinforcement coming from a source outside of ourselves. And, in the knowledge that we are not alone, that God is on our side, we manage to go on" (Kushner, 1983).

In other words, suffering puts us in our place. We have to be reminded that we're not the ones in charge here. Failure is often the result of not being in control of or being able to account for all the variables of a situation. A humorous line goes, "You want to know how to make God laugh? Tell her your plans." In being taken down a few notches, we find true humility. Once we realize we cannot control the universe, that not everything can be fixed, and that the world will not unfold according to our carefully laid out plans, we are forced to surrender that control to something larger, to that unseen order. Faith is giving up those plans, surrendering our ego identity, and letting The Great Unknowable Unknown take the wheel.

What is God? *Anything that disrupts your life.*

True Help

Many people's first word on their spiritual path is "help!" as they search for something larger or deeper to assist them in times of intense suffering. People turn to faith-based traditions when they have no one else and nowhere else to turn to. Like Winston Churchill joking, "You can always count on the Americans to do the right thing after they have tried everything else," many people turn to a necessary spiritual development only after exhausting every other secular and scientific method. When we drop to our knees and scream "help," we have finally surrendered our defenses and are open to something beyond ourselves. Faith then becomes the buffer that cushions the fall.

In almost all Eastern Spiritualities, a recognition of suffering is a prerequisite on the spiritual path. The path of the Buddhists, Yogis, Hindus, Jains, and others are the same: understand suffering and seek to become free from it. The Abrahamic approach is a bit more extreme: total darkness is often required for us to finally turn to the light. An intolerable sadness, a darkness of the soul, a sudden tragedy, these are all essential steps to progress on the spiritual path. The divine is found in the depths. As Thomas Merton put it, "Prayer and love are learned in the hour when prayer becomes impossible and the heart has turned to stone" (Merton, 2007). Only when one's world is in total ruins, do we finally turn to the divine and find the gift of God's infinite compassion. For some, God is a parachute that deploys right before we hit the ground. For others, the path of divine grace is a rope leading out of the abyss.

Some priests in the pulpit might say "God never sends you more than you can bear" or "He sends the greatest challenges to His greatest warriors." There is some logic to this idea, that God sends tribulations our way in order to test and strengthen us and knows exactly how capable we are. But I disagree, I think God would send us *more* than we can handle so that we are forced to gather up the resources of something beyond ourselves. God often chooses the smallest people for his biggest tasks; throughout the Bible there are countless examples of God giving strength to the weakest among us.

There are two paths to God: one through intense love, the other through intense suffering. Many of us will take both paths at once. I remember one client who expressed that the death of her adult son was the catalyst for her own spiritual awakening, as she was forced to reckon with whether or not there was an essence to our being that went beyond birth and death. Her experience gives truth to the phrase, "You will either be brought to your knees by despair or by devotion."

Just as our parents give us freedom to learn from our screw-ups, God allows us to make our own mistakes. We are like children begging to go play on our own, only to fall and scrape our knees and cry, "Why does this happen to me?" Despite being responsible for our own pain, we still run back to our compassionate and understanding mother, who wipes tears from our eyes. In suffering, we run back to the open arms of love. Like the person addicted to drugs who finally signs themselves into the caring and kind nurses in rehab, moments of intense suffering in life guide us back to the Ultimate Force of Love.

Forced Into Change

That "something larger" we search for doesn't have to be God; it could also be the soul. Even during times of incredible grief, despair and confusion, there is still an open channel to the soul, and our biggest betrayals can still serve its awakening. The therapist and ex-monk, Thomas Moore, wrote that the soul is the bridge between the parts of ourselves that exist in time and the parts that exist in eternity, and we can "remember the part that resides in eternity when we feel despair over the part that is in life" (Moore, 2016). Like the Buddhists practicing *not always so* in immense suffering, we can use intense pain as a gateway to find a greater order to the universe. It forces us to look for any aspect of ourselves that goes beyond our current struggle, any larger presence or eternal spark of the divine. Only when our life becomes so shrouded in darkness will we search deeply for a match.

"The deeper one's awareness of one's powerlessness and the more desperate, the more willing one is to reach out for help," says Father Thomas Keating (Keating, 2011). Human beings are notoriously resistant to change. Ask any therapist struggling with a client and they will tell you the biggest obstacle is their client's unwillingness to try something different. We all know that growth happens at the end of our comfort zone but fail to realize that we often don't leave that zone unless absolutely forced to.

When I asked one elderly monk who had spent his life in Buddhist Monasteries why he hadn't become enlightened yet, he replied, "Probably my stubbornness." Sometimes, to truly change our habits, in order to truly turn our life around, we have to be dragged, kicking and screaming. If we want to keep our hearts open in hell, sometimes that heart must be broken open, again and again, until it finally stays open.

God might give you more suffering than you can handle so that you offer it to the Universe to hold. So that you realize you are not alone at all in your wallowing, but have something, or somebody, to hand it off to. That somebody might be named Jesus, the one character most important, and most divisive, in all Abrahamic religions. To understand suffering and why God allows it, we can look to the one who perhaps has suffered the most. Because if we don't understand suffering, we don't understand Jesus, and if we don't understand Jesus, we won't understand God or our role in this life.

The First, Fallible, Human, God?

Interestingly, the earliest pictorial drawing we have of Jesus Christ is not an homage at all, but a mockery. Looking like a childhood doodle, what is known to historians as *Alexamenos graffito* depicts a roughly drawn figure of a man with the head of a donkey crucified on a cross. Next to this figure is a smaller person with a caption roughly translated to "Alexamenos worships [his] God."

This ancient graffiti, etched into marble, is believed to have been carved somewhere between the first and third centuries and is believed to be one of the first, if not the first, depictions of the crucifixion of Christ. It is thought to be the result of one student teasing another for his strange minority religion, where his supposed "God" was punished in a gruesome and humiliating way and defeated by the evils of man. This cheeky engraving might offend some now and it probably offended some back when it was etched, too.

The graffiti points to something that separated early Christianity from other religions at the time: a fallible God that suffered and died due to the actions of humans. Most Gods were only punished by other Gods, like Prometheus who was punished for giving fire to man, or Sisyphus, punished to roll a boulder up a hill for eternity. They are still considered to be better than, or above man, existing in a different realm altogether, often eternally.

Around 1300 years after the *Alexamenos graffito*, in the year 1521, Hans Holbein the Younger painted his own depiction of Christ. Known as *The Body of the Dead Christ in the Tomb,* Hans' depiction depicts the brutal, mutilated corpse of a crucified man. There are no halos or angels to be seen and no ceremonial fabrics across the body. With a grotesque expression and a gray-green coloring of skin, this painting often shocks those who view it.

When the famous Russian writer, Fyodor Dostoevsky, came across the piece, he became mesmerized, spending hours staring at the painting, his mouth as agape as the figure depicted in it. The painting would be a feature of his upcoming book, *The Idiot*, reading, "The face was depicted as though still suffering; as though the body, only just dead, was still almost quivering with agony. The picture was one of pure nature, for the face was not beautified by the artist, but was left as it would naturally be, whosoever the sufferer, after such anguish."

The picture shows an undeniably dead body, forcing Dostoevsky to ask how anyone who "gazed upon the dreadful sight" could ever believe "that He would rise again?" (Dostoevsky, 2008).

Indeed, the suffering and humiliation Christ went through don't seem very Godlike at all. Why would God put his only son on Earth to suffer at the hands of humanity? Why would anyone worship a fallible God who suffers and dies? How does the cross, an instrument of torture and a symbol of helplessness and pain represent the power, love, and wisdom of God?

Because, dear reader, as you have probably surmised, suffering is still the ultimate guru, the ultimate teacher, and getting into the nature of suffering will tell us about God, humanity, how to live our lives with grace, and the nature of love. Once we begin to answer these questions, like why God might send his Son to die or allow evil to spread, a life of meaning will sprout from this fertile earth of questioning.

The Ultimate Sacrifice

Without a doubt, Jesus suffered and died. In being faced with this truth, we are being asked to embrace the reality of suffering. We are presented with the duality of life and death, humanity and divinity. We are being shown how we might be able to live our lives: by keeping our hearts open, even in hell, including the hell that is torture and crucifixion.

Some say that as the son of God, Jesus didn't actually sacrifice anything. After all, he knew the Big Boss had his back and he was going to return from the dead anyway. But this stems from a misunderstanding that God is anything less than pure infinite love. Jesus Christ was rooted in love, above all, which gave him the confidence to meet any challenge. This is the lesson of the cross: love is stronger than death.

One of the most famous lines Jesus uttered on the cross was, "Father, forgive them, for they know not what they do" in Luke 23:34. Jesus, like the Buddha, knew that suffering is caused because people are unconscious, caught up in a dream. Sin, evil, injustice, all come from the unconscious self, while the true self acts with unconditional love.

God put Jesus on this Earth to suffer and serve as an example of what it means to have a pure heart of compassion, even for those who do and wish us harm. It is easy to love people that are good to us. When our life partner makes us dinner and tells us we are beautiful, who wouldn't love them in return? The real work of love is to extend it to those that do bad. We can start with those whose actions frustrate and annoy us, before potentially moving on to those that wish us harm.

The Scapegoat

In Christian studies, several theories explain the mechanism of Jesus' sacrifice on the cross and how it atoned for all of our sins. One is the *ransom theory*—that Jesus paid off a debt that we couldn't pay. Usually, that debt was paid to Satan, although some say it was to God the Father.

Another more modern theory of atonement is known as the *scapegoat theory*, which says that God sent Jesus down as a scapegoat to expose the lie that violence solves our problems. The scapegoat theory says that Jesus' death is a lesson of humanity's folly, pointing out our lack of evolution. Two Millennia before Hiroshima, Darfur, and Pol Pot, we were taught the lesson that we kill what we fear and don't understand. The symbol of the cross is a reminder that humanity will remain in the horizontal dimension of war and violence unless we put our faith in a transcendental dimension rooted in love. Jesus was not a sacrifice, but a *victim*, and our spiritual path is one of reconciling our violent ways by cultivating peace in our hearts.

Many believers waiting for the "Second Coming" fail to realize we would just crucify Jesus again for his radical teachings. We would look at the saint and only see his pockets. Even two thousand years After Death, peace is still a dangerous and radical act. While we praise the beliefs and legacies of non-violent peace activists like Mahatma Gandhi, Dr. Martin Luther King Jr., John F. Kennedy, and John Lennon, they were all killed for their teachings. For writing a poem wishing for peace, Tich Nhat Hanh was exiled from Vietnam for 40 years. Jesus' very own brother, James the Just, described as a righteous, honorable, and simple man, was tried and killed for defending the poor and weak against the wealthy and powerful.

A Moral Example

Beyond the scapegoat theory, there are other theories of atonement we can learn from. Another is known as the *moral influence* or *moral example theory*. This theory says two things. First, the death of Christ is meant to be a catalyst for society to live a life of love. Secondly, God made the incredible sacrifice of his own son to set an example. God demonstrated that He has skin in the game too. After all, what more can one sacrifice to the world but their own child? God is suffering too, right along with us, teaching us what it truly means to be a compassionate being.

Remember that the root of the word compassion comes from the Latin word *compati*, which means "to suffer with." We cannot be compassionate if we are not willing to face suffering, because compassion involves a shared feeling. So God sent his infinite Son to experience infinite suffering as a way to feel infinite compassion for all of His children. Jesus is God's act of solidarity with human suffering. God didn't want to be some outside, amorphous, abstract, separate power in the universe.

He wanted to live alongside and be with his creation as a deep expression of love.

Whether you firmly believe this idea or consider it a fairytale, the lesson is the same. *If we want to actually care for another person, we have to join them.* To truly know suffering, you must suffer too. To fully be with someone who is suffering, you must suffer with them. Nobody wants to be treated as a problem to be solved or a person to be saved. We can't rescue others, but we can walk with them. Often our rush to fix things reflects our inability to sit with suffering, when sitting is what the person needs the most.

There's a story of a woman who had a brain injury. As a result of the injury, she would sometimes collapse on the floor. Whenever that happened, people around her would rush to get her immediately back on her feet, but before she was ready. When asked about it, she would say, "I think that people rush to help me up because they are so uncomfortable seeing an adult lying on the floor. What I really need is someone to get down on the ground with me."

This story reflects the fundamental difference between sympathy and empathy. The common allegory is to see someone you care about at the bottom of the hole. They scream, "Hey, it's dark and I'm scared down here." Sympathy is looking down at your friend in the hole and saying "Wow, that's a deep hole. I'm sorry." Empathy is coming down into the hole and saying "Hey, wow, it is really dark in here. But you're not alone." Sympathy creates disconnection, while empathy breeds connection, the one thing that might actually make it better.

Love Connects Us

I first heard that allegory from Brené Brown, who also has an incredible description of the most fundamental essence of spirituality. "Spirituality is recognizing and celebrating that we are all inextricably connected to each other by a power greater than all of us, and that our connection to that power and to one another is grounded in love and compassion" (Brown, 2018). You will find this essential teaching of interconnectedness through love across every religion. Love transcends all traditions; it is the shortest definition of spirituality there is.

We saw this in previous chapters too: the Buddha taught that we are all connected, and still have an innate Buddha nature of limitless loving presence. Spirituality inspires us to cultivate such a strong inner peace that we are able to keep our hearts open, even in hell. We can witness any place that is hurting from the most open, spacious, wisest part of our being. Sympathy is *you* are suffering, empathy is *we* are suffering, and compassion is encompassing the suffering with spacious loving awareness.

While *empathy fatigue* is a real thing, particularly amongst healthcare and mental health workers, there's no such thing as *compassion fatigue*, because compassion comes from a place inside us of infinite love, a place of divinity. Compassion doesn't burn us out, it heals us, it opens us more and more to the limitless light of our being.

Facing the Pain

Brene Brown also wrote that when we meet suffering in our lives, we have three choices. The first is to live in constant pain and seek relief by numbing it or inflicting it on others. This type of person dumps their suffering everywhere they go. We treat our pain like a hot potato, the quicker we can unload it onto someone else, the better. The second choice is to deny the pain, which ensures that such repressive tactics are passed on to those around us, like our children. This happens when an emotionally avoidant father teaches his son that "boys don't cry." The third choice is what this book is all about: finding the courage to face the pain, own the pain, and develop a level of compassion and understanding that shifts our unique perspective of the world.

Brown spends a lot of time studying *vulnerability*, another word to describe keeping our hearts open in hell, which is "the birthplace of love, joy, trust, intimacy, courage—everything that brings meaning to our life" (Brown, 2020). From the Latin *vulnerare*, meaning to wound, vulnerability is our susceptibility to be wounded, which is the natural outcome of living with an open heart.

God came to Earth to be vulnerable, to share in suffering, and to inspire us to be there for each other in moments of suffering. God descended so humanity could rise; God became man so man could become God, pure love and the shining light of compassion. Many Christians, even the happiest ones, love the idea of a crucified God who walks with crucified people. When they go to church and see, front and center, a bleeding and suffering being, they know that God is not observing suffering from a distance but is at the center of it all. With them and for them. Whenever we experience failure, God is right there waiting for us, to be found in suffering. The divine is in the depths.

So why doesn't God save us from our suffering? Well, because He never promised to. But He did promise to join us in our suffering, which is a far greater gift than taking all of our difficulties away because we are given a new attitude and power to face whatever suffering life throws at us. This is exactly what good parents do. Rather than help their child avoid challenges, they help them move through them. God doesn't take away suffering, He takes away the fear of it, and since fear is the opposite of love, God gives us the power to face suffering with a wide-open heart. If suffering is the question, love is the answer. If violence is the question, compassion and forgiveness are the answer. If hatred is hell, being loved is heaven.

A Substitution

Christianity teaches that to love is to suffer. We suffer for and with another. God is suffering too, and not just because his own son has died at the hands of his creation, but because we are created in God's image. The cross is the ultimate archetype of suffering; it represents helplessness, pain, and surrender.

As the Son of God, it is part of the job requirement to take on people's suffering, and Jesus wants to be compassionate to those who suffer. As it is written in Matthew 11:28, "Come to me, all you who are weary and burdened, and I will give you rest." No matter how bad our own suffering is, it will never be as bad as the infinite suffering of Jesus, hence John 16:33 "In this world you will have trouble. But take heart! I have overcome the world." Jesus, in his infinite love, has taken on all the suffering of the world. He can therefore take on a bit more, including your personal struggles.

An important definition of sin is "missing the mark" and closely resembles even the Buddha's definition of suffering. Any time we aim at something and miss, like trying to be kind but getting caught up in reactivity, that is sin, which Jesus has taken on for us.

Some say Jesus suffers *with* us, others say Jesus suffers *for* us. In contrast to the moral example theory, there is the theory of *substitutionary* or *vicarious* atonement, which says that Jesus died as a substitute for others. The idea is that humans have sinned and we deserve punishment for our sins. For humans to enter the kingdom of heaven without punishment, Jesus takes on that punishment for us. It is almost like your own friend pretending to be you and living out your lifetime prison sentence so that you can be free in the world. How could one possibly pay back such a sacrifice?

Suffering in Place

This offers us a crucial example of how we might, too, embrace suffering in our own lives. Because it strengthens our hearts, because it is a way of being of service to others. Anyone who has ever ridden a train knows this. There are always signs on subway trains letting passengers know that if they see an elderly, disabled or pregnant person, they should give up their seat. Why do we do this? Because if we have some capacity within ourselves that makes it easier to withstand suffering, then it makes moral sense to put ourselves in their place. As the priest and poet, John O'Donohue writes, the question "How can I help?" is the eternal dialogue of spirit.

Often, we have the opportunity to suffer more so that someone else might suffer less. We can donate blood, plasma, or an organ to someone who needs it. As parents, we undergo immense suffering and sacrifice when raising children, often hiding our pain so that our children can continue to be happy. Selfless sacrifice is often held as one of the greatest virtues, like the soldier fighting for their country, the firefighter running into the burning house, and the parent pushing their child out of the way of the oncoming car. Divine love is sacrifice.

But we don't need to literally sacrifice our lives, we can also sacrifice our own egoic desires for the greater good. Just like the Bodhisattva who acts with selfless service, so too there is a Christian path of moving from selfishness to selflessness. While many people dream of heaven as an escape from the suffering of this Earthly realm, when you look at great saints like Mother Teresa, it immediately becomes apparent that deeply human work—helping the poor, tending to the sick and dying, practicing forgiveness—is profoundly spiritual and meaningful work. Keeping our hearts open in hell means being a healing presence in an often traumatizing world. It means cultivating a love so strong, so deep, that we are able to bring that love to the places that need it most, the places with the most suffering. Remember: suffering in ourselves is a call to awaken, suffering in others is a call to help.

Paradoxically, the path of selfless service is one of the most personally rewarding paths there is. By releasing all desire for your own personal fulfillment, you end up being fulfilled more than you could ever imagine. The great Bengali poet, Rabindranath Tagore, put it beautifully, "I slept and dreamt that life was joy. I awoke and saw that life was service. I acted and behold, service was joy."

Nonviolence

There is a well-known story of a Tibetan Lama by the name of Lopon-La. He was imprisoned by the Chinese for 18 years and tortured many times to try to get him to denounce his religion. When finally free, he came to India and was asked about his experience. The Dalai Lama asked if he was ever afraid, to which Lopon-La replied, "Yes, many times." Asked when he was afraid, he replied, "I was afraid I might lose compassion for the Chinese."

Many great saints, including Lopon-La and Jesus, provide a strong moral example of keeping their hearts open even in hell. Their inspirational stories take the question one step further, perhaps asking, "Can you remain present to this moment, even in a violent and traumatizing world?"

It is not easy to extend love to those who wish us harm and do us harm, but it is possible. The Buddha noted that even a tree offers shade to the axeman who wishes to destroy it. Keeping our hearts open in hell is the essence of nonviolence, known as *ahimsa*. One of the most powerful forms of civic action there is, nonviolence is a form of resistance that requires us to face immense suffering and often the threat of death, with no desire for retaliation.

Nonviolence is an all-or-nothing game, requiring us not to have a single ounce of hatred for others. Whether we are going on a hunger strike, living for months in a sacred tree, or marching to the Arabian Sea for salt, nonviolence requires us to face suffering with a simultaneous love for all humankind. It is not born out of thinking one is right, but that one is rooted in truth. Hence Mahatma Gandhi's Sanskrit word for nonviolent resistance—*satyagraha*—with *satya* meaning truth and *agraha* meaning "polite insistence." There is the truth that all human beings have an innate loving nature, and others will not be won over through violence, but through love.

The Buddha said that hatred will not cease through hatred, but only by love alone will the world be healed. Jesus, like the Buddha, wanted to empower all human beings, no matter their sex, race or social status, because he saw the essential divine identity in us all.

He didn't just tell us to love our neighbor, but to love our enemies too, to bless the ones that curse us, do kind acts for those that hate us, and pray for those that persecute us (Matthew 5:44-45).

Gandhi also taught that *ahimsa* arises from the truth that we are all connected and that violence to another is violence to ourselves. Getting to that truth, *satya*, requires ceaseless striving. The quest for truth requires *tapascharya*, or self-suffering, sometimes all the way to death. We will further explore the idea of *tapas* in Chapter 5; the point to understand here is that *nonviolence* does not mean *nonaction*, and a nonviolent life will almost always require intense suffering. Whether it is going on a hunger strike, getting beaten by police during a peaceful protest, or getting crucified on a cross, the path of nonviolence is a path of suffering.

Developing Our Capacity to Suffer

Dr. Martin Luther King Jr., another champion of nonviolence who was deeply inspired by Gandhi's activism, also recognized that nonviolence requires a willingness to suffer with an open heart that sees the good in another. In his famous correspondence that also featured the quote, "Hate is too great a burden to bear," Dr. King wrote:

Somehow we must be able to stand up before our most bitter opponents and say: "We shall match your capacity to inflict suffering by our capacity to endure suffering. We will meet your physical force with soul force... We will not only win our freedom for ourselves; we will so appeal to your heart and conscience that we will win you in the process, and our victory will be a double victory".

We shall match your capacity to inflict suffering by our capacity to endure it is perhaps one of the most powerful statements I have ever heard. In that same correspondence, Dr. King speaks to the enduring truth that unites us all, and no amount of violence to another will change it (King, 1967).

It is said that Jesus was the way and the truth, and he took on all the suffering of the world, finally overcoming evil. Regardless of whether you believe Jesus to be the Son of God, the Son of Man, or simply a deeply compassionate human being, the lesson here is that if we can conquer suffering, we can win any righteous cause. The practice of *self-immolation*, the nonviolent protest of burning oneself by fire, is perhaps the most profound example of the willingness to face suffering for the awakening of others. Like Kuan Yin sacrificing herself for the executioner and Jesus sacrificing himself on the cross, giving one's life for others is the greatest act a human can do.

There once was a story of a famous general who had recently come to power. He went from town to town to make sure that all the villagers bowed down to him and acknowledged that he was the one in charge. As he traveled, he heard of one monk who had refused the order. So he went to visit this monk in his hut, to find him sitting in the meditation posture, still and unmoving. The monk did not even acknowledge his presence. The general, angered, began to shout, "Don't you know who I am?!? I could slice my sword through your belly, without even batting an eye." Hearing this, the monk replied, gently, softly,

"Don't you know who I am? You could slice your sword through my belly, and I wouldn't even bat an eye."

To an enlightened being who has already faced every demon of this world and others, nothing can knock them off their pedestal of peace. If we can face death, we can face anything—any tyrant, government, or force of oppression. Power is not to be found outside, but inside. Jesus knew well in advance the rejection, arrest, torture and execution he would have to face and went to Jerusalem anyway, becoming an inspiration for all of humanity. The fundamental lesson of the cross is this: divine love demands us from us total fearlessness and boundless courage to become an instrument of peace and justice.

Rebirth in Every Moment

All spiritual and religious teachings can be interpreted on many levels: literally, metaphorically, allegorically, and more. For example, the idea of karma and reincarnation is often presented as spiritual fact. Our actions in this life literally decide our birth, lifespan, and life circumstances in the next one. Yet even in this Eastern cosmology, a human birth is still seen as a precious and fortuitous one, because we humans have the greatest potential for awakening. The reason for that? Humans suffer, and fairly uniquely out of all the creatures in the animal kingdom. A lizard warming itself the sun isn't worried about the inevitability of death, nor are the mice making offerings to appease the cheese Gods.

Because humans suffer, we are motivated to walk the path to alleviating that suffering, in turn, awakening to the truth of who we are and attaining liberation. Life is an adult education class and if we do not learn its lesson, we will have to retake the test again. If you don't learn the truth of love and freedom from suffering now, don't worry, you have as many chances as necessary.

But we can also interpret the law of karma quite literally as the law of cause and effect. Actions have consequences; you reap what you sow. If you skip a few meals, you will be hungry. If you rob a bank, you will get arrested and end up in jail. If you have too many beers and hop behind the wheel of a vehicle, your actions might result in your death. Karma reflects how the past has led to the present moment.

Our personal karma is simply the mental patterns from our accumulated thoughts and actions, called *samskaras*, or mental conditioning. The law of karma and the psychological principles of science both agree that we are controlled by impulses we cannot see and do not often understand. If we do not learn how to control our own minds, they will end up controlling us. To paraphrase Jung, if we don't understand our karma and unconscious patterns, it will rule our life and we will call it fate.

We can interpret the idea of reincarnation differently too. We can see the reality of reincarnation as a recognition that we are changing and transforming all the time. The person who boarded the train will not be the same person who arrives at the destination; the person who finishes this book will not be the same person who started it. We died as a child and were reborn as a teenager, we died as a teenager to become an adult, we lost our innocence and are reborn with a new understanding of the way things are. None of the atoms in your body now were there seven years ago.

In the Zen tradition it is said that in the time it takes to snap your fingers, there are 900 cycles of birth and death. Every moment and every breath offers an opportunity to let go of old selves and patterns and step into the person we wish to be. This is the essence of transformation, asking "Who do I need to become?" and taking that leap, no matter how hard it may be.

Suffering Leads to Rebirth

Many people believe the Bible to be the infallible word of God, and every word must be considered literally and factually true, interpreting the text differently is blasphemous. This is a shame, as we can gain a lot to consider the story of Jesus' resurrection metaphorically and allegorically. We can see life, death, and resurrection happen at every moment of life. Every time you breathe, an inhale is born, dies, and is resurrected again after the exhale. We die every night and are resurrected every morning.

In the face of intense suffering, we are called to let old selves die to be reborn, or resurrected, into more life and love serving versions of ourselves. Nature teaches us that one form must decay so another can grow. Just as the seed dies to become the tree, or the tadpole dies to become resurrected as the frog, we can face intense suffering that kills a smaller self that isn't serving, and be *resurrected* as a more whole, and healed, version of ourselves. We can let the false self get tortured to death and let our selfish egoic love suffer and die, in order to resurrect the True Self that endlessly emanates a love and compassion for all beings.

"Accept the pain involved in recreating yourself afresh," writes Naguib Mahfouz (Mahfouz, 2016). The resurrection represents that suffering can be transformed, that pain can be part of our path. No matter our past, each moment is an opportunity to resurrect a new life for ourselves. Like the cracking of a shell, we might have to completely fall apart to get there.

In his transformational book on trauma, *Waking the Tiger Within*, Peter Levine writes, "The paradox of trauma is that it has both the power to destroy and the power to transform and resurrect" (Levine, 1997). The difference in whether or not our trauma transforms or destroys us is whether we choose to move through it or avoid it altogether. Just like our sage from before asking, "What are you unwilling to feel?" we might also ask ourselves, "What am I unwilling to face?"

Levine's use of the word *resurrect* is quite telling here, and perfectly matches how the trauma that Jesus experienced was able to be transformed. We, seeing that trauma, a bleeding crown of thorns and a suffering entity on the cross, are encouraged to face our own traumas, to be reborn and transformed into more healed and whole versions of ourselves. Redemption, renewal, and resurrection are all found through an openness to suffering. Within our feelings, even the most intense ones, lies our very humanity.

Jesus is the ultimate archetype for a human death that gets reborn as divinity. This gives us the encouraging message that we too can experience an ego death to reveal our own divine nature, which we could say is the purpose of humanity itself. As St. Anthony of the Desert encouraged, we can all have a resurrection of our own hearts from the very earth itself. No matter our deepest wounds, and often including our deepest wounds, we can still live from the place of our deepest love.

Rejoicing in Suffering

Pain is a friend, suffering is an ally. For these reasons and more, many of the Christian faith are told to actually rejoice in the midst of suffering. "Blessed is the man who has suffered; he has found life," says Jesus (Gospel of Thomas 58). After all, Jesus isn't the only one who suffered or underwent extraordinary tribulations in the Bible. Numerous saints like Job, David, Paul, and Abraham, all suffered greatly. Paul the Apostle, who was imprisoned, beaten, lashed, shipwrecked, and more, tells us so. "More than that, we rejoice in our sufferings…," he says in Romans 5:3, and also, "Now I rejoice in my sufferings for your sake…," in Colossians 1:24.

We rejoice in our suffering because it strengthens us and awakens something deep inside us. We rejoice in suffering because by surrendering to it, it turns into a symbol of the divine. We rejoice at the test of our faith. We rejoice in suffering because it allows us to be of service to it. We rejoice in suffering because it increases our own empathy for others who are suffering. We see the child suffering under the weight of neglect and because we ourselves experienced that neglect, we know how important it is to embrace them, love them, and tell them what they need to hear. Moving through our own grief gives us a greater ability to help others in theirs. By getting in touch with our own suffering, we get in touch with the suffering of God on the cross.

Compassion is a two-way street, God suffers with us, and we suffer with God. As the Nobel laureate and Holocaust survivor, Elie Wiesel, writes, "the day will come when we shall understand that suffering can elevate human beings. God help us to bear our suffering well" (Kornfield, 2011).

The Universe will send us all sorts of things we don't want. These times are opportunities that ask us, what will we do with this suffering? Will we transform and use it? Will we choose love, or let it destroy us? We cannot selectively choose what to be present for, we must be present for the bad times to also be present for the good times. Any therapist will tell you the same: we can't pick out just the positive feelings and leave out the rest. Despite our best efforts to numb and avoid only the bad feelings and enhance only the good, it doesn't work that way. We have to feel it all. If we want to experience the ecstasy of holding our firstborn, we must be present with our fear when the doctors take them back to run some tests. If you try to keep pain away, you will keep the love away.

If we deny our depths, we won't reach our heights. Suffering is to be celebrated because meeting it accentuates the good times. In a Christian sense, it also prepares followers to really appreciate the kingdom of heaven and the end of suffering altogether. For everyone else, being present during the bad times helps us to appreciate the good times.

A Caveat

All this talk about Jesus might make some readers uneasy, or outright object to everything in this chapter. And for good reason too. There is often a gap as large as the Grand Canyon between many of the precepts Jesus taught, like *loving thy neighbor* or *judge not lest ye be judged*, and those that say they represent Jesus.

When I interviewed the life coach Kat Harris, who has spent years helping women have a healthy, biblical sexual ethic rooted in freedom, truth, and grace, she exclaimed, "The Church has blown it, over and over again!" She specifically referenced how Christians have used the name of Jesus to justify slavery, oppression of women, and abuse of the ostracized, but you do not have to go far into history to find incredible atrocities committed by those who say they follow Jesus. Rather than tolerance and love, there has been intolerance and persecution, like the Spanish Inquisition or the Crusades. Rather than a use of scripture for peace, many used religious doctrine to justify war and genocide.

If history has anything to show us, followers of Abrahamic religions have generated as much violence in the name of their Prophet as they have love. This is why shadow work is so important. The shadow loves disguises, like when a parent hits their child and says it is "for their own good." Sometimes the shadow wears spiritual robes and shrouds entire centuries in darkness.

For many people, the big, institutionalized religions have become houses of bigotry. The Church seems to have lagged far behind both sexual and feminist revolutions, focusing a lot more on castigating physical pleasure and oppressing women than helping the poor or practicing forgiveness. The philosopher, Alan Watts, observed that the Christian Church has "institutionalized guilt as a virtue" and turned mostly into a "sexual regulation organization." Jung called it a "misery institute." The monk and religious studies professor, Thomas Moore, observed how most people "automatically think of religion as a suppressive, anxious, top-heavy institute that tells you not to enjoy those very things you enjoy the most."

The hypocrisy of priests who preach about sexual shame for women and homosexuals while secretly abusing altar boys is not lost on the general public. Being told the beautiful, pleasurable, connecting, healing, God-given act of sex is shameful and dirty ostracizes most people.

We have all seen people who are supposed to be "loving their neighbor" but instead expressing hatred and vitriol for people who are queer, black, poor, immigrants, or getting an abortion. Father Richard Rohr, the founder of *The Center for Contemplation and Action*, similarly observed that Jesus' clear teachings on nonviolence, simplicity, forgiveness, loving enemies, mercy, and inclusivity have been overwhelmingly ignored, while elitism, classism, torture, homophobia, poverty, and the degradation of the Earth remain unaddressed by most monotheistic believers (Rohr, 2009). The popularity of faith-based religions is at an all-time low, and their proponents have only themselves to blame.

In my experience, the root of the problem goes to the very first few centuries of monotheistic development where faith, belief, and rote ritual superseded reasoning, contemplation, participation, and action. It seems as long as you *believed* in the right thing, any violence was justified, even if it created great suffering. Right *belief* became more important than right *action*, and what you *thought* became more important than what you *do*. Rather than see spirituality as changing oneself, it was used to force change upon others. Spiritual practice shifted from an embrace of mystery to an enforcement of certainty.

Returning Within

For our world to heal and religion to regain its reputation, we must return to action that alleviates suffering and practices that cultivate compassion, kindness, and forgiveness. We must move from *belief*-based religions to *practice*-based religions. We must move from an *outer authority* that castigates behaviors and creates in-groups and out-groups, to an *inner authority* of abiding peace and acceptance.

The activist, Valerie Kaur, is equally critical in her book, *See No Stranger*, arguing that white supremacy is intertwined with Christian supremacy. "Any theology that teaches that God will torture the people in front of you in the afterlife creates the imaginative space for you to do so yourself on earth" (Kaur, 2020). Having to believe and obey one omniscient power paves the way for authoritarianism and fascism, while a contemplative spirituality always blossoms into a life of freedom and compassion.

True spiritual practice encourages spontaneous love and a lifetime of unselfish work. If religion does not make us better people, if it does not transform our consciousness to one of compassion, then it is part of the problem, not the solution. If our practice doesn't help us be in tune with the goodness in all people, and instead divides up the world between good and bad, then it is a method to be abandoned.

Cultivating a Loving Heart

Intention and action are needed to change the world. There is very little correlation between *knowing* what is right and *doing* what is right. One of the best experiments to prove this point was the Good Samaritan Experience in 1973 by John Darley and Daniel Batson at Princeton University's Theological Seminary. Participants went from one building to another to give a speech. One group went to give a speech on helping people, while another went to give a speech on job opportunities. On the way to the other building, they passed by a stranger who had fallen into an alleyway, coughing and moaning. And yet, even the participants who were primed to think about helping people didn't help any more than the control group.

What did help was telling people they had plenty of time, which is exactly what spacious, meditative, spiritual practice is designed to do. This study reminds us that nothing is more important than cultivating a calm mind and open heart that faces suffering and seeks to alleviate it. An incredible example of such cultivation is the practice of *centering prayer*, a modern movement in Christianity. Abbot Thomas Keating, one of its founders, saw the growing interest in the 1960s and 1970s in Eastern meditation methods, like the cultivation of unconditional goodwill and loving-kindness. Seeing the usefulness of such practices and the importance of turning intention into action, Keating and a couple of other Trappist monks developed centering prayer, a practice of quieting the mind and returning to the heart, where the presence of God is discovered.

Centering prayer transforms our relationship to suffering, because it encourages us to change our way of thinking about it. Keating explains, "God approaches us from many different perspectives: illness, misfortune, bankruptcy, divorce proceedings, rejection, inner trials. God has not promised to take away our trials, but to help us to change our attitudes toward them" (Keating, 2014). Consciously choosing our attitude is holiness. The source of true happiness is shifting our attitude toward reality, if we can meet this moment, and whatever suffering it may contain, with a wide-open heart.

Turning To Something Else

There is another perspective on Jesus we can take, one that doesn't quite elevate him to the level of divinity but instead elevates us all to a world of divine possibility. If the idea of following Jesus, Buddha, Mohammed, or any person, historical or not, makes you a bit uneasy, there is another path to consider. This path does not require any faith or belief in an outside authority. It requires no intermediary, no institution, no filter between you and the divine. It is as inspirational as it is joyous, as real as it is revelatory. This path that has inspired billions of humans across time is known as the path of the mystic.

Chapter 4

The Love of God

There is no way of telling people that they are all walking around shining like the sun. Thomas Merton

There is a profound human experience that is quite common, but rarely talked about. Many institutions would prefer for people to not know about it.

During this experience, an affliction comes upon us, the same way we might catch the flu. It is something that envelopes us and takes us with it, like falling in love or a tidal wave washing over us. I have experienced it, there is a good chance you have too.

It has been described as sitting in a dark room and having someone turn the light on. A sudden realization washes over a person, as a radiant ultimate reality shines before them in sharp contrast to how dim, dull, and perhaps dirty things were before. Some say it is more like being a frog that has spent its entire life in the dark recesses of a large and deep well, only to be then pulled from the well and put on top of a mountain to see the sun rise over radiant hills. Others describe it like 10,000 watts suddenly going through a 60-watt bulb. The body, senses, and mind are that 60-watt bulb.

Sometimes this experience happens after months or decades of intense disciplined practice and effort. Sometimes it happens after undergoing a day and night of arduous and exhausting repetitive movement. Sometimes it happens totally at random, as it can happen to anyone for any reason at any time.

You might call it divine inspiration, sudden revelation, or spiritual ecstasy. You might call it an inner arising of wisdom, or the realization of our primordial or original mind. You might call it the realization of cosmic, universal, unitive, or God consciousness. You might call it the complete and total ecstatic union with God with a capital G or Self with a capital S.

But I prefer the term *mystical awakening*, and have found that this experience has a lot to teach us about what love is, how we might bring it into our lives, and how suffering might help get us there.

The Path of the Mystic

The word *mystical* has many edifying etymologies. It is close to *mystery* and thus connotes getting in touch with what many call "The Great Mystery" of the universe. It also comes from words relating to *secret*, as if the universe has been keeping this a secret all along, and we are finally let in on it. There is also the Greek, *mústēs*, meaning "one who has been initiated," implying that once you experience the mystical, there is no going back. Almost all mystics speak of their awakening as an initiation into the ultimate secrets of the world.

Those who experience mystical awakening often incorporate their understanding into a slightly different belief system than the common institutionalized narrative. In Judaism, this path is known as the Kabbalah, in Islam it is Sufism, and in Christianity it is most often simply referred to as Christian Mysticism. Some of the early Christian mystics include St. Augustine and Basil the Great, while later mystics include St. Teresa of Ávila and St. John of the Cross. Some say Abraham Joshua Heschel and Martin Buber were Jewish mystics, while Sufi mystics include Hafez and Rumi. The land of India is full of mystics, like Sri Ramakrishna, Sri Nisargadatta Maharaj, and Anandamayi Ma.

While much is not understood about this mysterious path, one thing is clear: those who have had the mystical experience report back an all-encompassing, overwhelming, and overflowing love that permeates God, consciousness, and all things. A love that is like air; one that surrounds us, flows through us, that is distinct from us but never separate. Thomas Keating simply called it *presence,* describing it as "immense, yet so humble; awe-inspiring, yet so gentle; limitless, yet so intimate, tender and personal" (Keating, 2002).

The mystics have much to say about what the divine is and how we might discover this unifying love within us all, and we have much to learn from them in our journey through the wisdom of love and suffering.

Fundamentals to the Mystical Experience

In *The Varieties of Religious Experience,* psychologist, William James, noted four distinct qualities of the mystical experience. First, the experience is *ineffable,* in that it defies expression in our typical language. Secondly, it is *noetic,* in that it provides an overwhelming experience of knowing, or understanding. Thirdly, it is *transient,* meaning it lasts a short time, although the afterglow may persist for a lifetime. And finally, it is *passive,* in that a person feels grasped by some sort of superior power, something much larger than the individual self or ego.

The mystical experience is impossible to describe; the only way to get remotely close is with metaphor. One popular analogy is to imagine the individual human experience as being on the tip of a wave. *I,* in ego consciousness, look around and see other waves, thinking they too are separate. The mystical journey takes us down the wave, to an "Ocean of Being," or Paul Tillich's term, *the ground of being.* On the way down the wave, we meet our *soul,* which acts as a bridge between our individual self and the Ultimate. Finally, we find the great ocean, upon which we discover that everything is connected and that human beings are caught up in a delusion of isolation. We also realize the fundamental essence of it all is the same: ego, body, soul, humanity, time, world, universe, the light hitting your cup of tea, it's all water. It's all divine. Whatever we were seeking was inside of us all along.

In the *Ramayana*, a great Hindu text, the great Rama asks his devotee Hanuman, "How do you look upon me?" The great monkey God offered a three-part answer: "When I believe I am the body, then I am your faithful servant. When I know I am the soul, I know myself to be a spark of your eternal Light. And when I have the vision of truth, you and I, my Lord, are one and the same." These three layers—body, soul, and truth—represent those three layers of the wave. We see ourselves as an ego trapped into the body, until we discover the spark of the divine that is the soul. Finally, we enter the ocean to discover nothing was or is ever separate from anything else.

The Christian Mystic, Thomas Merton, wrote clearly that we can all experience God, awaken to and become aware of this presence, and in so doing, become whole. While there are many different Sufi sects, they too believe in the truth of divine love and knowledge through a direct personal experience with God. The Sufis attempt to reach that state of temporary ecstatic intoxication of divine love, as well as a lengthened condition of complete indwelling with God.

Different Experiences, One Reality

Many people attracted to mysticism today tend to be of the *spiritual but not religious* type and prefer not to associate the great mystics with institutionalized religion. Modern translators have received reasonable criticism for erasing the religious aspects from their commentaries of mystical writings, replacing words like *celibacy* with *moderation*, *Allah* with *the Divine*, and *sin* with *missing the mark*.

We need not reject the teachings of the mystics because their religious words conflict with our own; it is easy to contextualize what is happening here. The mystical experience is universal and available to anybody at any time. It is a sudden realization of the Ultimate Truth that could never be verbalized to another. Like trying to describe the color blue, the mystic knows *who* God is but finds it impossible to express *what* God is. Due to this ineffability, when the limited human mind comes back down to normal waking awareness, the mystic can only make sense of what happened with the words, symbols, and beliefs they have on hand. Depending on what they have been exposed to already, they will follow up the realization of "I am…" with words like God, Brahman, the Son of God, Source, Allah, or consciousness. The mystics might have different instruments and different styles, but they all play the same song.

The key piece here is that all mystics seek to *experience* God, rather than just sit around and talk about the divine, which gets you nowhere. It would be like talking about the taste of chocolate. You could read every book about chocolate and get a PhD in cacao studies, but you won't ever "know" the taste of chocolate until you actually experience it, nor will you understand its pleasure. The word *water* will not quench your thirst, nor will the word *hunger* cure your cravings. No word about God or from God can meet one's eternal longing for the divine. Only real, lived experience can satiate our innermost desires. In doing so, we move from *belief* to *knowing*. Mysticism, fundamentally, is experiential knowledge, it is participatory.

Some religious scholars theorize that the mystical experience is the same across history and peoples, and there is good evidence to say that Jesus and Buddha could be considered mystics. When the Buddha was asked who he was, he simply replied, "I am awake." Such an answer is not very different from Jesus saying, "I am a son of God." Thomas Merton uses similar Buddhist imagery, referring to the mystical experience as awakening, becoming aware, being born again, finding a new level of reality, and a new life of the self, no matter the presence of suffering in this life. "No despair of ours can alter the reality of things; or stain the joy of the cosmic dance which is always there," he writes (Merton, 2007).

Proponents of the idea of a unifying mystical experience point to the similarities between *Christ Consciousness, Krishna Consciousness,* and *satori,* the sudden awakening in the Zen tradition. There is also considerable evidence for experiences like enlightenment or the use of psychedelics to be similar to the mystical. Sometimes referred to as *the perennial philosophy,* a term popularized by Aldous Huxley's book of the same name, the similarities in reports of transcendental experiences across time and peoples are extremely encouraging. Just as Jesus could bear all the sufferings of the world, upon mystical awakening, so can we.

The point is the gate of heaven is everywhere. Everything is already here, you are already all that you need to be. We are like beggars on the street unaware our pockets are full of diamonds.

Poetry of the Mystics

Despite the ineffability of the mystical experience, those who have seen the Ultimate Reality often cannot stop talking about it. Many express a desire to go running through the streets shouting, *Wake up! We are what we seek! You and I are THAT! We're IT! The divine is in me, in you, and all things! Right here, already knowing, loving, and serving all that is! Space is Spirit!*

In seeking union with God, the mystic becomes like the scientists who discovered DNA: they find that at our deepest essence, we are all connected, one and the same, made of all the same stuff. What seemed separate—material and spiritual, mind and matter, subject and object, inner space and outer space, human and divine, soul and spirit, finite and infinite—become one. God, consciousness, being, are all the same. There is no place to go or get to, we are already home and whole, an illuminating sun radiating through every part.

The art that springs forth from those who have experienced the mystical is often some of the most beautiful pieces ever created by humans. Wishing for others to see reality the same way they have seen, extraordinary works, often of poetry, spring forth. And of course it does. The word *inspiration* is closely tied to *spirit*, just as *original* is to *origin*. If you get in touch with the Origin of the Universe, great original and inspirational works will come forth from you too. The same creative force that made all the creatures of the world flows through the mystic to create beautiful songs and scriptures.

Hindu mystic poets like Mirabai and Kabir come to mind. Hafez's body of work is considered to be one of the highest pinnacles of Persian literature, while St. John of The Cross' poems are considered among the greatest works of all Spanish literature, and their words continue to inspire people today. Already quoted a few times in this book, Rumi is one of the most cited and popular poets in modern times; his words have made their way into movies, pop songs, books, and countless weddings.

One way to think of the mystical experience is a sudden awakening beyond our usual egoic identity to discover union with the universe, which Rumi (Rumi, 2004) describes marvelously in his poem, *The Worm's Waking*:

There is a worm
addicted to eating grape leaves.
Suddenly, he wakes up,
call it grace, whatever, something
wakes him, and he is no longer a worm.
He is the entire vineyard,
and the orchard too, the fruit, the trunks,
a growing wisdom and joy
that does not need to devour.

That short poem eloquently describes the experience of mystical awakening. We find ourselves meandering about our lives—going to work, driving home, eating dinner, and kissing our children good night. We seek material pleasures, social connections, daily comfort, a few hobbies, and a bit of entertainment, without much more to think about. But then something happens—we are pulled out of our experience and the veils of illusion dissolve. This might be random or might occur by the grace of God. Our sense of separateness disappears and a connection with all beings naturally arises. This ultimate experience puts our entire life in a new context and afterwards, there is no turning back. The dirt covering the windshield has been cleaned off and there is a bright world of possibility in front of us.

The Christian Mystic, Thomas Merton, had his infamous awakening in Louisville, Kentucky, sitting at a park, "at the corner of 4th and Walnut." He writes of waking up from the dream of separateness to finally see the secret beauty in everyone's heart and being overcome with an incredible love for all the people there. As the veils of illusion dissolved, he writes that he saw each person as God sees them, and if we all saw each other in this way, there would be no more war, hatred, cruelty, or greed, and we would all fall down to worship each other (Merton, 1968).

Whatever you might call the mystical experience, its nature is sublime. The Bhagavad Gita, arguably one of the most beautiful long poems ever written, speaks of such mystical awakening (Easwaran, 2007):

He is forever free who has broken
Out of the ego-cage of I and Mine
To be united with the Lord of Love.
This is the supreme state.

Those four lines speak again to the essence of the mystical: an illusion of isolation disappearing to find ourselves resting in an ocean of divine love that has been there all along. The mystic discovers the innermost core of the soul to be the divine center of the whole universe.

Heretics

Despite the incredible literature and insights that arise from mysticism, most institutional religions in the West would prefer not to talk about it. Part of the reason is that followers with their own relationship with God—no initiation, affirmation, or authority necessary—are not good for business. A larger reason the mystics are often marginalized is that the information they report back after their union with God is often contrary to the current relatively rigid, dogmatic beliefs. Mystics rarely toe the line. During their own time, mystics are often seen as blasphemous radicals, but are almost always vindicated through history, which goes to show how the truth they uncover is timeless.

One of the most striking examples is Julian of Norwich, a Christian mystic born in 1343. At the age of 30, she fell gravely ill and had what we would call several near-death experiences which contained visceral visions of Christ. In writings that would fit in perfectly with the modern feminist revolutions, one of the radical messages she received was that there is no such thing as sin at all. "But the truth is, I did not see any sin. I believe that sin has no substance, not a particle of being," Julian wrote (Starr, 2013). Sin is like a drop of rain on a hot furnace, it instantly evaporates when met with the fire of love. If there was no sin for the body, then it too was sacred, including its deepest desires and erotic pleasures. Rather than view the body as something to be distrusted, Julian saw the body as something to be celebrated.

If rejecting sin and loving the body wasn't heretical enough, Julian also came to the fundamental conclusion that Jesus Christ, the second part of the holy trinity, was undeniably, irrevocably *female*. Only a mother would do what Christ did, completely break herself open to the world and give birth to wisdom. It is the female body, after all, that bleeds and gives birth. Thus, God is power and masculine, Christ is wisdom and feminine; together they are encompassed by the Holy Spirit, all as one.

The mystics have no qualms about seeing God as feminine, or to see the Father in the Mother. Some write that we all exist right now in the womb of creation, and what we call death is actually birth in the afterlife. After all, the human species is propagated by a great act of making love. Life is brought into being by mothers. Is it so far-fetched to see God as a great feminine creative force that loves us into being?

Such revolutionary revelations of an embodied and free feminine reality in the fourteenth century were quickly hidden by the Church, and Julian of Norwich's writings would not be revealed until centuries later. When it was, people found that for Julian, "The fruit and the purpose of prayer is to be 'oned' with and like God in all things."

When that oneness is achieved, we find the same fundamental essence to God that we see in other mystical revelations: *love*. Ecstatic, joyful, oozing, undeniable, sweet, sweet love. Julian closed out her aptly titled, *Revelations of Divine Love*, with:

> *I desired many times to know our Lord's meaning. And fifteen years after and more, I was answered in spiritual understanding, and it was said: What, do you wish to know our Lord's meaning in this thing?*
> *Know it well, Love was his meaning.*
> *Who reveals it to you? Love.*
> *What did he reveal to you? Love.*
> *Why does he reveal it to you? For Love.*
> *Stay with this, and you will know more of the same, you will never know anything but love, without end.*

Simply put, love was at the heart of everything that Julian of Norwich learned. "Our life is all grounded and rooted in love, and without love we may not live," she wrote, plainly and clearly. A truth she found not by seeking the light, but by going into the darkness, even expressing, "our wounds are our glory" (Julian of Norwich, 2006).

Julian isn't the only one to find love as the Ultimate Reality. An ineffable feeling of love is the unifying theme behind almost all mystical experiences, across any religious background. The poet, Mark Nepo, wrote, "Enlightenment is the moment we realize that we are made of love" (Nepo, 2013). Mirabai, a Hindu Mystic, complains in a poem, "I am mad with love, and no one understands my plight." After all, why is the human experience so captivated with love? Why do we speak of love in our stories and sing of it in our songs? Because, *like knows like*. We are what we seek. Our own heart is calling us back home.

The Love and Suffering That Leads to God

The mystics' lives were almost always ones that embraced both love and suffering. Meister Eckhart, a Christian mystic born in 1260, wrote of the importance of darkness in finding the light, expressing that even in our deepest sorrows, the light is nearest to all of us. He spoke of the universality of the mystic experience, saying that while religious scholars might quarrel, all the mystics of the world speak the same language. Eckhart spoke of the stillness of God, the wisdom of *not knowing*, and the importance of a peaceful heart. Rather than an isolated personal God, he wrote of God as the Ultimate, that "God and I are one" and "Every creature is a word of God."

For writing such inspiring words of the heart such as "my eye and God's eye are one eye, one seeing, one knowing, one love," Meister Eckhart was tried for heresy, accused of being a pantheist, and died before his verdict was received.

Meister Eckhart and Julian of Norwich were not the first, nor would they be the last persecuted mystics. The controversial ninth-century Sufi Mystic, Mansour Al-Hallaj, would fall into trances and say he was in the presence of God. Criticized for teaching mysticism to the masses, Al-Hallaj would tell his followers that God was in his turban, his cloak, and could also be found inside their own souls. Acknowledging the ineffability of the mystical experience, his books included many line diagrams and symbols. For his continued heresy on unification with the divine, including his most famous line, "I am the Truth," he was tried, lashed until unconscious, decapitated, and set on fire.

Centuries later, the Italian Philosopher, Giordano Bruno, wrote of a similar union with God, not as a luxury, but a necessity. With words like "Unless you make yourself equal to God, you cannot understand God," he was put on trial for blasphemy and heresy, imprisoned for seven years, and finally executed by the Church.

St. John of the Cross, in the sixteenth century, might have had it the worst. Due to his work supporting the Counter-Reformation, St. John was jailed and tortured in a monastery. His punishment included severe isolation in a tiny cell, public lashings before the community, no change of clothes, and a diet of water, bread, and scraps of small fish.

Being imprisoned by the faith and tortured in front of his religious community made St. John question his relationship with the Church and its teachings. During that time, he was passed small pieces of paper by a friar who was guarding his cell. Only able to see by a small light passing through a hole in the adjoining room, St. John wrote some of the most beautiful poetry of all time.

Tying together many of the themes we talked about in the previous chapter, St. John wrote that suffering is necessary to reach spiritual maturity and finally attain union with God. His experience was the inspiration for this meaningful work, "Dark

Night of the Soul" which describes how hardship—the dark—is necessary to reach the light of the Creator.

"The endurance of darkness is the preparation for great light," he wrote. St. John wrote that an inner contemplation, "is nothing else but a secret, peaceful, and loving infusion of God" that "will set the soul on fire with the Spirit of love." He also coined the term "luminous darkness" to describe the intense joy that coexists with deep suffering. If only we could all see our darkness as luminous. The dark night destroys the ego and in its barren ashes, the love of our true nature is born.

It's All Love

St. John of the Cross' experience mirrors that of many inspirational people of the modern day. Viktor Frankl had a similar experience that he wrote about in *Man's Search for Meaning*, describing his own version of keeping one's heart open in hell. Frankl's hell was that of a Jewish concentration camp, where in the midst of suffering, he realized everything can be taken from us except our freedom to choose our attitude. In so doing he discovered the truth, "that Love is the ultimate and highest goal to which man can aspire… The salvation of man is through love and in love." The suffering and evil deeds of the world are redeemed by the spirit of love. It is our duty to redeem it.

There is something very magical happening here. No matter how bad this world gets, the beauty of humanity will always shine through the suffering. You can put the body in prison but not the spirit. The human spirit is *in* this world but not *of* this world. The body may suffer, perhaps even die, but the spirit endures. At the darkest depths of the human experience, still, there is grace.

Inside of us, we have the capacity to touch our suffering with love, and to keep touching and keep touching until there is only love. The heart is like the finger of King Midas, except instead of everything it touches turning to gold, it turns to love, and not by forcing it to change but by inviting it to transform from within, like a bud into a flower. The mystical experience breaks our hearts completely open, and an undying eternal love floods out, covering every square inch of the Earth and every particle in the universe with its love.

The heart is the point of contact between humanity and divinity and breaking it open is like a dam finally breaking for an eternity of love to flow through it.

Touching everything with love might seem like a tall order, but we do it all the time. We walk through beautiful woods and admire all the trees. We lie down at night in wonder at the stars. We sit around a fire and watch it dance before us. We lie on the beach and see the waves come in and out. What if we saw each other the same way? We don't look at one tree and think it is better than the other. We don't see crookedness as wrongness. We don't look at the night sky and try to improve it, instead, we appreciate it for what it is.

We can do the same to each other; see each other as that dancing pattern of matter and energy, part of and one with everything else. Rather than be so discriminative about individual differences, we see what Thomas Merton calls *the secret inner beauty* that lies at the heart of every human being and how everyone is walking around shining like the sun. We can see this world as God sees it: good. The mystic knows that the ground of being puts us deeply in touch with the four transcendentals: truth, unity, beauty, and goodness.

We can approach our own feelings the same way. One of the most important lessons I have learned from trauma-informed training is that there is no such thing as a "wrong" feeling. Once we find the courage to face it and hold it with love, any feeling becomes like a meteor that simply wishes to make its way across our sky. That's what we all are: bubbles blown from the breath of the divine, floating across this green earth before we pop and return to that divine space. The fundamental substance of everything—both our inner and outer—is love.

Gone, Gone, Gone Beyond

The mystical experience is not one of gaining anything, but a taking away of everything that is not our most fundamental essence. We expose ourselves to destruction to discover the indestructible. It is a nonconceptual experience that goes beyond thought, so we can only point to this moon with the imperfect metaphors of our fingers.

St. John of the Cross used the metaphor of a dark night to describe how transformation involves perpetually dying to anything less than love. Albert Camus described an invincible love, invincible smile, invincible calm, and invincible summer that is to be found in the midst of hate, tears, chaos, and winter.

This is something every human being must consider: is there anything to our existence that goes beyond your body, sense, mind-complex? Self-discovery is not finding ourselves, but removing everything else. You take away what is *sometimes* you to discover what is *always* you. This process of unlearning mirrors the Vedantic practice known as *neti, neti,* meaning "not this, not this." In the same way a sculptor will uncover the image from the raw marble, you discover your own essence by chipping away at your cultural and societal conditioning. As one popular joke goes, "Am I a Hindu? No, I am an undo."

We might think of spiritual practice as a series of things to do, like pray, meditate, and study scriptures, but mystical spirituality is one of *non-doing*. It is a matter of stopping, in order to access the inner being within us all. It involves diving deep into the realm of interiority. We look deeply and recognize that we are not our thoughts, our emotions, or passing sensations. By recognizing all that we are not, we are left with what we truly are, something that goes by many names. Consciousness, awareness, divinity, bliss, the True Self. An immortal diamond that is untouched by ups and downs, coming and going, hot and cold, birth and death.

We must become empty. We must empty ourselves so the divine can fill us up, just as the clouds disappear to reveal the light of the sky, just as a water-wheel empties out to be filled up again at the next turn. The more we pour ourselves out, the more the light of God is revealed in us. Hence in Matthew 12:25–26, "Anyone who wants to save their life must lose it. Anyone who loses their life will find it."

In Christian theology, emptying ourselves is known as *kenosis*, in Buddhism, *sunyata*. Fasting, silence, spiritual retreat, these are all kinds of emptying, just as we can let go of all conceptual thinking and rest in the larger mystery. Only by surrendering our false, small, conditioned self, will we find the True, Eternal, Unconditioned Self.

In Sufism, negating all that we are not is the practice known as *fana*, an Arabic word meaning "passing away" or "ceasing to exist." It involves a kind of spiritual death where one renunciates all human attributes, and instead meditates on and contemplates the attributes of the divine, until finally losing oneself in the love of God. The individual ego is literally "annihilated," or the sense of an isolated self disappears. In its place, there is nothing but a divine loving presence. Thus after *fana*, the dissolving of the self into the divine truth, comes *baqa*, the subsistence of the individual in God.

The thinking mind won't get us there, and most spiritual guides say that the less thinking you have, the more progress you will find. As the Sufi, Idries Shah put it, "Knowledge is not gained, it is there all the time. It is the 'veils' which have to be dissolved in the mind" (Shah, 2002). This is the *apophatic* path, also known as the *via negativa*, that finds what is real and true by negating all that is false. While we rarely take this path willingly, if we open to it, it will be a path of reward beyond measure.

What we are goes beyond words, so perhaps more appropriate than "I am awake" or "I am a son of God," all we can say is "I am *that*." The great mantra, *tat tvam asi*, translated as "That art thou" or "You are that," is one of the most sacred verses found in ancient Vedanta texts, and the title of Sri Nisargadatta Maharaj's wonderful work. In it, Maharaj writes, "In seeking, you discover that you are neither the body nor the mind, and the love of the self in you is for the self in all."

Love is *via positiva*, the path of everything, while suffering is *via negativa*, to the path of nothing, and our life flows between them all the way to heaven.

Mistaken Identity

The major finding of all mystical experiences is that we have it all wrong. *We are not who we think we are.* Our constant search for some deeper and larger meaning is like a wave looking for water. While you might think of yourself as a separate ego, an internal "I" caught up in an external world of "other," you are an expression of an unfolding eternal infinity. We do not need to learn the truth, *we are the truth*. There is no need to *be present* or practice *paying attention*. We are not a separate self that must focus and practice experiencing this present moment. *We are the present moment.*

Many people go through life feeling like they are only skimming the surface, sensing as if there is some deeper experience somewhere just out of reach. Discovering who we are is that deeper experience. We must let go of our small selves by finding a deeper security in a larger love. Right now, in normal waking consciousness that separates "I" and "other," you feel like you are responsible for moving your arm, but not the compressor in the fridge.

But in mystical awakening our consciousness slips in such a way that we become that player of all the parts, and all the parts play us. While you think of yourself as the "doer" in a universe where things "get done," the mystics say that it is all just happening, all part of a divine play. Life is not about us, we are about life itself. God is not a separate creator, nor even a personal God, but the actor of the world.

You might say that we are all Buddhas at a great costume ball, the divine in drag. Every person is just a mask, behind which is the divine shining forth. Even the word *person* comes from the Latin *persona*, meaning mask. Rumi complained, what use is it giving honey to bees or sparkling jewelry to the sun? Kabir laughed at the idea of going on a pilgrimage to find God, saying it was like a fish complaining they are thirsty.

In sharp contrast to the belief that all people are flawed and will never be good enough for a perfect God, the mystics see the perfection of it all. They understand why everything is exactly the way it is, and that everyone is playing a part in this cosmic drama.

The essence of the mystical awakening is *non-separation*. Your self, God's self, and the self of the Universe are the same. You might call it *advaita* or *nondual*, meaning *not-two*, or *not divided*. The dual mind finds knowledge in exclusion and *either/or* thinking; true wisdom is always *both/and*. It is as inclusive as it gets.

St. Francis

In true mystical fashion, twelfth-century Catholic friar, St. Francis of Assisi, refused to exclude anything and anyone from his teachings. Known as the "nature mystic," Francis described trees, worms, and lonely flowers by the side of the road as saints gazing up into the face of God. He was said to preach to the birds and the fish. In his aptly titled poem, *The Canticle of Creatures*, St. Francis expresses a deep love and respect for every aspect of the natural world. Rather than claim that God gave man dominion over the Earth's creatures, St. Francis' teachings were born out of a mystical consciousness of our interrelatedness. He embraced the inherent dignity and value of all of creation, in what is often referred to as a "creation of kinship."

In a startling act of humility and connection to the natural world, St. Francis chose for his "deathbed" the bed of the earth, asking to be stripped naked and laid on the barren earth in the last days of his life. St. Francis chose to die the same way we are all born: naked, embraced fully by a great divine and natural feminine force.

St. Francis taught the same principles we see in so many other mystics: our life is based on what we have given and how well we have loved. Rather than divide up the world into holy and unholy, happiness and suffering, sinners and saved, St. Francis included every aspect of life in his work. By kissing the leper, loving the poor, and wearing patches on clothes, he worked with the common person and presented himself as one too. St. Francis saw the power of *intentional* poverty, not as one of renunciation of material wealth, but as a deep act of love and liberation.

While decrying abject or involuntary poverty as evil, St. Francis saw voluntary poverty as a conscious protest against injustice and an act of solidarity with the poor and all those who suffer. Poverty is not the problem, it is the solution. We must live simply and equally with each other, and share all that we have until everyone has what they need. As the Peruvian philosopher and Catholic theologian, Gustavo Gutierrez, observed, voluntary poverty is a way of joining ranks with the exploited to help them with their cause on the path to liberation and justice. Only the wounded truly understand the wounded, and if you want to love someone, you have to join them.

Nonviolence

Mirroring the Bhagavad Gita, St. Francis prayed to be an instrument of peace, "Where there is hatred, let me sow love." St. Francis represents how the mystics are almost always pacifists, committed to justice, peace, and reconciliation. They are anti-war, pro-civil rights and supportive of social justice. This activism is born not out of some abstract belief in doing the right thing, but rooted in an understanding that we are all connected through divine love. Violence to others is the same as violence to ourselves. Nonviolence is not an attempt for unity, it is an expression of a unity already achieved. Peace is fundamentally human, while violence is dehumanizing.

Imagine yourself walking down a street. A child comes up to you and says, "Here, take my hand, I want to show you something." They then take you to prison and show you the innocent people languishing. They take you to the single mother living on the street, divorced after domestic abuse. They take you to the patient in hospice care. This is what mystical love does. It takes us by the hand directly to those who are suffering the most and asks us to tap into kindness, compassion, and understanding for all. It asks us to take down any barriers we have put up between ourselves and others that prevent us from entering into authentic and meaningful relationships. Gandhi taught that before every action we should "recall the face of the poorest and weakest man you have seen, and ask yourself if this step you contemplate is going to be of any use to him." Keeping our hearts open means seeing those that require the most compassion. Jesus too was quite clear his mission was to be with the poor, broken hearted, blind, and bruised (Luke 4:18).

The ultimate mystical reality is fundamentally free of all dualities, including birth and death, being and nonbeing. We don't get there by avoiding suffering, but by embracing all of life.

There is a story of a Zen teacher who taught, "To end suffering, you must touch the world of no-birth and no-death." His student then replied, "Where is the world of no-birth and no-death?" The master answered, "It is right here in the world of birth and death." In the messy, painful, traumatic, hidden heart of it all, there is freedom and there is love. Life is a series of possibilities to awaken, and the hardest times are the ones with the greatest potential.

Humanity should always be moving towards greater acceptance and inclusivity. The more we do, the happier our hearts will be. Our love wants to grow, it is meant to grow. Our heart calls for an endless widening and deepening to encompass all beings. Decades ago, many people were not included in the heart of humanity and were not even seen as people. Women, people of color, queer and trans folks, indigenous peoples, and other marginalized populations all had to fight and win to be considered just as human as those in the dominant culture. In certain places in the world, many of these groups are still fighting, still crying out to be seen and honored for who they are.

The journey of the human heart is always towards more togetherness, and there is much more to go. The mystic knows that everyone, and everything, belongs. They say *yes* to everything, encouraging us to say yes to more and more too.

Brothers and Sisters in Divine Love

Once the mystic sees the Ultimate Truth, a natural kindness, kinship, and love arises. We are all siblings of the infinite, brothers and sisters of infinite love, all bonded together in a fabric of love. The mystic doesn't become holy, they realize we are all holy. Holiness is wholeness. Everything is already forgiven. The gift of sainthood is to see the beauty of everyone else. Our bodies are temples, within lies the altar of the heart where the fire of love burns eternally.

There is a warm feeling of seeing the divine in everyone's eyes, and a desire to help them. When Mother Teresa was asked how she tended to so many needy people, she replied she pictured them as "Jesus in a distressing disguise." This is why the washing of another's feet is such a spiritual practice, we get to bow down to the divine in another and wash the Beloved's feet. To paraphrase Tagore, we are only dreaming we are strangers. Waking up, we become dear to each other.

The Jewish mystic and philosopher, Martin Buber, describes this process wonderfully in his seminal 1923 work, *I and Thou*. He says the normal human experience sees the world as "I" and "it." The *I-It* mode of relating treats others as mere objects to be used for our own end, as separate and distinct from ourselves. But if we want true fulfillment, if we want satisfaction in our relationships, we must shift to an *I-thou* mode that views others, God, and nature as unique subjects. The I-thou relationship is sacred, it is reciprocal, it is literally "being together." It is love (Buber, 2000).

Knowing the mystical perspective allows us to go back to the sacred texts and read them again in a new way. St. Teresa of Ávila's writings of the mystical experience, "you find God in yourself and yourself in God" are mirrored in John 14:17, "You already know: the spirit is with you and the spirit is in you." St. Teresa also wrote about the misconception that discovering our divine nature is like digging for a well. We may think it requires a lot of arduous work to only then find a bit of water to have to continually pull up, when in reality it is like finding the actual spring and letting it flow to you, through you, and from you.

This perspective gives a whole new meaning to "there is no way to me. I am the way."

Even the word "Catholic" comes from the Greek *katholikos*, meaning "universal," and religion comes from the Latin *religare*, meaning to bind. This points to the true meaning of religion as binding ourselves together in a universal love. Jesus saying, "follow me" really means, "follow me to die at the hands of love, until there is nothing left of us but love, which alone is eternal, real, vast, and true."

For a long time, I wondered the meaning behind the famous line from Matthew 18:20, "For where two or three gather in my name, there I am with them." That was until I learned more of the mystical experience, and it dawned on me that God works through us in our presence to each other and is known through that loving presence. Anytime two people meet, see each other, and are kind, supportive, and forgiving to each other, that implies the presence of the divine. God is manifesting through every human relationship. Being there for each other is divine work, divine work is relational work. Loving our neighbor is loving God.

Thomas Merton observed, "Life is this simple: we are living in a world that is absolutely transparent and the divine is shining through it all the time." What makes the world so opaque? "It is care," says Merton. Our love for another and our interest in their divine humanness. The presence of God is in between people.

From Unknowing Ourselves to Fully Knowing Love

The messages from mystics across time are the same. Love is God. We find God through love because God is Love. We must live a life of compassion and discover our underlying unity. Empty yourself fully to let the Divine fill you. The longing for God and longing for our True Self are the same. There is a False Self to let go of and a Real Self to discover. We must completely die by letting the sense of separate self-dissolve away to become one with the Ultimate Reality. We can, at any point, suddenly experience what the ancient Roman philosopher, Boethius, calls "the completely simultaneous and perfect possession of unlimited life at a single moment." The times of intense suffering in our lives, where everything is falling apart, are opportunities to finally let go of our false selves and pretenses. Death will do it eventually, so we might as well get ahead of the game.

Almost all spiritual paths say there is as much *unlearning* to be done as there is learning. When our ego becomes so inflated, and we think we know it all, we have to be taken down a few notches, often unwillingly. True learning begins with humility; it's almost impossible to teach someone who has no desire to learn.

There is a well-known Zen story of the professor who goes to the master to learn the nature of Zen. The master begins pouring a cup of tea but doesn't stop pouring, even when the tea is full and overflowing. When the professor protests, the master replies, "Your mind is the cup, overflowing with knowledge. You must empty it first before I can teach you anything." It is that humility, that ego death, that puts us on the path towards the mystery of the divine. As Henry Adams put it, "For after all man knows mighty little, and may someday learn enough of his own ignorance to fall down again and pray." To know nothing is everything.

A text that exemplifies these teachings in a poetic and beautiful way is the fourteenth-century Mystical Christian text known as *The Cloud of Unknowing*. The text tells us not to find God in the light, but to go right into the darkness, and to "wait in this darkness as long as is necessary." Like St. John of the Cross's dark night or Julian of Norwich's near-death experiences, the text describes how the darkness is where we find our true longing for the light. The dark represents suffering, but also ignorance, because we don't know who we are and the nature of the divine. Hence the name of the text, we can't *know* who we are until we *unknow* who we think we are.

An important component of any spirituality is a recognition that there is more to the world than what we can know. Just as water cannot rise above its own level, the mind cannot rise above the level of thought, making it not of much use on the spiritual path. Genuine faith embraces the full mystery of life, which must include both halves: love and suffering, birth and death, certainty and doubt. This is true wisdom, both knowing and unknowing. While genuine spirituality embraces mystery, too many people of faith are overly rigid in their certainty.

What is most clear from *The Cloud of Unknowing* is that the divine cannot be found through rational discourse. Rather than the mind, the text says that God can only be found with the heart, in perhaps one of the best rallying calls for love:

> *I encourage you—bow eagerly to love. Follow its humble stirrings in your heart. Let it guide you in this life and it will bring you safely to eternal bliss in the next. Love is the essence of all goodness. Without it, no kind work is ever begun or finished. Simply put, love is a goodwill in harmony with God.*

Since God is love, the more loving we are the more aligned we are with God. *The Cloud of Unknowing* is written across 75 chapters, which read more like letters to a young student than a scholarly work. We are that young student, and we can take the author's advice, remembering that any genuine spiritual path begins with love. We must make that infamous 18-inch journey from the head to the heart, where we will find the spark of the divine, and ourselves not as separate, but as the ultimate indivisible whole (*The Cloud of Unknowing*, 2018).

Treating Others Well

What would life be like if we recognized the mystical reality and started treating each other as manifestations of the divine?

There is a story about a wise Rabbi, told by Megan McKenna in *Mary: Shadow of Grace* (McKenna, 2007). One day, his friend, an abbot, came to him and complained that his community of monks at the monastery was dwindling, and fewer and fewer people were attending mass. Weeping, the Abbot asked the wise Rabbi what he should do.

The Rabbi, comforting him, said "There is nothing I can do to help you. But I will tell you one thing, we have long known in the Jewish community that the Messiah is one of you." The Abbot was surprised, "What? the Messiah is one of us? How can this be?" But the Rabbi insisted that it was so, and the Abbot went back to his monastery wondering who it could be. Once back in the monastery, he would pass by a monk and wonder if he was the one. Sitting in the chapel, praying, he would hear a voice and look intently at a face and wonder, is he the one? The Abbot had always been kind but now began to treat all of his brothers with profound kindness and awe, ever deeper respect, even reverence. Soon everyone noticed. One of the other brothers came to him and asked him what had happened to him.

After some coaxing, the Abbot told him what the Rabbi had said. Soon the other monk was looking at his brothers differently, with a deeper respect and wondering. Word spread quickly: the Messiah is one of us. The monastery was suddenly full of life, worship, love, and grace. The prayer life was rich, passionate, and devoted, and services were alive and vibrant. Soon the surrounding villagers came to the services, listening and watching intently, and many joined the community of monks. The monastery grew and expanded into house after house, and the monks grew in wisdom and grace before each other and in the eyes of God.

Factual or not, it is an incredible story. We all know beauty is in the eye of the beholder but fail to recognize how the beholder's eye can be a mirror, so the person reflected sees their own beauty. How wonderful it is to find someone who reflects back our light and what an incredible opportunity it is for us to become someone's mirror.

Love, Love, All Love

You might call our natural essence divine, awakened, or simply "that." Any word is limited and we are limitless, so no word could describe our true essence. But if I had to choose just one word that best encapsulates who we are, it is *love*. Sweet, sweet love. For the mystics do not speak of loving, falling in love, or being in love, but simply *being love itself*. Thomas Merton (Merton, 1979) put it so wonderfully I can only repeat his words here:

> The true Christian rebirth is a renewed transformation, a 'passover' in which man is progressively liberated from selfishness and not only grows in love but in some sense 'becomes love'. The perfection of the new birth is reached where there is no more selfishness, there is only love ... there is no more ego-self ... only the Spirit acts in pure love.

Our true essence is love; our spiritual path is one of walking toward the light of unconditional love to discover it has been here all along. We don't need to get, receive, or find love; we are love.

Love is awakened in the midst of suffering and is what carries us through times of immense suffering. Suffering forces what is false within us to die so the realness of love within us can be realized.

Through torture and isolation, St. John of the Cross knew that "In the evening of life, we will be judged on love alone." While St. John of the Cross managed to escape from prison after 8 months, Nelson Mandela was jailed for 27 years in prison for opposing South Africa's apartheid system. He never stopped his efforts to achieve equality for all people, because he knew that while hate is taught, "love comes naturally to the human heart."

Life can often feel like a burden, but love is what lifts it. Love gives us the capacity to endure the unendurable. Toss a rock into water and it will sink. Fill your pockets full of rocks and you would sink too. But you can sit in a boat with many rocks. Love is that boat, allowing us to carry the burdens of suffering to the other shore.

The Loved and Beloved

Mystical writings are so applicable to the modern person today because their language mirrors that of our most intimate relationships, of the connection between loved and beloved. I had a friend who would carry around a book of poems by Hafez and read it to people at parties. Kabir himself referred to his poems as one soul meeting another. One of my most precious memories was during yoga training, where I found myself lying in a pile of people reading Rumi to each other. Lines like, "Lovers don't finally meet somewhere, they're in each other all along" and "Your love lifts my soul from the body to the sky" fit just as well in a romance novel as they might in an ancient mystical text. The natural language describing the union of loved and beloved, while typically referencing God, is so easy to extrapolate to our own, intimate relationships.

There are some scholars who think it is disingenuous to connect a mystic's love of God with a regular person's romantic relationship. Hence the humorous line, "I think Rumi also wrote, 'My poems are about God, not your boyfriend'." But this perspective forgets that the love we have for each other is divine love. There is a point when our love gets so deep it becomes a spiritual experience. There is also the moment when our spirituality becomes so expansive it turns into a transformative love for one person. After all, where does this desire for love and union come from? It was already planted inside of us by the divine. When we finally look up to the sky, God is winking back, "Yep, it was me all along." Divine love and personal love are mirrors, and one will often lead to the other.

Our love for one another is an echo of God's love for us. We seek intimacy with another the same way God seeks intimacy with our souls. Just as St. Augustine says that the divine is "more intimate to the soul than the soul itself," we seek to become closer to our lovers than they are to themselves. The mystics speak of a *naked love* and a *naked now*, that simultaneously refers to the bare intimacy of two lovers in bed and the vulnerability of emotional connection. Even Buddhist practice encourages cultivating a *bare attention* that brings us close to this moment without the separation of our judgmental mind.

Everything in our most intimate moments—intimacy, specialness, ecstasy, wishing, mystery, being pulled close—are the exact qualities we associate with the mystical. In romantic partnership and our relationship with the divine, we seek an entity that knows us and loves us more than we know and love ourselves.

Out of all the metaphors to describe the mystical experience—a frog finally getting out of a deep well, a sculptor taking away all that is not to reveal all that is, a droplet of water finally becoming one with the ocean—the most common one of all is the meeting of two eternal lovers. If you think Rumi was romantic, see the sultry words of Mechthild of Magdeburg, a female Christian Mystic born in 1207:

> *Then the bride of all delights goes to the Fairest of lovers in the secret chamber of the invisible Godhead. There she finds the bed and the abode of love prepared by God in a manner beyond what is human.* (Jensen, 2013, p.59)

And the erotic dialogue that follows would fit into any romance novel and probably be removed from school shelves. Like many other mystics, Mechthild faced fierce opposition and her writings were called to be burned. But Mechthild continued to write even after becoming blind and having to dictate her mystical visions of God. Such "nuptial mystics" talk of falling madly in love with God, being married to God, of a boundless desire fulfilled in limitless lavishness. An infinite wellspring of love inside the heart reaches towards an infinite existence with an infinite love that has always been falling in love with them. God is love, the verb, not the noun.

Nature teaches us that nothing survives without a continuous influx of nutrients. Plants need the sun to shine and water to flow. For human beings, love is what sustains us. If our closest relationships are to survive, we must also continuously nurture it with our kindness and love. And it is God's continuous influx of love that sustains the whole universe. Many people see God as the Creator, what would it look like to see God as Lover? What if we all saw scripture as a love letter, and our own poetry as a reply?

The mystics know: *love is always loving us.*

The Ecstasy of Falling in Love

We must understand; we are already infinitely understood, and the infinite light of this understanding will carry us through any darkness. The heart is designed for infinite love and the mind for infinite truth.

But the mystical experience doesn't just stop at the love and union with another, there is joy to be found too. Anyone who has fallen in love with another human being and comes to learn that that person is also falling in love with them, knows that it is an ecstatic experience. There is joy and wonder in such romantic meetings. Hafez speaks to this in his poem, "For no reason / I turn into a leaf / That is carried so high / I kiss the sun's mouth / and dissolve." Which could be the experience of the mystical as much as the writings of someone who has fallen madly in love. Hafez writes like a young lover speaking to their beloved; you can almost imagine Romeo telling Juliet, "I'm happy even before I have a reason / I'm full of Light even before the sky / Can greet the sun or the moon."

Kabir often speaks to this ecstatic joy of the mystical. Open any page and you will find many lines that talk of love and joy, like "I hear bells ringing that no one has shaken, inside 'love' there is more joy than we know of" and "How lucky Kabir is, surrounded by all this joy he sings inside his own little boat."

The ecstasy of falling in love is almost universal. Once it touches us, we too sing a song in our own little boat, skipping home from that magical date with that magical someone.

Why is true love full of so much joy? Because our isolated sense of separateness finally dissolves, and we teach the real for the first time. The British writer, Iris Murdoch, wrote that "love is the extremely difficult realization that something other than oneself is real" (Murdoch, 1959). The human experience is one of separation; we feel ourselves to be a separate "I" almost caught up in a bag of skin in a lonely and indifferent universe. Everything, to us, is subjective. That is until we finally and fully understand in the meeting of another there is another subject, another light just as beautiful and tragic as our own.

We all know the experience of falling in love and realizing that something other than oneself is real. It is this self-forgetfulness that is so key to understanding love, and why no amount of ego or willpower will get us there. Falling in love is when we finally stop putting ourselves at the center of our own universe and instead think about someone else, what they want, and what their inner world is like. We become obsessive about them and have butterflies in our stomachs just thinking about them. Like the mystical experience, it just happens to us, and we are asked to surrender to it. To fall into love, trusting it will catch us.

This inner joy, this inner bliss, is in fact our true nature, the nature of the universe. Iris Murdoch went on to say that love "is the discovery of reality." Our sense of separateness is an illusion, it is not reality, and when we pierce the illusion and experience reality as it is, we feel a sense of love and joy. When we gaze into a person's eyes, they become real. Looking deeply into a flower, it becomes real too.

To a mystic, falling in love with one person is a great introduction to the love that is part of everybody, and the realness that there is to everybody. It's like a sample of heaven.

Stare at the sun and we would go blind. Lay under a tree, however, and we can watch the rays pass through the leaves all day. We are those trees, acting as filters for the divine light, so we may gaze at each other and see the light shining through everything.

The Cessation of Longing

A key piece to the mystical experience is the cessation of longing. We drop out of ego-based desires that separate "I" and "other" and seek to turn everything into "me" and "mine." In our self-forgetfulness, nothing is missing, everything is exactly as it is supposed to be. The mind that finds fault has ceased and now not a single atom in the universe is out of place. The mystical experience penetrates the truth of our desires to find that happiness is not found through material fulfillment, but rather by being free of all desire. Spiritual communities are abound with stories describing an enlightened person as being totally unperturbed by the changing vagaries of life, like the monk who faced the General from the last chapter.

Mystical bliss is so transcendent and glorious that most spiritual paths begin by dissuading spiritual practitioners from looking for happiness in anything material since the lasting spiritual joy we all have far surpasses any temporary experience of pleasure. Once you experience what is real, the unreal becomes a mere distraction. The Katha Upanishad says only the ignorant choose passing pleasure, while the wise rest in perennial joy. The Mahabharata says we finally become free when a handful of corn is the same as millions of carts of grain, and a small hut is no different than a palatial mansion.

Although these texts were written thousands of years ago, not much has changed. Most of us desire a big house, a new car, and the fastest, slimmest, lightest phone. Such desires bind us to the material world and simply create more suffering. True freedom is being just as happy in a small shack as in a huge mansion, just as content with a small bowl of food as a large, luxurious buffet.

Freedom is not having everything we want at our fingertips; it is a lifting of the burden of endless craving. Freedom is not doing whatever we want whenever we want, freedom is liberation from all wants. In yoga philosophy, it is said true yoga is the state of needing nothing. In Taoism, Lao Tzu tells us that "the truth waits for eyes unclouded by longing." Only by letting go of all desire—including the desire to get rid of desire—will we ever know the truth and ever be at peace. As one teacher said to me, *when the mirror of understanding is cleansed of the dust of desire, the light of pure consciousness is reflected in it.*

The fundamental lesson we might apply to our own lives here is another equation:

Happiness = Have / Wants

While we try to maximize happiness by increasing our haves, this method is not very effective. Accumulating money and material things takes time and effort, while their impermanence means those things will always be slipping through our fingers like sand. Meanwhile, as anyone who has taken Calculus will tell you, when you reduce the lower half of a fraction towards zero, the value approaches infinity. Reducing your wants tenfold will increase your happiness tenfold. Desireless-ness is true heaven.

One interesting symptom of depression is known as *anhedonia*, which is the inability to experience pleasures in ordinary things. The first sign of depression is usually when a person doesn't enjoy all the activities they once did: watching sports, doing a hobby, eating delicious food. This can be a painful and debilitating symptom, and if you are experiencing it, I encourage you to seek therapy.

However, so many of the sacred texts say that we should consider ourselves lucky if our mind is fed up with worldly objects, because the truth of love and light is not to be found outside of us. A *fedupedness* with the world represents the state of suffering that puts us on the path to God. All suffering, even the abyss of depression, is divine, and can be transformed. Through such dark nights, where material things no longer bring us the pleasure they once did, we can renounce the materialistic path and turn to something deeper, something larger, something more real, to carry us through to the joy of lasting love. Pleasure comes from the outside, but joy from the inside. Know thyself first, and all else will follow.

Never Stop Loving

There is a bit of chicken and egg going on here. Which came first? Do we experience union with the divine and then an overflowing of love? Or do we follow a river of love that guides us to the divine? While the former might be possible, the latter is much more practical. There is an undeniable love and joy in mystical union, but it is not something we can force to happen. We can do things that might increase its likelihood, but it is not up to us.

The final teaching that you will find in the mystics is that we must cultivate our potential to love as much as possible. Hafez encourages lovers to ask each other, "How can I be more loving to you; How can I be more kind?" In Mark 12:30 we are told to "Love with your whole heart, your whole soul, your whole mind, and your whole strength." We also have the reassurance of Thomas Merton, "If you have love, you will do all things well."

Religious or not, spiritual or not, the inspirational writings of the mystics inform our own lives. Kahlil Gibran, while not a mystic himself, was heavily influenced by the mysticism of the Sufis. One of his most moving poems, *On Love*, speaks to the reality of a love that is both beautiful and agonizing, both expansive and reductive. "When love beckons to you, follow him, Though his ways are hard and steep," writes Gibran. Although love asks for nothing and takes nothing, and love alone is sufficient, if you wish to love, Gibran writes that you must be ready:

> *To know the pain of too much tenderness.*
> *To be wounded by your own understanding of love;*
> *And to bleed willingly and joyfully.*
> *To wake at dawn with a winged heart and give thanks for another day of loving;*
> *To rest at the noon hour and meditate love's ecstasy;*
> *To return home at eventide with gratitude;*
> *And then to sleep with a prayer for the beloved in your heart and a song of praise upon your lips.*

Even in the ecstasy of love, there is still sorrow. Sorrow that the love will not last, sorrow at how banal life had been before the ultimate love parted the skies over the soul. So we keep our hearts open in hell, bleeding, willingly and joyfully.

It's All Here

There's a story of a young woman who recently got married. As she was cleaning up the house, she couldn't find her diamond wedding ring. Panicking, she looked everywhere she could. Finally, she got onto her knees and prayed. "God, please help me. I know I don't attend church very often, but if you help me find this ring, I swear I'll be much better." At that moment a breeze came in through the window, pushed aside the curtain, and a ray of light shone right behind the couch to highlight exactly where the ring lay. The woman, seeing her ring again, exclaimed, "Never mind God! I found it."

These are the lessons from the mystics: we don't see the all-pervading presence of God, we don't recognize the divine within, we don't experience every moment as precious, and we don't see life as sacred. Suffering can be a gateway, and perhaps the most powerful one of all. We don't realize that the world and time are a dance of divinity, moving to the music of love. And yet, here it is, right here in front of us. Clear as day, no doubts about it. The mystics with such authority, with such confidence on the subject because they themselves have experienced it. If only we could open our hearts and minds and tap into the soul. May we all be inspired by their work and words, as we tune into the mystical love that is always available, everywhere. May we take that love with us like a flag as we storm the gates of hell.

Chapter 5

The Suffering of Humanity

What is to give light must endure burning. Viktor Frankl

If you haven't seen the original 1999 sci-fi masterpiece *The Matrix*, I might ask what rock you are living under. If you do not want any spoilers for the movie, you can go ahead and skip these next two paragraphs.

While the movie seems to be set in the present moment, the movie is actually set 200 years in the future. Machines have taken over the world, and they have put the entire human race into a simulation that resembles what life was like in the year 1999, "the cusp of civilization" according to the machines. There is a moment where the villain, Agent Smith, is explaining to one of the protagonists, Morpheus, why the simulation was designed to mimic humanity at the turn of the millennium.

In one of the most iconic dialogues written for film, Agent Smith, essentially representing an advanced Artificial Intelligence, says that the current Matrix was not the first iteration. Originally The Matrix was designed to be a perfect human world, where no one suffered and everyone was happy. However, according to Smith, no humans accepted the program, because "human beings define their reality through suffering and misery" (Wachowski & Wachowski, 1999).

Agent Smith's determination that human beings could never stand to live in a utopia is an interesting one. Two centuries earlier, Schopenhauer came to the same conclusion. He predicted that if humanity was transported to a perfect world where every desire was satisfied and "turkeys fly around ready-roasted," we would either die of boredom, kill ourselves, or kill each other. We would inflict more suffering on each other than the world already inflicts on us (Schopenhauer, 2004).

Are we human despite our suffering, or because of it? If life was perfect, would we reject it, perhaps create suffering to fill what was lacking? Last chapter we explored the idea that divine ecstatic love is part of human nature. Is suffering part of human nature too? Is it part of human nature to bring suffering into every situation?

What Would You Do?

In my own workshops on compassion, I like to offer a thought experiment. Let's say you had a button where, if you pressed it, you would never suffer again for the rest of your life. You would never experience pain ever again. Would you press it?

Almost everyone says no. There is an intuitive sense that pain and suffering play an important role in our lives. First of all, pain warns us of danger. Without that warning signal, we often can't discern what is harmful to us. A wound left untended can easily get infected; would we rush to attend to it if there wasn't any discomfort? Would we give our broken ankle time to heal if we could walk freely on it? There is an extremely rare mutation where a person's pain receptors don't reach the brain. Jo Cameron, known as the "woman who doesn't feel pain," has this condition. She says she often burns herself on the stove and only realizes her skin is burning when she smells singed flesh. While people associate leprosy with a loss of one's limbs, the disease itself does not cause the loss. Rather, those with leprosy experience damage to the nerve endings that makes the fingers and toes go numb. They then don't feel or experience injury, and small burns and cuts often go unnoticed until an infection spreads.

When we do get in touch with pain, we realize there are two main types. The first, what I like to call *good pain*, asks us to lean into it. Good pain is when we get a deep tissue massage that "hurts so good," or bring some whips and chains into the bedroom. The second, *bad pain*, is a warning sign that we should stop what we are doing. Bad pain is when we move our neck in an awkward way and feel shooting pain. Bad pain tells us that something is wrong and we should do something to make it right.

While no one likes bad pain, it is a very incredible motivator. We might have a hard time getting out of a hammock on a beautiful sunny day, but when we feel a bee sting our back, we immediately get up and start running. When we accidentally put our hand on a hot stove or begin to step on a nail, our pain receptors send an instant message to immediately stop whatever it is that we are doing and get out of harm's way. Pain says we are in contact with something that is detrimental to our well-being. Negative feelings aren't that different. Because we all need love, connection, and belonging, our mind makes loneliness feel painful to tell us that disconnection is bad for our health too.

The same applies to those so-called "bad" emotions like sadness or anger. Few would choose to eradicate a feeling like anger. When I ask why, participants often give answers about how anger can be useful. Some say anger tells us when our boundary has been crossed, others cite that anger gives us the energy to protect ourselves or others. Some participants say that anger can be a teacher about what we value. It is normal to get angry at injustice or environmental destruction because we value equality and the world, and this anger can be an important motivator to right certain wrongs.

Rather than look at any emotion, label it as negative, and try to eradicate it from our life, we can see it as a teacher too. The emotion of grief is a testament to our love, the emotion of frustration encourages us to look for a better way. Even feeling discomfort after being in the same reading position for a while will force us to turn over to the other side and bring balance to the body.

We can consider another thought experiment. Let's say you were God and were in total control of the entire universe. What would you do? Many of us would have everything we desire at the snap of a finger and spend time fulfilling all of our fantasies. We would participate in a wild excess of sensual delights and journey to the far edges of the universe. But then what? After we have tasted, touched, and seen everything there is to experience, done everything there is to do, then what? After a certain amount of time when the entire universe was under our complete control, we would get bored. If we already know everything that is going to happen, why even bother living it? Then we would want to release a certain amount of control and ask to be surprised.

At that moment we would find ourselves awakened in our current body, right here in this moment, reading this book, not knowing how it, or life, is going to end.

Risk Means Excitement

Humans oscillate between suffering and boredom. Suffering is not having what we want, boredom is actually getting it. Our pleasure at getting something lasts for a brief moment before we find ourselves disinterested with it, like a dog catching his tail and not knowing what to do with it. It doesn't take long before that shiny new thing becomes yesterday's news. Just as the Buddha recognized that nothing lasts, neither does our experience of exciting and pleasurable things. Our mind is an incredible habituation machine, always seeking homeostasis. It doesn't matter that most people in the industrialized world live more lavish and decadent lifestyles than the richest kings did a few centuries ago, we are all stuck on what psychologists call the *hedonic treadmill*: exhausting ourselves running after pleasures but ultimately going nowhere.

Even if we artificially flood the brain with feel-good chemicals from ingesting certain drugs, our brain will respond by closing off the receptors for those feel-good neurotransmitters until it reaches the same baseline again. We call this *building a tolerance*, which applies just as much to cars, money, or fancy new outfits as much as it does to cocaine. Even dictators with more power and wealth than anyone else in human history still aren't satisfied and seek to increase their domain.

Fortunately, as any parent will tell their screaming child begging for more ice cream, there is more to life than just getting what we want. Human beings need friction, surprise, uncertainty, and challenge. We know the road less traveled makes all the difference. We need something to push back against us from time to time. We need to be knocked down to find the courage to get up. We need resistance, it excites us and we thrive on it. Mystery, unknown, and uncertainty, are all erotic and highly seductive.

After surveying hundreds of people about their sex lives, the sex therapist, Jack Morin (Morin, 2012) found the erotic equation to be:

Attraction + Obstacles = Excitement

The more obstacles there are in the way of what we are attracted to, the more excited we get. We can even "hack" this equation by intentionally putting obstacles in the way of our attraction to build excitement. Often, intentionally restricting pleasure in the moment makes the future payoff better. Rather than just show up naked in front of our partner, we do a little strip tease. Practitioners of neo-tantra or sacred sexuality will encourage the importance of restraining and building up to orgasm. What is sometimes called "stacking," those engaging in this practice will get very close to orgasms only to back away at the last minute. Eventually, the final orgasm feels like five or six all at once.

Often *not* getting what we want is more exciting than actually getting it; few people feel happy when the thrill of the hunt is over. Hence the joke: The masochist requests of the sadist, "Please torture me," and the sadist teases, "*No.*" But the erotic equation doesn't just include being blindfolded and not knowing what sensual delight is going to happen next. When we look at a mountain and think about how difficult it is to climb, we get excited. When we walk into the arena and see our competition, we can't wait to demonstrate our skills and training. Wanting, longing, desire, these are all extremely motivating.

Desires and obstacles in the way of those desires take us on an adventure, a voyage of discovery. In finding out what is possible, we risk going up against what is not possible. In looking at how the current struggle will provide us with a future payoff, we see how almost all future payoffs require suffering in order to get there. This is due to a particularity of the human experience: suffering is a source of growth.

Suffering Is a Source of Growth

As we have mentioned in previous chapters, if you want to gain flexibility in a muscle, you have to stretch it. You have to put an external force that will create an internal stress on the system, and the system will respond to build resilience against that force. This applies not just to our physical bodies but to our mental and emotional lives as well. Human beings grow through struggle.

If we truly want to grow, we have to face our shadows. We have to go into the places that scare us. That is the only way to heal. The poet and sexual assault survivor, Vironika Tugaleva, put it this way, "Emotional pain cannot kill you, but running from it can. Allow. Embrace. Let yourself feel. Let yourself heal." Healing involves welcoming in all the unseen, unwelcome, unheard, parts of ourselves with the open hands of the heart.

Many of our life goals are hard won. People that are dedicated to growth are dedicated to struggle. Commitment to growth requires a commitment to suffering. This shift in consciousness no longer looks at the world through the lens of good and bad, but rather sees everything as grist for the mill. Because growth requires struggle, our capacity to grow is directly tied to our capacity to meet suffering. This especially applies to growing our compassion. Our ability to be compassionate, both to others and ourselves, is directly tied to our ability to be with suffering. To be compassionate we have to be able to sit with the suffering; to be present with the darkness of others we must know our own. If you don't understand suffering, you won't understand compassion.

We have to face suffering not just on a personal level, but a global one as well. Humanity is facing unprecedented challenges right now. A warming planet. Political divides. Attacks on women's rights. Late-stage capitalism. But it would be naive to think that any problems we are currently facing are greater than any of those in generations before us. Humanity's place in the universe has always been one of struggle, both against each other through endless wars and against a universe that seems largely indifferent to our survival.

If we are to solve any problem, we have to have the courage to face it, especially when it comes to injustice. The biggest impediments to justice in the world are those that claim nothing needs to be done. Those who deny injustice exacerbate suffering and make the situation worse. Acknowledging and being with suffering is not a path of complacency. Rather, once we accept suffering, it becomes a catalyst for action. For peace. For justice. For protecting the most marginalized people in the world. James Baldwin said, "If I love you, I have to make you conscious of the things that you do not see," which applies just as much to the evils of societal oppression as it does to being a mirror that reflects back the beauty of another person (Baldwin, 1985).

One of the most fundamental human experiences is to be given a set of constraints with full freedom to explore the possibilities within them. Like a potted plant, we need to find the outer barriers that support and encourage our upward growth. The painter is limited by the size of their canvas, the musician by the notes on the scale, and the sculptor by the size and material of their marble. Any sport is going to have a strict set of rules, but beyond that, you can do whatever it takes to win. Constricted situations often fuel the most growth and motivation. Even knowing we only have one life to live forces us to get off our butts and try to make it all mean something. While kids will push and test their parents' limits and boundaries, fundamentally they want and thrive on them. That's how they learn.

We don't want everything to go exactly the way we want it, where is the fun in that? We all need a bit of suffering and frustration to put us back to the drawing board or the workout room, see what went wrong, and correct ourselves to succeed. Of course, seeing others go through immense suffering and coming out the other side also gives us hope that we can do the same. Helen Keller noted her source of optimism was the observation, "Although the world is full of suffering, it is full also of the overcoming of it" (Keller, 1903).

The Song of Suffering

Suffering shapes us. There are many sayings that express the need to bump up against things from time to time, like:

> *Rejection is a chisel for perfection.*
> *Smooth seas don't make good sailors.*
> *There is no failure, only feedback.*
> *The master has failed more times than the novice has even tried.*

These nuggets of wisdom express how strength and courage are not formed in isolation, but forged through intense battles, vulnerability, and often, major failures. In response to a question about his missteps, Thomas Edison once famously said, "I have not failed 10,000 times—I've successfully found 10,000 ways that will not work" (Hendry, 2013). There is no such thing as failure if we learn something from the experience. This is the way life is. A lot of the time we don't know we have a boundary until it has been crossed. We often have to experience things we don't want on the path of discovering what we do want. Many "bad" relationships are there to teach us what we don't want.

We need to hear the word "No" not just once, but often, to force us to either muster up more strength and motivation or change our way of doing things. When one businessman was asked what the secret to his success was, he replied "Two words: right decisions." When asked what led him to the right decisions he replied, "One word: experience." When asked what leads to experience, he replied, "Two words: wrong decisions." It might be easy to admire a talented actor, famous musician, or successful businessman and think they must have it all figured out, but when we look into their life path, we will see numerous failures that put them on the path to success. Mistakes are rarely a problem; they are almost always learning opportunities. We learn and grow more by doing things wrong than by doing things right.

Earlier we talked about the very important teaching that "every human being wants to be happy and no one wants to suffer." This idea provides the foundation for secular ethics and one that can be a guiding force in our own lives. We all have a moral imperative to not intentionally cause or increase suffering in the world. Where there is suffering, a meaningful life is committed to lessening its burden. This teaching helps us come to an understanding of our common humanity—we all want to be happy and not be in pain.

However, one big caveat is that human beings consensually and willingly enter into painful situations all the time.

Sometimes we want to, sometimes we have to. Rather than shy away from pain and suffering, we often choose to head straight into it, armed and ready. There is intense power in being able to be with and sit with suffering, and there are numerous reasons why this is the case. The more we get in touch with these reasons, the more we learn about suffering, the more we will learn about ourselves.

The Future Reward Surpasses the Current Struggle

One of the biggest reasons we embrace suffering is because there is a perceived future reward that surpasses the current struggle. If we do not meet a little suffering now, we will meet a lot of suffering in the future. Many problems are like a leaking roof in our house. Fixing it now will require a bit of effort and money, but if we ignore it, repairing it in the future will be much more expensive and extensive. We must remove the cancer before it spreads, no matter how painful the process. Jung pointed out that all human life requires a certain amount of necessary suffering, and if we try to avoid the necessary suffering, we will encounter 10 times more in the long run.

During the writing of this book, a famous celebrity died of an overdose a week after his father died, because he was using drugs to cope. Whatever we use to avoid necessary suffering will simply add to it in the long run, especially the coping strategies we use to not feel what we are meant to feel. "There is no way around the Cross" wrote the fourteenth-century Catholic priest, Thomas à Kempis.

Overcoming the current challenge will often make all future challenges much easier. *No pain, no gain.* From elite athletes pushing their bodies to the brink of exhaustion to the average person going to the dentist for that long-awaited root canal, suffering is a part of life and often a requirement for us to get what we truly want. Growth happens at the end of our comfort zone, and it also widens our comfort zone. Lifting a 50-pound weight will make all future weights seem lighter. We labor to enjoy the fruits of our labor. Any dancer who has gone through countless hours of rehearsal will tell you it takes a lot of effort to appear effortless.

There are many times when feeling worse is the first step to feeling better, whether it's taking a bad-tasting medicine, detoxing from drugs or alcohol, or those first few therapy sessions. Sometimes we even need to take a little poison, in the form of a purgative or laxative, in order to get all the other poisons out. The Chinese have a saying, "bitterness is good fortune," which applies just as much to the healing properties of bitter medicinal plants as it does to hardship being a good thing, and how a little pain can end much greater pain.

We have to be able to cross that large peak of a mountain before we can coast down the other side. Whether we own a business that struggles for years before finally becoming profitable or are dealing with a child through their "terrible twos," much of the human experience involves months or years of struggle to finally be where we want to be. Fortunately, many battles, once fought, will never have to be fought again for the rest of our lives. Like digging a well, once you hit the water, you're done, there is no more digging to be done.

Many birds must make a tremendous effort to begin flying but once they're up in the sky, they can travel thousands of miles by simply spreading their wings and letting the wind take them. In spiritual practice, much work is needed to attain inner peace, but once that inner peace is attained, one becomes anchored in it. Peace then becomes the means.

In the Bhagavad Gita, Krishna explains to Arjuna that what seems like poison at first often becomes nectar later, while what seems like nectar now often turns into poison later. We can see how easily nectar turns to poison with immediate sensual pleasures, as smoking gives us lung cancer, sugar rots our teeth, or a poor diet gives us heart disease. Nectar also easily turns into poison when we get overly attached to behaviors that hurt us in the long run.

Psychologists define *maladaptive patterns* as behaviors that result in short-term gain but long-term problems. As the yoga master, B.K.S. Iyengar, warned, "Pleasure seekers end up as pain finders" (Iyengar, 2006). Addictions are perhaps the quintessential example of these patterns, as the short-term pleasure of gambling, shopping, overworking, or drugs gives long term negative consequences.

Delaying Satisfaction

Moments of suffering now, whether it's extra years of education, saving money, eating healthily, or exercising, turn into nectar later. The psychological term for investing in ourselves is known as *delayed gratification*, which means an ability to withstand present discomfort to reach a future reward. This is much of schooling and education in general. Doctors have to struggle for years of additional education and residency in order for them to fulfill the requirements to practice. Delayed gratification is a lesson in investing, whether in oneself or a mutual fund. The better the child is at delaying their gratification, the more successful in life they will be. Contrary to popular sayings like "live each day like it was your last," by forgoing immediate satisfaction now, we are often able to attain greater satisfaction in the future.

This brings us to another equation we might apply to our lives:

Struggle + Achievement = Satisfaction

The bigger the struggle and the bigger the achievement, the more satisfaction you will find. Climbing Mount Everest will be a lot more satisfying than the hill behind your house. This equation is why everywhere around the world, you will find humans competing with each other, from sports to chess to poetry and beauty contests. We want to prove ourselves. We want to win, but only fair and square. Advanced players in sports don't particularly enjoy playing against novices. We don't want our competition to just submit. We want the risk of losing. There is no challenge and thus, no fun. No struggle and therefore no satisfaction.

Years ago, I quit my corporate job to follow my heart and fulfill my life mission of bringing more love into the world. During this time, I have helped many others listen to their hearts to find and follow their purpose too. I have found time and time again that we have a very romanticized vision of following one's purpose as all sunshine and rainbows. When in reality, living our truth is often extraordinarily inconvenient. Our hearts might tell us that we have to change jobs, move away from our hometown, end our current relationship, take a huge pay cut, or cease all contact with a family member. All these transitions are exceptionally challenging to do. Unfortunately, the truth often makes us miserable before it actually sets us free.

Grow Now or Suffer Later

In yoga we have a saying: *listen to your body's whispers now, so you don't have to hear it yell later*. Often when we have a creak in our knee, or the doctor warns us of high cholesterol, or our partner tells us they are unhappy, we think we can ignore those gentle nudges to change. That is until it all explodes in our faces later with the knee replacement, heart attack, or divorce papers. The universe is always sending us wake-up calls, but we are so quick to click the *don't answer* button. That is until one day the universe knocks down our front door and takes a tornado through the living room for us to finally get up and do what needs to be done.

Pain, like us, wants to be heard. Our wounds contain valuable information. As kids, if our parents didn't hear us the first time, we just got louder. If we don't respond to life's gentle nudges now, we will face tremendous suffering later. Fortunately, that tremendous suffering will also transform our lives. It's like the parent teaching their kid to drive, "Ok there's a stop sign coming up, you're going to want to press on the break ... ok slow down. Slow down! STOP STOP STOP!" Hopefully, we can stop before the brick wall, but if not, the crash will stop us anyway.

Many of us aren't even aware of our bodies until there is intense pain. But if that's what it takes, so be it. Pain is a messenger, pain in the body is an opportunity to learn about the body. We lead sedentary lifestyles, largely ignorant of our own inner workings. Whenever I teach anatomy classes, it is surprising how little people know of their own bodies. People with PhDs in chemistry or philosophy often don't even know what muscle is used to breathe (the diaphragm) and how many bones are in the adult body (206), or could tell you what the ligaments, tendons, bursae, labrums, and menisci are up to. The suffering of a herniated disc, torn ACL, sprained ankle, or broken clavicle are all incredible opportunities to learn about these parts of the body and their surrounding structures. With that deeper understanding, we can better love and take care of our bodies.

If we are unable to say no, the body will say it for us. I remember one client who worked so hard and was so stressed that her hair started falling out. Still, she felt unable to ask for even a few days off from her job, because according to her, "the place would fall apart without her." And yet, a few months later when she got so ill she had to take six months off to recover, guess what, her workplace went on just fine.

When we get sick, we often lament that we aren't able to do things, when being sick is often a result of always needing to do things. Our body finally screams, "Stop!" as we lay in bed unable to get up.

Meeting a bit of suffering now often prevents much more intense suffering in the future. We go to the dentist to fill a cavity so it doesn't turn into a root canal. The therapist, Resmaa Menakem, writes. "Healing involves discomfort—but so does refusing to heal. And, over time, refusing to heal is always more painful" (Menakem, 2017). Suffering is always pointing to where we are out of alignment, where we can move from *dis-ease* to *ease*, and it's up to us to listen and make those adjustments before things get even worse.

A powerful question to ask ourselves is, "If the pain could speak, what might it say?"

In chapter one, we learned the equation *pain times resistance equals suffering*. One of the biggest things we resist in our lives is change. We desperately crave security and stability to the point where we often remain in terrible conditions rather than venture out into the unknown.

There's the old joke, "How many therapists does it take to take a lightbulb? Just one, but the lightbulb has to want to change." Common to many therapy clients is the desire to get better, coupled with fear of trying. We want to change and are simultaneously deeply afraid of it. Maybe our job stinks but we are scared to look for a new one, or our relationship is in the gutter but at least we know what to expect. Change requires some pain, but the ego hates both. Our attempts at improving ourselves will be thwarted by the part of ourselves that wants to stay the same. This is where questions like, "What would I do if I knew I would not fail?" and "What do I fear would happen if I made the change I need to make?" are so useful.

In order to step into better, more whole, or more real versions of ourselves, we have to let our old selves die. And there are some older selves that really, really, do not want to die. This is the essence of *self-sabotage*: when that part of ourselves we are trying to let go of prevents us from becoming the person we want to be. We get close to our goal but then quit, or never start at all and keep procrastinating. Negative self-talk, poor boundaries, and getting off track are all survival tactics that keep us in patterns that don't serve.

Intense Suffering Forces Internal Transformation

We don't just need to listen to our bodies, we need to listen to our heart's whispers too. Otherwise, we will have to hear it yell later when we find ourselves two decades into a loveless marriage or a purposeless career.

Humans can be so stubborn, so headstrong, and so set in our ways, the only way for our course to change direction is to ricochet off rock bottom. We often have to fall down to even know which direction upward is, and many people have to hit the bottom a number of times to finally get the message. People struggling with mental illness will often need to relapse into multiple depressive or psychotic episodes before finally seeking treatment or taking their prescribed medication. To welcome something new into our lives, we often have to be forced out of the old. We can't lie to ourselves forever, and when our house of deceit finally collapses, we can begin the real work of rebuilding it from the ground up with a more solid foundation.

I coach numerous individuals going through the grief of heartbreak. As they move on they realize they weren't dumped, they were set free. Their now ex-partner saw something that they didn't; they knew it wasn't going to work out, that there wasn't a match, and simply ended it before the other partner came to the same conclusion. As Lao Tzu put it, "New beginnings are often disguised as painful endings." In the same way, breakthroughs are often disguised as breakdowns. Every human being experiences a number of breakdowns and breakthroughs in their lives. We must experience them; it is part of growing up and stepping into new versions of ourselves.

When I interviewed the Divorce Coach, Karen McMahon, she shared with me the pain and devastation that her clients go through when a relationship ends. There are few things as difficult as going through a challenging divorce, when the person you once loved the most ends up being a source of incredible anguish. But Karen shared with me the profound resiliency of her clients, particularly the ones that do the work, roll up their sleeves, refine their shortcomings, and begin to see how that miserable year of life was the best thing to ever happen to them.

If we welcome suffering as a great guru in our lives, breakups can turn into the best thing that can happen to us, as it puts us on the fast track of breaking free of unconscious patterning and poor attachment strategies and on the way to healthy and whole love. When our systems break down, we have the opportunity to build them back better than they were before. In the earth right now are seeds waiting for the next forest fire to come alive. There are also abilities and possibilities inside of us that are waiting for our life to burst into flames in order to awaken.

Bouncing Off Rock Bottom

Believe it or not, rock bottom can be a trampoline. When, after all of our careful planning and well-thought-out decisions, we find ourselves at our absolute lowest, we realize we have to change something absolutely fundamental about ourselves. As the addiction recovery slogan says, "All you have to change is everything." Our current operating system, or state of consciousness, brought us here, and we will have to completely transform in order to get out of it. This can put us on the transformational path of the heart.

Times of suffering often teach us we can endure anything. Once we make it through the tunnel to the other side, we no longer fear the tunnel. We go from "There's no way I could ever do that" to "I did it." Maybe we think there is no way we can raise our children alone, or that if we get fired that means our life and career are over. Those are limiting beliefs and life circumstances might happen to force ourselves to let go of them. We often have to lose something to realize we didn't even need it in the first place, or that it was holding us back.

Growth is life, stagnancy is death. As Nietzsche put it, "A snake that cannot shed its skin will not survive." We must meet our edge, push through it, go beyond what we are, and discover who we can be. We muster up everything we have to hack our way through the forest, before finally finding the clearing at the end.

Being with suffering can be a catalyst for that necessary internal revolution. Intense suffering awakens something incredible deep inside of us. There is even a psychological term for it: *post-traumatic growth*. We have all heard of post-traumatic stress disorder (PTSD), but post-traumatic growth is when what we went through becomes an incredibly fertile ground for a profound personal transformation. While we should never wish intense suffering onto anyone, most often it is a wake-up call. Those who have a brush with cancer often report having a renewed perspective on life. Such traumatic growth experiences are rarely wanted or expected, but in retrospect, almost always needed.

The poet, Rupi Kaur, wrote: "i am not a victim of my life / what i went through / pulled a warrior out of me / and it is my greatest honor to be her" (Kaur, 2020). Often, our deepest pain can turn into our deepest power. Even great superheroes go through an intense loss that puts them on a path towards courage and truth. Batman witnessed the death of his parents, the same goes for Spiderman and Uncle Ben, Luke Skywalker and Uncle Owen. These traumatic events shook them to the core as they realized the old rules no longer applied, and they would have to discover and cultivate a new fortitude to prepare for what is to come.

Entering a New Stage

Sometimes, when the suffering we experience becomes so extreme, it turns into something else entirely: a rite of passage. Rites of passage are almost ubiquitous across all cultures, as participants undergo extreme feats of endurance in order to attain new levels of consciousness. Immense suffering gives us the opportunity to prove ourselves, whether to ourselves or others. Once we cross some intense and painful barrier, not only do we know we can cross it again if necessary, but also know we can beat any trial of any lesser intensity.

Perhaps one of the biggest examples of pain as a rite of passage involves the bullet ant mittens of The Sateré-Mawé people of Brazil. The name bullet ant comes from the fact that being bitten by just one of these ants is so ungodly painful that it is akin to being hit by a bullet. There are stories of travelers unknowingly laying down in a nest of bullet ants, to find the stings so unbearable they end up committing suicide. The Mawé believe that any boy who wants to become a man must experience the worst pain the jungle has to offer and stick their hand inside the bullet ant glove. In the ritual, hundreds of bullet ants are rendered unconscious with a natural sedative and woven into gloves made of leaves. The boys must keep their hands in the glove for five minutes, enduring the stings, and then be with the pain for hours afterwards, sometimes experiencing paralysis and hallucinations. A young boy must do this ritual up to 20 times over the course of a few months (Paoletti, 2017).

Rites of passage might involve days of fasting or lonely vision quests in the jungle, desert, or on top of a mountain. In the Lakota Sun Dance, participants will dance around a pole staring into the hot sun. Pierced through their chest are strong metal hooks, which are tied to the center post. Dancing in a circle, they have a thin whistle pursed between their lips, unable to speak. Only once they become so exhausted they cannot go any further do they collapse, and the weight of their own bodies tears the hooks from their muscles.

Boys aren't the only ones that undergo intense experience as a rite of passage into manhood. In the Apache tradition, there is the practice of The Sunrise Ceremony, or *Na'ii'ees*, which takes place in the summer of a girl's first menstrual period. During this ceremony, the young girls dance for days to the chants and drumming of the community. After four full days of nonstop dancing, it is believed that the girls temporarily become an incarnation of the first lady and mother of their people, known as Changing Woman. The girls must fight through their own pain and fatigue, while battling the elements of the weather, to transition to womanhood. Some women say the demands of the dance are more challenging than childbirth, but the suffering is transformational. Not only is it considered necessary to build strength and character, and the path to cross from adolescence to adulthood, the tradition bonds the community together. Like soldiers becoming brothers through the communal suffering of war, the community is joined together through the ritual that has been passed down since ancient times (Wagner, 2014).

Waking Up

When suffering takes us to the very edge of our existence, it forces something to die, so that something new is born. What we think will destroy us is what reveals us. Going through an intense experience to be reborn is the essential symbolism behind a sweat lodge ceremony, practiced by many Native American and Mayan cultures, known in Nahuatl as a *temescal*. Usually, the sweat lodge is encased in darkness as one enters the great womb of Mother Earth. Intense physical endurance is required to stay in the lodge as it gets hotter and hotter. When participants think they can't go on any further, they continue to sing divine songs and offer divine prayers to build inner strength. The sweat pouring off the body is like a shedding of skin and old layers of self that no longer serve. Finally, like a newborn child, the red and wet participants are reborn into more purified selves. The Lakota term for sweat lodge is *Inípi*, which means "to live again."

Sometimes rites of passage involve heat, other times cold. A tradition of the Coast Salish people of the Pacific Northwest is known as the "spirit bath." At 5 a.m., in the winter cold, participants strip naked and plunge themselves into the freezing rushing waters of the river. Guides offer prayers of strength and connection while striking them with sharp and abrasive cedar leaves. The ceremony wakes up a person both physically and spiritually, and this rite is for anyone in need of healing.

While some rites of passage might be thought of as tests of someone's fortitude that the participant would either pass or fail depending on their ability, more often they awaken something deep inside. When you can't think you go on, when the mind and heart fully reach their limit, something else inside awakens. Like the runner finding their second wind, you cross a precipice you have never crossed before to find something incredible awaken within. You might call it God, soul, or Spirit. Almost always these rituals are done in a spiritual or religious context, and for good reason: the meeting of pain and suffering is a deeply spiritual practice.

Discipline

The Sanskrit word for the practice of physical discipline for spiritual attainment is *tapas*, a concept with multiple layers of meaning. The first is discipline, which most people misunderstand as punishment meant to discourage bad behavior. Decades ago, a teacher would hit their students with a ruler if they weren't paying attention, or a parent might put soap into a child's mouth as punishment for saying "dirty" words. The idea of discipline as a kind of punishment was developed in medieval times along with the chastisement or self-mortification that Christians might do to repent. In perhaps one of the most extreme examples suffering bringing us closer to God, the practice of self-flagellation is one that was as controversial back then as it still is today.

Most religions, and even the Buddha himself, reject self-mortification as a legitimate spiritual practice, expressing it as having the right idea but the wrong method. We can use the suffering that is already present in life as fuel for our awakening, rather than specifically perform acts to inflict even more suffering. Suffering will happen to us, no matter what, so we might as well use that, rather than specifically seek it out. Life already offers plenty of opportunities to suffer. If we go even further back in time, we learn that discipline does not mean inflicting pain and punishment to encourage good behavior (which rarely works anyway, as it just breeds anger and resentment). It comes from the same words as *discipulus*, meaning student; *disciplina*, meaning knowledge or instruction; and *discere*, meaning to learn. Discipline, and *tapas*, is more closely related to the discipline one needs in order to gain knowledge and become wise. If students are running around the classroom shouting and throwing things, they will not learn much from the teacher at the front of the class. The students first need discipline, the ability to sit down at their desks and pay attention.

Tapas teaches us that we have to sit in one place in order to gain wisdom. Only by being still for long periods of time will we be able to get in touch with the wisdom that lies within each and every one of us. As St. Augustine recommended, "Do not go outside, return to within yourself; truth dwells in the inner man" (Libreria Editrice Vaticana, 2008).

Tapas teaches us that in order to get in touch with the truth of who we are and reality as it is, we need discipline. *Tapas* also teaches us that the path to what we want is a deeply challenging one, that often requires incredible suffering. If you want to start a business, you might have to undergo years of uncertainty and hard work. If you want to lose weight, you will need a lot of *tapas* to avoid eating bad foods and to stick to your exercise regime. Discipline is the necessary structure that allows something to happen. As the yoga teacher, Donna Farhi, put it, discipline is any practice that contains our thoughts, energy, and actions so that we may use it in a potent way (Farhi, 2005).

Discipline is saying no, such as, "No, I will not open my phone for no reason. No, I will not see what's in the fridge for the twelfth time. No, I will not fill every moment with this and that. I say no to a thousand things, so I can say yes to the things that actually matter and nourish my soul." Discipline is needed to focus on the heart, to enjoy the simple things, to be there for each other, and to awaken.

Fire

This brings us to another definition of *tapas*: fire. Fire can refer to our motivation, just as an artist might have a burning fire within them, or an athlete might get "fired up" before the big game. In *Mindfulness in Plain English*, Bhante Henepola Gunaratana used the word *gumption* to refer to the energy, grit, determination, and discipline required to sit for hours at a time and cultivate mindfulness (Gunaratana, 2009).

But what happens when we bring a lot of motivation to our practice? We meet resistance, we meet friction, and an internal heat begins to occur. Just as holding a challenging physical posture will heat the muscles and the body, any kind of discipline will heat the mind. Just sitting in meditation for 20 minutes, a practitioner might experience the burning desire to get up and check their email. As the mind reaches and grasps for things to hold onto, we might experience anger within ourselves. But still, we use *tapas* to discipline the mind and let these temporary urges go. It is like pruning the smaller branches of a plant so the bigger ones can grow.

Fire can also purify. Just as you would put a raw metal into the fire to burn everything else away, we put ourselves into intense spiritual practices in order to burn away impurities, leaving only what is strong and true. Walking slowly will burn away the impurities of always needing to rush and run from one thing to the next.

Like putting a pot into a kiln in order for it to harden, a yoga teacher might say that pain is weakness leaving the body. The fire of tapas has the capacity to remove impurities inside ourselves. A fever is the body's response to fighting a virus, an attempt to heat up the body and burn the infection off. This is *tapas* too. A genuine spiritual practice must have some internal difficulty to burn off the impurities of hatred, ill-will, and egotism. While the Western mind easily associates the word purity with sexual purity, in the East, a pure mind is one of love, kindness, and compassion. Purity has nothing to do with one's outward sexual activities, rather it is the inward activity of the heart. Envy, resentment, jealousy, judgment, and bitterness are impurities that obscure our true loving nature, and we must face difficulty for them to burn away. Our spiritual practice then is like a large forest fire that burns everything away except the strongest and most resilient trees.

Many mystics describe divine love as a purifying or destructive fire. Catherine of Genoa, in her *Treatise on Purgatory*, writes, "The love of God does to the soul what fire does to material things: the longer it remains in this divine furnace, the purer it becomes. This fire, ever making it more pure, ends by annihilating it in all imperfection and all stain, leaving it wholly purified in God."

In St. John of the Cross' aptly titled, *Living Flame of Love*, divine love is described as a fire that purifies the soul. St. John uses the metaphor of a damp log on the fire that becomes cleansed and stripped of its moisture and ugliness, before burning cleanly and completely. He writes that the soul will endure great suffering in this purge of evil spirits and bad habits, but upon completion, we become united in sweet, peaceful, and glorious love.

The Ability to Tolerate Suffering

Think about it: what activities in our life involve fire? We experience fiery passionate love. We also get red hot with anger. Fire itself can produce a lot of pain. We find all of these references in the ancient scriptures that describe *tapas*. In the ancient *Upanishads*, life is said to be perpetuated by *tapas*, referring to the sexual heat and desire that keeps our species going. This idea is intimately connected to the fact that life requires warmth itself, just as the hen keeps her eggs warm, all of earthly life is supported by the sun's *tapas*.

In some of the earliest texts, *tapas* refers to the heat necessary for biological birth. Childbirth might be the quintessential example of times in our life we must undergo intense suffering in order to get something we want, and in this case, will love deeply. Birth is also an incredible metaphor for humanity's ability to bring anything new into the world. Hindu scholars have extended the metaphor of human birth to the idea of hatching new bodies of knowledge. In the ancient yogic texts, *tapas* is also described as the process that led to the spiritual birth of the *rishis*, sages of spiritual insights. Just as a scientist or writer will barricade themselves in the lab or writer's room, it takes discipline to bring forth new theories and ideas. This brings us to another incredibly important formulation of the word *tapas*: the ability to tolerate suffering and impose austerities upon oneself.

Just as we give birth to new ideas, at certain times in our lives, we are also reborn into newer, better versions of ourselves, which can be painful too. Eventually the pain to remain as a bud overcomes the pain required to blossom. Many of the darkest times in our life are simply gestation periods, after the final push we are reborn. The womb after all is a very dark place, and we often find ourselves in dark times before extraordinary transformations.

The practices of *tapas* show us the earliest forms of modern yoga that focused on physical postures, where ancient practitioners would challenge themselves to be in challenging positions for many hours or days at a time. When Alexander the Great invaded India, his army witnessed 15 men standing in different postures, sitting or lying down naked in front of the baking sun. Another man they found stood on one leg with a piece of wood three feet in length raised in both hands, in a position that today we would call tree pose. When one leg was fatigued, he changed to support the other, and thus continued the whole day. Some practitioners would never sit down for years sleeping slumped on a swing (Simpson, 2021).

There is also the recent example of Amar Bharati, who in 1973 chose to raise his hand and hold it up for the rest of his life in order to show his faith and appreciation toward Shiva. After two years of pain, he eventually lost any sense of feeling in his arm as the connective tissue hardened it in place. Amar Bharati's intense spiritual exercise taps us into the true meaning of tapas: to get closer to God.

Training in Suffering

Look across almost all religions and spiritualities and you will find trainings in austerities, an intentional letting go of desires and taking on of physical sufferings. Fasting is one of the most common ways people refrain on the physical level in order to get in touch with a more spiritual level of existence. Rumi likened humans to flutes that must be emptied so sweet music can flow through us. St. Francis said we must become empty so the divine can fill us up. The tenth-century Sufi, Abil-Kheir, said the less desire we have in the mind for the material world, the more room there is for the beloved.

During the month of Ramadan, Muslims observe a strict daily fast from dawn until sunset. Participants are not allowed to eat or drink, not even water. The temptation of Christ is described in the Gospels where after being baptized by John the Baptist, Jesus fasted for 40 days and nights in the Judaean Desert. The practice of Lent commemorates this time. Strikingly similar to how the Buddha was visited by Mara on his dawn of enlightenment, Satan appeared to Jesus and attempted to tempt him towards sin. Satan's temptations were hedonism, egoism, and materialism. John the Evangelist in his epistle categorized these temptations as "lust of eyes, lust of body, and pride of life," which might be the ultimate example of delayed gratification, forgoing any pleasure in this life for the sake of the ultimate heaven of an afterlife.

While fasting might seem like a rejection of the material to focus on the spiritual, the main reasons to fast are actually very human. Refraining from eating puts everyone on the same level, both rich and poor. It reminds the more fortunate of those who have less, putting the rich in touch with the suffering that the poor experience every day. It's an extraordinary act of solidarity.

When one has nothing, one is not afraid of anything being taken away. In this way, authentic human love naturally arises, as consciousness shifts from an isolated oneness toward a more mutual relatedness. The Franciscan Sister, Ilia Delio (Horan, 2014) explained it this way:

> Only those who can see and feel for another can love another without trying to possess the other... Poverty is that free and open space within the human heart that enables us to listen to the other, to respect the other and to trust the other without feeling that something vital will be taken from us... Conversion to poverty and humility is the nucleus of Christian evolution because it is the movement to authentic love, from individualism toward community.

Fasting is another way to cultivate the nonattachment that allows us to love all beings unconditionally. Fasting isn't just not eating. It also means removing the distraction of eating, which takes up a lot of our time and energy, in order to focus the mind on what is actually important.

Silence is another kind of fasting, as is the spiritual retreat, of removing ourselves completely from society in order to discover deeper aspects of our inner life. In today's modern world full of more distractions than ever before, it becomes even more important to intentionally remove those distractions to focus on personal and spiritual development.

Feeling Better

While monastic retreats tend to be a test in austerities and minimal living, modern-day yoga retreats tend to be the opposite. Although historically yoga was also rooted in a rejection of sensual pleasures, in modern times yoga is associated much more with health, wellness, stress reduction, and following one's bliss.

When my colleagues and I run yoga retreats, we put an incredible amount of effort into ensuring everyone is happy. There is pampering and indulgence. We choose fancy retreat centers in beautiful, exotic locations. We work closely with the kitchen to ensure three abundant meals that cater to Western tastes. We plan an awesome schedule of waterfall hikes, beachfront yoga, chocolate tastings, and community gatherings of play, song, and dance. People pay for everything ahead of time and for one or two weeks, they have no responsibilities, no work to do, and nothing to stress them out.

Yet, no matter what we do, there will be suffering. Despite glorious buffets, there is always a litany of food complaints, whether it is the carnivores complaining about the lack of protein or the vegans complaining about the lack of vegan, gluten-free, organic, locally sourced options. I see the suffering the Buddha mentioned on a daily basis if the pool is too cold, there's no coffee after 12 p.m., or the masseuse didn't press hard enough. People coming from more developed countries have high expectations and meet major disappointment when they see the reality of less developed countries that don't have fast internet, super-hot water, or electricity 24 hours a day.

Whether it's stray dogs, scorpions in the rooms, or loud music from a hotel nearby, there's always something to complain about. I have learned that no matter how much you try to accommodate and please someone and try to make them happy, there are some people in the world who will never be pleased. While growth happens at the end of our comfort zone, for some people, misery is their comfort zone, and they revel in it. Their ego thrives on the resistance it puts up against the world.

But after doing many trainings, I realized the reality of such suffering goes deeper than simply first-world problems. It's not that people are sad, it's that they are seeing their sadness for the first time and don't know what to do with it.

There's a joke about a man who goes to therapy because he is angry and frustrated all the time. The therapist recommends that he go on a meditation retreat to feel better. While on retreat, he feels even more angry and frustrated, and goes back to complain to his therapist. The therapist smiles and says, "See, I told you that you would feel better. You're feeling your anger better, you're feeling your frustration better!"

As mentioned before, it's normal to feel backdraft when we finally release that pressure of all the emotions we have been suppressing. It's normal to feel worse on the first steps to feeling better. So on day three of meditation when people's complaints increase, I know what is actually going on and can practice compassionate understanding.

True Connection

But it's more than just backdraft too. It's that *I am actually hearing about people's suffering*. Before any large retreat, I read people's health forms and learn all about their personal struggles. Many have experienced physical accidents and the resulting injuries have plagued them for years, if not decades. Others have deep childhood trauma and a lifetime of therapists and medication trying to work through it. I've learned there's not a single person on Earth without any mental, emotional, or physical problems.

Living in a community, you become deeply connected to others, emotionally, energetically, and spiritually. If Jessica doesn't show up to class because of a stomach bug, you feel it. If John didn't sleep last night because of the barking dogs, he shows up disheveled to class and makes more sardonic comments than usual. In our atomized individualistic world, it's easy to hide our suffering behind closed doors and social media filters. But sitting in a circle with a question prompt like, "What are you most afraid of?" you learn deeply about other people's struggles and that you are not alone in yours.

It's not that people are needy, it's that people are suffering. Everyone is suffering. Me, you, and that coworker who seems super bubbly and happy all the time. Once you really connect to people you see the suffering, big and small. In just a few weeks, we will have physical injuries, mental breakdowns, and interpersonal conflicts. Students will get mosquito bites, stomach bugs, and bacterial infections. I've seen trauma triggers, including the practice of fasting challenging those with eating disorders, and the use of plant medicine bringing up childhood trauma from a student whose parents were addicted to drugs. I remember one student would fall to tears in almost every class because English was her second language, and when she didn't understand what was going on, she felt abandoned and alone.

Because we live in a world that doesn't see weeds as treasures, we hide away our vulnerability and put on a face to go to work and pretend everything is ok. But living in close proximity to 20 other adults, sharing rooms, meals, and activities, you know exactly who is sick, who is injured, and who just went through a hard breakup. It is one thing to know "everyone is fighting their own battles" but another to be in the battle with them. Sometimes we will have trauma-informed trainings designed to specifically equip teachers with the tools to work with trauma. While the training is open to anyone, the people that attend will usually have a history of deeply traumatic experiences. While we often hide our darkness, learning to see it, share it, and hear it from others is deeply healing.

Hell, in Paradise

When we can share our story in a safe and non-judgmental space, it lessens its hold on us. As social beings we help to regulate each other; being seen and accepted puts us on a path to healing and belonging. I remember leading a training at a luxury center on the shores of a gorgeous lake. Incredible food, perfect weather, and big, comfortable beds. After a few days, one student, struggling with her own depression, shared with the group her morning thoughts, "Well, another crappy day in paradise." And we all understood. It doesn't matter where you go to try and escape your problems, because you will be taking that same mind with the same problems along with you. There is no escape from our own selves. As the saying goes, "Wherever you go, there you are," the same patterns of reactivity and trauma. While many people go on retreats to avoid their issues, getting away is really just an opportunity to meet our stuff in a calm, safe, and supportive environment.

Another reason people are suffering in spiritual communities is because they are self-selected that way. Many have come to this spiritual path in the middle of their own dark night, often having recently quit their job, lost their business, sold the house, gone through a messy breakup, or all of the above. They've come disillusioned and are searching for that "something more." They're finally seeking the light.

When I go on a meditation retreat to be confined to a small cell and not talk for days, I often ask myself, is this worse than prison? After all, in prison, the inmates get to watch TV and socialize with one another. We don't get any media or the ability to socialize. Prisoners get three square meals a day, sometimes we get a single morning meal of rice and papaya. For a long while, I wrestled with the difference between intentionally going into suffering and having it forced on us. After all, the main difference is that prisoners are forced into their conditions, while practitioners on a meditation retreat can leave whenever they want. Is there a difference between consensual and nonconsensual suffering?

I had a lightbulb moment in a talk by the Venerable Ajahn Brahm who said, "A prison is any time you are somewhere you don't want to be" (Buddhist Society of Western Australia, 2023). If you don't want to be in your body, your body is a prison. If you don't want to be in your job or marriage, those will be prison too. If your mind is stuck in the past, your past is a prison. If you are at a luxury retreat center but have food poisoning, sunburn, and your skin is breaking out in hives, paradise will seem like a prison. If you believe that you are a small, isolated, fragile, and lonely self, that belief becomes a prison.

One time, two prisoners of war went back to their country. After a few months, one asked the other one, "Have you forgiven your captors?" When the second POW replied, "Absolutely not!", the first one said, "Well, then you are still in prison." Hatred, anger, an unwillingness to forgive, these are prisons too.

Freud's greatest insight was that unconscious patterns keep our lives stuck in the prisons of our own behavior. Like the nectar that turns to poison, many times the castles we spend our lives building end up being prisons. We go to school for years and the first day of the job we worked so hard for, we hate it. Or we upend our life and move to a new city to be with our partner, only to discover they have been having an affair for years.

The only true and lasting home we have is in the heart. Nowhere else. In all circumstances in life, if you are where you want to be, you are free. As Tara Brach put it, "The boundary to what we can accept is the boundary to our freedom" (Brach, 2011). The fact that we can feel crappy even in paradise is actually quite promising, because it also means we can feel paradise even in crappy situations. If we make our heart our home, it doesn't matter where life puts us. Maybe we are sent to prison for a crime we didn't commit, or for breaking an unjust law as part of a peaceful protest. No matter what, our practice is the same: to keep the heart open even in intense suffering.

Believe it or not, some people are grateful to be in prison. There are many valid critiques of the prison system, and while we shouldn't ignore those problems, some people do come out of incarceration with greater wisdom and understanding. Some use the opportunity to reflect on their actions and deepen their spirituality, to transform the suffering into light. Nothing can change the love that is our true nature, and the peace that can be found in the present moment.

Heaven

One day a samurai went to a monk and asked him "Teach me the nature of heaven and hell." The monk picked up his chin and looked down his nose at the samurai, saying, "Teach you about the nature of heaven and hell? Your robes are dirty and your sword is rusty, you don't even have the intelligence to comprehend such things." The samurai, hearing this, became enraged. He stood up, pulled out his sword, and was ready to strike the monk down. At that moment, the monk said, "That's hell." Hearing this, the samurai realized the monk was about to risk his life just to teach him a lesson. He dropped his sword, fell to his knees, and began kissing the monk's feet, heart full of compassion and tears streaming down his eyes. "That's heaven," the monk whispered quietly.

For many people, religion is their "evacuation plan" from the tribulations of this physical world. But this powerful story teaches that heaven and hell are not to be found in the afterlife, they are states of mind we can experience in the present moment. As Richard Rohr put it, "The gate of heaven is first of all in one concrete place, better if carried with you, and best when found everywhere" (Rohr, 2013). These are the phases of our spiritual development. Heaven and hell aren't geographical places, they are eternal states.

Fortunately, by the end of the training, the woman's depression lifted and she was singing and dancing with the rest of us in our own little heaven. While professional therapy can be useful and some people do need medication to lessen the burden of anxiety and depression, any psychologist would also agree that daily exercise, mindful movement, being in nature, eating well, and being seen and held by a loving and supportive community can be extraordinarily healing as well. Talk to anyone who has been in solitary confinement and they will tell you that loneliness and isolation is hell. Union, belonging, and connection is heaven.

The fact of the matter is, us humans didn't evolve to regulate our own emotions. We evolved to co-regulate each other. We can move our arms up and down, we can move the pitch of our voice up and down, but we can't move our sadness or anger down. For that, we need someone else to listen to and hear us.

Heaven is here when we can see each other and hold each other, and ourselves, with compassion and understanding. "All the way to heaven is heaven," says St. Teresa of Ávila. We can't fix each other's suffering, but we can share the burden, and deepen our love and compassion for each other. This is the power of community, what we call the *sangha*, one of the three refuges in Buddhism, a true place of support when life is hard. Whether it's your Church or AA group, your extended family or a group of close friends, having community is key to belonging.

In the introduction to this book, I mentioned all that it took to get to a training in the Peruvian Andes. Long flights, days of travel, bad airplane food, health forms, passport checks, taxis, trains, and more. Then on day two of that training, a student approached me with tears in her eyes. "I just got a call that my father passed away," she said to me. I was shocked, I had never had this happen on a training before, and my immediate response was "Time to get you home." It didn't matter that she had spent thousands of dollars, months of planning, and a week of travel to get here, we both knew she had to go back home to be with her loved ones. Before she left, we sat our group in a circle, saying goodbye to someone that we just met. She cried. I cried. We all cried. It was a moment of intense suffering, and also intense beauty. By not shying away from our suffering, we are able to hold it, face it, and support each other through it. Being loved is heaven.

The poet, Jane Hirshfield, observed that "Suffering leads us to beauty the way thirst leads us to water," reflecting how the challenging times in our life not only accentuate the good times, but also force us to look for a saving grace (Hirshfield, 2015). I think of this quote a lot when I hear an agonizingly beautiful song, the kind that expresses the sorrow of the human condition in a beautiful and moving way. Who wants songs that only sing of sunshine and rainbows? There's a reason we love listening to the blues. "It is no surprise that danger and suffering surround us. What astonishes is the singing," wrote the poet, Jack Gilbert (Academy of American Poets, n.d.). Like stars in the sky, the darkness enhances the light. We can dance to the music of our tears, write poems to the movement of our grief, and sing with the sorrows in our hearts.

Another Kind of Suffering

Going on a retreat for many to fast, sleep on a hard bed, and not talk to anybody isn't easy. Yogis might lay on a bed of nails, walk on hot coals, or stand on one leg in the hot sun for days. Some Himalayan monks will climb mountains and sit in the snow, wet towels on their backs, cultivating an internal heat that makes the water steam. Bodybuilders will go to the gym on "leg day" and be unable to walk out on their own afterward. Humans suffer for a lot of reasons. To test ourselves, to learn, to grow, to awaken something within, to get closer to God, to get something we want in the future, to empathize with others who are suffering, and more.

But there is something else we haven't mentioned that is much, much harder. There is another container a person can enter into that will put them face to face with their own shadows, unconscious patterning, fear, and anxiety. A container that provides more suffering and agony than perhaps even a mitten full of bullet ants. That container would be what we call an intimate, romantic partnership.

Chapter 6

The Suffering in Love

You are the knife I turn inside myself; that is love. That, my dear, is love. Franz Kafka, *Letters to Milena*

Every step of the way, love has the potential to ruin our mental and emotional lives.

We get ghosted, ignored, dumped, or cheated on. We express our deepest feelings in a state of total vulnerability, only to find our love unrequited. We set up our entire life with someone—children, house, finances—to watch it crumble before us in a mess of tissue, tears, and litigation.

Listen to any number of songs on the radio, and you will inevitably come to the conclusion that the presence of love is pure ecstasy, while a lack of love is nothing but pain. Mutual love is joy, unrequited love is anguish, and one is rarely far from the other. The transition from "you complete me" to "now you're just somebody that I used to know" can happen in a very short period of time.

As relationships progress, the stakes get higher, along with the pain of ending. The deeper the intimacy, the deeper the vulnerability. Love feels like giving our tender hearts to somebody who could crush it on a whim. "Soul-mate" quickly turns to "soul-hate" when that person we love leaves us in a crying heap on the bathroom floor, and everything breaks: our heart, our home, our faith in love. If a long-term relationship ends, we don't just experience heartbreak; we experience grief—over the loss of the relationship, over the loss of another person who was an essential part of our lives, and the loss of a future that will never come to be. Dr. Judith Lewis Herman, who has done extensive work on trauma recovery, says that breakups are one of the biggest traumas that we will ever have to go through (Herman, 1992). You read that right: the end of a relationship is traumatizing.

One of my most popular blog posts is entitled *How to Love Without Attachment*. A lot of visitors come from Google after searching that very phrase. It seems like many people try to avoid the inevitable pain that comes with loving another human being. Lovers everywhere want to love without risking the emotional turbulence of it all.

Losing a relationship is hard, but being in a relationship isn't all sunshine either. Ask a couple if they are happy together, and they will say yes. Ask them if there are occasional moments when they want to be out of the relationship that they're in. Again, they are likely to say yes. Ask them if there are times when they want to strangle their partner. Ok, don't actually ask them that.

Struggling in love seems almost fundamental to the human experience. Who hasn't had an intense crush on someone, only to mournfully watch them fall in love with someone else? Who hasn't thought they found their true love, soulmate, other half, their twin flame, only to have the relationship go up in even bigger flames? We can lie in bed next to our partner of decades and feel totally lost, disconnected, and alone.

There's a joke with a number of different setups but the end is the same. It begins with two men talking, and one says, "I had the worst Freudian slip the other day. I meant to ask the female teller for a train ticket to Pittsburg, but instead said 'Tittsburg'." The other man replies, "Oh, don't feel too bad. I had one the other day. I was having dinner with the wife and meant to say, 'Please pass the salt' but instead said, 'Gosh darn it woman you've ruined my life!'" While the joke isn't the most tasteful (and some versions are much more vulgar), it does point to the reality that if you peel back the veneer of many relationships, you will find bitterness and resentment. Behind the smiling photos and perfect social media accounts, we occasionally despise the ones we supposedly love.

Relationships are a great source of happiness, joy, intimacy, and ecstasy, but also home to betrayal, abuse, heartbreak, and emotional upset. When we desire to keep our hearts open, even in hell, we can recognize that our most intimate relationships can be a kind of hell. What would it be like to keep our hearts open, even when anger threatens to consume us? The human heart longs to be open, we want to live with a wide-open heart. But when we try, our heart gets hurt. Not wanting to be hurt again, we close down and armor ourselves. This is a natural and understandable inclination, but is it necessary?

Love and suffering are our greatest teachers. An intimate relationship puts us face-to-face with both. Until we stop resisting and begin to get in touch with these great gurus, our relationships won't reach their ultimate potential. Once we come to learn that the suffering is there for a reason and are able to face it to learn what lessons it has to teach us, we will finally find and keep the love that we seek.

The Art of Letting Go

Love is hard to hold onto for the same reason life is hard to hold onto: it changes. In previous chapters, we talked about how recognizing the impermanent nature of reality asks us to learn how to let go. An intimate relationship teaches us to let go on so many levels. The most obvious one is when "til death do us part" finally reaches its fruition. In acknowledging impermanence, we recognize the fleetingness and thus the preciousness of everything; that a moment missed is a moment unlived, and to love another means to enjoy every moment because you never know if it will be your last. To love and let go is the meaning of life. Few people who watch their loved ones pass away would trade for anything in the world. It is the risk we all take when loving.

The Buddha taught that there is suffering in life, and even during the good times there is a nagging concern in the back of our mind about how long it will last. Love is no different. There is no love without loss. "Grief is an ingredient in every love potion," writes the poet Andrea Gibson. The deeper the love, the deeper the grief. We have to be willing to lose if we are willing to love. People often want to get over the end of a relationship as soon as possible, rather than see heartbreak as fundamental to the human experience and recognize that we are here for all of it: the laughter and the tears, the joy and the pain, the bearable and the unbearable. We are here to love what is mortal, to love what does not last, and to be the love that floats among these waves in complete awe of the miracle of it all. When we recognize the impermanence of all things, it gives us the courage to face suffering, knowing that it will come and go like everything else.

Death Is a Great Teacher

Suffering is our greatest teacher, and death is often a source of great suffering in our lives. Thus, death is a great teacher too. If we don't understand death, we won't understand life. Death teaches us to appreciate this moment, to savor the time we have with each other. Birth and death are the edges of the canvas, love is the colors we add to it. Would we appreciate this life as much, or seek to give and find love with such intensity, if we all lived forever? Embracing death magnifies the importance of life.

Unfortunately, we live in a death-defying and suffering-phobic society that prefers to hide death away in retirement homes and hospitals. We don't challenge each other to keep our hearts open in the hell of losing one another, we try to hide the hell altogether. As a result, we are missing out on one of the most important aspects of the human experience. There is nothing more human than dying. Like a puzzle piece, we will never be whole without it.

Much of our attachment to youth stems from our fear of death. We spend billions of dollars on anti-wrinkle creams, plastic surgeries, and hair dyes to look younger, to stave off the feeling of our impending decay and demise. Unfortunately, by rejecting death we reject life, and by avoiding how everything changes we cut ourselves off from the creative aliveness of this moment.

Imagine you wake up in the morning with a hundred things to do. You then receive a phone call that someone you love is dying. Putting down that phone, you are in a new world. Beforehand, your mind was in a million places. Afterwards, we can count on one hand what truly matters, and love is perhaps the biggest one. You cancel your plans and go to the hospital and sit next to them. At that moment, would you be checking your phone? Of course not. Death's lesson is to love each other now, never knowing if the words we say now will be the last ones they hear. In trying times, your capacity to hold the pain will be equal to your capacity to love.

I'm going to die, you're going to die, your cat, dog, mother, father, and spouse, are all going to die. In that space between the maternity ward and the mortuary, we all need all the help we can get. Recognizing death brings us closer to what matters. In Bhutanese culture, a country that routinely is at the top of the world happiness index, one is expected to think about death five times a day. Rather than lead to a nihilistic view of the world, acknowledging death brings one to an innate happiness of life. The Buddhist practice of *Maraṇasati* explicitly encourages mindfulness of death and even meditating on nine stages of corpse decomposition. After attending a five-day summit on *Death, Love, and Wisdom*, at the top of all my notes I wrote my biggest takeaway in bold letters: *we are all living in the light of death*. Death shines on what matters, reminding us that while the days to our life are limited, there is no limit to the life we can bring to our days.

When I talked to the therapist and caregiver, Daniella Marchick, who works in end-of-life care, she said for almost everyone she works with, a profound depth of compassion is found while witnessing someone going through death. The death of a loved one gives us the opportunity to offer the greatest showing of love imaginable. Keeping our hearts open in hell means loving and being committed to love throughout all of life's challenges. This might include the last few days, weeks, or years that someone we know is on their deathbed. This will often be the final test of our character, showing up for someone who might not even be the person that we knew. But we still offer our loving presence, the hand to hold, the shoulder to cry on, the humor in dark moments.

Loving Means Risking Losing Love

This brings us to another reason why we choose to bring suffering in our lives. Deep down, our hearts know: it is better to have loved and lost than never to have loved at all. We risk suffering at the chance of experiencing one of the most beautiful emotions known to human beings: falling in love. We sometimes suffer a lot, a whole lot, to experience that one brief moment of such pure ecstasy that it makes it all worth it. It is not a rational decision where we weigh the costs and benefits. We have no choice. There is something deep within us, an unquenchable desire, that will not stop until it is fulfilled. Our soul is here to love, to feel, to risk it all, and we know it. Keeping our hearts open means not letting our suffering overwhelm us, which is why most people don't want to love again after being hurt. It was too much.

There's a saying, "Ships are safe in the harbor, but that's not what ships are made for" that seems so essential to the human experience. Humans are a risky bunch. We often do insane things just to experience the thrill of it. People jump out of airplanes, climb snowy mountains, and fight each other in boxing rings. We love to compete, even if that means losing half the time. Yet no matter how crushing the loss, we head right into the next game, because the joy of winning and satisfaction of overcoming our own weaknesses is worth it.

A lot of human endeavors are propelled by a predictably irrational hope. We buy lottery tickets with terrible odds and start businesses that have a 90% chance of failing. We enter into these situations thinking, "That won't be me" and foolheartedly go deep into danger. The statistics of relationships are not too different. Many people cite the fact that over 50% of marriages fail as a sign that love is doomed. They forget the statistics are actually much worse. People will go through a number of relationships and breakups before they find their "one." When you include all the first dates, brief flings, first relationships, and months of promises of those in the first throes of love, we have to admit: almost all loving relationships end. Yet we keep trying because in the depths of the human heart there is a longing to connect. After countless bad dates, we might swear love off altogether, but only a short amount of time passes before we find ourselves knowingly and willingly walking off the plank again to fall deep into love's waters.

Love is hard. Even the great couples' therapist, Stan Tatkin, says that "the hardest thing for a human being is to be in a loving relationship with another" (TEDx Talks, 2016). Love in relationships is almost as ubiquitous as struggle. Why is that? If we are wired for love, born for love, and all yearn for love, why aren't our relationships easy?

Loving Someone for Who They Are

I spend my life going around the world teaching people to love everyone and everything. Inevitably, people will always object with the exact place they are stuck. Love everyone? What about that politician that I hate so much? What about pedophiles and murderers? As we learned in previous chapters, all resistance is an opportunity to grow. Love will reveal everything standing in the way of love, and it's up to you to face those obstacles and release the tension that keeps them there.

But a very interesting "what about..." comes up when people ask, "What about my partner when they're being a total jerk?" How can I keep my heart open in hell, when my partner is the source of that hell?

Well, that's the next step on the path. Loving relationships are hard because there are other, more subtle forms of letting go that have to happen. In order to truly love someone, we have to love *all* of them. The good parts and the so-called bad parts. If we only love part of a person, we don't really love them. This is the true essence of love, letting someone be who they are, in all that they are. Many people misunderstand the Sarte quote, "hell is other people." Because what Sarte was really saying is that being stuck with the judgmental gaze and criticism of others is a kind of hell. Being loved and accepted for who we are is heaven.

This is another reason we suffer in the world: things come in packages. The rose and the thorn grow together. You have to take the good with the bad. Nothing and nobody is perfect, so to fully engage with life and love we must embrace the imperfections. If we want to be in partnership with someone who is attractive, nice, humorous, creative, and wealthy, we also have to deal with their short temper, childhood trauma, and how they never put their toothbrush away. Rather than see these personality quirks as something to be fixed, we see them as essential to who they are and how they came to be.

Being present means letting go of trying to change the past and letting go of trying to control the future. In a partnership, this means recognizing that our partner is always changing, so we invite, not demand, them to blossom into their most beautiful selves. One of the most common complaints in couples' counseling is, "You're not the person I married." Of course they aren't the person you married! They aren't even the same person they were yesterday. This is to be expected and welcomed, as a true loving relationship is one that encourages us to become the absolute best version of ourselves. One would hope that couples in partnership are learning and growing, shedding old parts of themselves that do not serve love.

Not only is everything in the physical world constantly moving, shifting, coming into and out of existence, but so too is our perception of it. This is why the early phases of a loving relationship are so ecstatic: we have met someone new, someone exciting, someone who has made us feel like nothing else before. But this feeling doesn't last either, as nothing can stay new forever. Our mind automates the routine and repetitive factors of our lives, and our partner is not immune to this effect.

Relating

In meditation we say, if you are bored, you are not paying attention. Every day is a brand new one, never to happen again in the history of all time. Reality is the best show there is, constantly reinventing itself. This flower will never appear the same as it is right now. We can apply this attitude to our relationships too. Anthony De Mello wrote, "You cannot love what you cannot see afresh" (De Mello, 2011). If you think you are in a routine stuck with the "same-old" partner, you are not paying attention and noticing how each day is new, never to happen again in the history of the universe. Your partner is changing right before you, learning new things, gaining new experiences and memories, shedding old parts of themselves. You are too. The person who finishes this book will not be the same person who started it.

The future is unknown. We don't know what is going to happen five minutes from now, let alone tomorrow or next year. This gives us a new vision of how trust is actually built in a relationship. From the words of Dr. Rachel Botsman, trust is "a confident relationship with the unknown" (Botsman, 2018). There will forever be mystery to relationships and to the other, which is a source of joy and eroticism. You can never truly know somebody, and love is the process of deepening that knowledge as much as possible. Any elderly couple will tell you the same: you will never run out of things to learn about your partner.

Of course, there might be boredom in a relationship if both partners are committed to not growing, not changing, and not discovering anything anew. If there is no space for people to grow, there will be no space for love to grow either. While it might be easy to blame our partner for not growing, it is our responsibility to grow, to discover ourselves anew, and to grow the relationship as well. Boredom is like food going stale on the counter, a great relationship is still on the vine.

After all, what is a relationship? It is not something that you have, it is something that you do. You cannot save your relationship by putting it in a safe or upon a pedestal to look at. You cannot show me your relationship. A relationship is something we use to describe a continuous process of relating. It is not one thing; it is a million tiny things across many years. Every day we have dozens of opportunities for tiny expressions of love. From writing little love notes to embracing for 30 seconds before running out the door to work, love is a continual call to action to be loving. Nature teaches us that the only way to grow something is to nourish it, so we must always be feeding our relationships.

By shifting from "me" to "us" we enter what the couples' therapist, Terry Real, calls "relational consciousness," shifting from being reactive individuals to proactive teammates. Relationships are hard because they are a dance. They require a continuous calibration, an iterative process of harmony, disillusionment, and repair. You cannot rely on the same methods all the time, you must bring an attuned and loving attention to another shifting being, respond to their needs with tenderness, while managing your own habitual reactions.

One of the most common pieces of advice I hear from couples' therapists and coaches is to "never stop dating your partner," a process known as *re-romanticizing*. Rather than get married and then think that you "have" a marriage, you never stop exploring new things, going to new places, showering each other with gifts and love and affection. I can't tell you how many couples I coach that do not tell their partner that they love and appreciate them because "they already know." But love doesn't exist in some ethereal medium. It exists in all the moments, big and small, where we express that love for one another, in words and in actions.

If you want to up-level your relationship right now, it's easy. All you have to do is turn toward your partner and ask them if they have a quick moment to chat. Then fill in the blanks of the following statement:

"Honey, I just want to say, I love and appreciate how [*personality trait*] you are when [*specific action they recently did*]."

For example, "I love and appreciate how kind you are when you read to our children." Or, "I appreciate how thoughtful you are when you make me a cup of coffee in the morning." Or even, "I think you're so sexy when you wear those pants." Watch how they respond. We can be mirrors that reflect back our inherent goodness. When our genuine love touches someone else, they bloom like a flower.

One of my favorite lines of inquiry goes, "If you were going to die tomorrow, who would you call, what would you say?" and the follow-up line, "And why haven't you done that yet?" I can't tell you how important it is to reach out to a friend and tell them you appreciate them. Or how good it feels to receive a message that says, "You matter. You are enough. You are lovable. You are loved." You can reach out to someone who needs some appreciation; you can also reach out to someone who might deserve an apology. When you're hurt, few things are more important than being recognized by the person that hurt you.

Of course, when you are stuck in patterns of habits and reactivity, resentment and criticism, stonewalling and defensiveness, expressing love and appreciation for your partner is hard to do. During times of relationship suffering, we have to deepen our understanding of why such suffering is happening in our relationship.

Why Is Love So Hard?

In my first book, *The 7 Lessons of Love*, I tried to be as scientific as possible, looking deep into the neuroscience, sociology, and evolutionary psychology of relationships. Despite citing all my sources and offering findings from great researchers, I still had a reviewer who said my book was "full of cliches and empty platitudes." While I initially got defensive, the truth is, it is hard to talk about the science of love without simply confirming what we know and hear all the time. Because science absolutely confirms that we are born for love, born to love, have evolved to love one another, and that everyone needs love from birth until death. Human beings are social beings; we need connection and belonging above all else. Our deepest and greatest desire is to love and be loved. We long to belong. Because love is our deepest longing, the lack of love is the source of our most intense suffering. Solitary confinement is torture, so is waiting for a text back after you say, "But I love you."

Call the science whatever you want—interpersonal neurobiology, attachment theory, social baseline theory, internal family systems, relationship synchronicity, relational neuroscience, relational-cultural theory, co-regulation—the lesson is the same. We have social brains that form in relationships, are wounded in relationships, and can only heal in relationships.

Disconnection causes suffering; we need healthy relationships to grow. Integration creates well-being.

As children, we are extraordinarily dependent on others to survive. Unlike many species that can live on their own soon after birth (sometimes even before the little ones hatch from their eggs), the human species absolutely takes the cake when it comes to the breadth and depth of care our newborns need. Our mental development has become *externalized*: rather than an instinctual brain running the show, we have more of a sponge brain designed to absorb all sorts of knowledge about how to live and exist in the modern world. It takes a lot of mental development and learning from others before we can make a doctor's appointment, drive there, communicate our gastrointestinal distress, and pay for it all on our own.

Many people don't realize that our dependency for love continues through the rest of our lives and exists on every level: physical, emotional, mental, and spiritual. We didn't evolve to *self-regulate*, but to *co-regulate* each other with attuned and caring attention. Being in a loving relationship boosts our immune system, lowers our stress hormones, helps us regulate emotions, and makes life less painful. People with strong social connections are at a lesser risk of death from *all* causes, from heart disease to cancer to suicide, while poor social connection is just as bad for overall wellness as smoking a pack of cigarettes a day or being obese. Even a cancer patient who joins a monthly support group will recover faster than someone not part of any community.

For the human species, it was never survival of the fittest, it is survival of the *most nurtured*. Life is like climbing a mountain, you might be able to make it to the top by yourself, but you're much more likely to succeed if someone is roping you up. And with all the worries and perils of the world, we might need a lot of people with a lot of ropes.

Deep Needs

Love runs deep. To a child's brain, "Am I loved?" and "Will I survive?" are essentially the same question. To an adult, "Does she love me?" and "Is my life over?" are the same question too. Rather than the physical survival of our body, we are attached to the survival of our own egos, our thoughts, opinions, and beliefs that we so tightly hold onto. We are no longer attacked by wild animals, but instead feel "attacked" in conversation when our partner points out our narrow ideas or shadow selves. When our partner says, "You're wrong," "I disagree," or "That's a silly way to do things," we experience a deep fear: a fear of our own death, of who we think we are. In this way, being willing to love means being willing to die. We can't love another person and still live life completely on our own terms. We must be willing for the ground to disappear underneath our feet, as the ideas we cling to for safety and security are seen as falsehoods.

Relationships put us face to face with our own conditioning and patterns. It's incredible all the little things that couples deal with that turn into big arguments. As a friend joked to me, "Before I got married, I didn't even realize there was a wrong way to put the milk back into the fridge." That's because we all have attachments, we all want things to be a certain way, whether it's the cleanliness of the house or what time we want dinner. When another person challenges our attachments, we suffer, being put face to face with our own stuff. Love asks us to let go of our need to be right all the time, stop arguing to be right and start listening to understand. What keeps most couples stuck is each person's inability to see their own contribution to the problem that plagues them.

If you look at any argument in a relationship, it is never about the topic at hand. Partners may argue about money, household chores, the frequency of sex, and which school to send the kids to, but that's never the real issue. The real issue is underneath, it is those core needs that those things represent, like the need for freedom, agency, and most importantly, the need to be seen. Questions like "Am I wanted? Am I being heard? Am I appreciated? Do I matter? Do I have freedom here?" underlie most conflicts.

James Baldwin, observed, "One of the reasons people cling to their hates so stubbornly is because they sense, once hate is gone, they will be forced to deal with pain" (Baldwin, 1993). Underneath our big aggressive emotions, there is always a small vulnerable one. But underneath that vulnerability, there is a wound to be healed. It's almost like a giant dragon protecting a small rabbit and beneath that rabbit, there is a seed that needs planting and nurturing. In a relationship, this often looks like shifting from "I can't believe you forgot my birthday, you jerk!" to "I'm so sad and frightened." Upon deeper reflection, we see the core wound, the core belief, "No one will ever love me." It takes some diving to get to that wound, and a lot of support to feel safe actually going there. We can never express ourselves fully until we feel safe.

Love taps into the most primal and essential parts of our being, and we will have all sorts of alarm bells set up to ensure we go out and seek love if it is lacking. One of the most important findings from neuroscience is that emotional pain and physical pain are not different from the brain's perspective. When we say, "She stabbed me in the back" or "he broke my heart," these aren't just metaphors, but ways to describe our lived and very real experience. To the brain, the pain of rejection is just as real as that of getting burned by fire.

This primal love puzzle has another piece: just as rejection, criticism, or dismissing comments will tap into our evolutionary survival needs, so too our adult relationships will tap into whatever conditioning we received a long time ago. Our brain underwent incredible changes in the first few years of life, and during this development it was also the most sensitive to the love and lack of love that was in its environment. Loving relationships are hard because guess what: our relationships as adults will tap into, target, and press onto those old childhood wounds we would have preferred to forget about. Falling in love turns our life into a snow globe—all of our old stuff, everything from childhood to our last intimate relationship, gets stirred up.

This sounds bad, but all that suffering and all that stuff is there for a reason: for us to heal and grow from it. Intimate relationships are absolutely the best container for transformation because they give us such rich content to work with. Because partnership brings up so much of our stuff, so often and so quickly, it is the best route for personal evolution, as long as we are open to it. Suffering in relationships reveals doors to deeper love, if we have the courage to walk through them.

Old Wounding

The brain undergoes its most development in the first few years of life, building and pruning trillions of neuronal connections. It forms all sorts of models about the world in order to use those models later on in life to navigate life. These models include what love is, how it is offered, and what we need to do to get it. *Tell me how you were loved, and I'll tell you how you love*, the saying goes. We develop *attachment styles*, a kind of emotional blueprint for how to operate in intimate relationships. We form what Katherine Woodward Thomas calls a *core love identity*, an unconscious understanding of love. Our core love identity might say "I'm loved just the way I am," or something worse like "I need to prove myself to be loved." Perhaps it even says, "I'm alone in this world."

It's become a cliche that as soon as you walk into your therapists' office they ask, "So, tell me about the relationship with your mother." But unfortunately, the research consistently shows that our feelings of being loved or unloved as children have an undeniable effect on our adult romantic partnerships.

The basic idea is this: children need to feel seen, soothed, safe, and secure. For that to happen they need *attunement*—a person that is *in tune* with their emotions and needs. Attuned caregivers reflect back our negative feelings, "You look grumpy, do you need a nap?" and mirror our positive ones, "Wow! You put the square peg in the square hole, well done!" If our caregivers were too intrusive on the one end or too neglectful on the other, we will grow up to have our own avoidant or anxious tendencies.

In her poem, *Origin Story*, Claudia Cortese (Cortese, 2016) describes the mis-attunement of a young child:

Lucy reaches her arms up for a hug, and her mother pats her on the head. Lucy tells her father that she made it to the final round of the school-wide spelling bee, and he mumbles something she can't hear. When she asks her mother for more apple juice, her mother hands her a glass of milk. When she asks her father to play Legos with her on the living room rug, he nods and leaves the room.

Reading these lines, you can feel the pain of not being seen. Relationship experts, Dr. Harville and Helen Hendrix, write that this ruptured connection in childhood is literally the source of all human problems and restoring this connection is the source of all healing (Hendrix & Hunt, 2019).

When such disconnection is a particularly challenging one, psychologists categorize it as an *Adverse Childhood Experience*, and there is a robust body of research showing how one's ACEs dramatically affect adult mental and physical health. Examples of ACEs include being around substance abuse, having a parent in prison, witnessing violence, and experiencing a divorce. Those with high ACE scores are more prone to health and behavioral problems when they become adults. People with childhood trauma are particularly prone to addiction problems, as they seek to soothe their stressed-out and hypervigilant nervous system with drugs or alcohol. "A hurt is at the center of all addictive behaviors," writes addiction specialist, Gabor Maté, as adult addicts seek to fill a very deep hole of childhood rejection (Maté, 2010).

Such childhood trauma represents a fundamental disruption in connection, and its adverse effects can be buffered by any kind of healthy, loving, and connected relationship. Whether it's a loving grandparent or a trusted friend, close relationships help us build resiliency to the challenges—and suffering—of life.

New Hurt

Researchers haven't just found that our adult relationships stir up old childhood wounds. They have actually found *we unconsciously choose the exact partner that will stir up our old childhood wounds the most*. The reason we fall in love with someone is because we believe this person can heal all of our hurts, especially those we experienced growing up. In a terrible twist of fate, mental patterns we aren't even aware of help us to choose the people we enter into a relationship with.

That "twin flame" you think you met in a "previous life" might just be a copy of who you met first as a child and will soon be stirring up all your old stuff. While we may think it is the physical attraction, their sense of humor, or that "we just clicked," in reality, our mammalian brain is seeking a partner that most resembles our own caregivers, usually our parents, in hopes that we can exert a sense of agency and control in order to heal our wounds. As the saying goes, *we all marry our unfinished business*.

Sometimes we repeat patterns, like continually entering into relationships with emotionally unavailable people, because they are familiar and thus seem safer than someone who might actually be good for us. Other times we repeat them because there is an unconscious desire to make it right. As an adult, we hope to fix the things that hurt us as a child. Our childhood seems like an unfinished movie. We think if we can start filming again, we'll be able to finish it with a happy ending, but usually, it ends up just being another rerun of crashing and burning.

We suffer and undergo a rollercoaster of relationships because there are unconscious patterns at play, and if we aren't willing to face and hold our suffering enough to listen to it and understand it, we will find ourselves entering into the same toxic cycles again and again. This is another lesson we can take from the suffering we experience in loving relationships: it is there to show us exactly where we need to grow the most. Partners in successful relationships recognize that every "upset" is a "setup" for personal work. Conflict in a relationship is always a call to go deeper. If our life is a snow globe, a loving relationship turns it upside and shakes it all up. All of our stuff comes up, our past patterns, childhood wounds, and limiting beliefs, and it's there for us to heal and grow from it.

Relationships are mirrors, but it's easy to forget that. Relationships keep the old adage alive, "We reject in others what we can't accept in ourselves," when partners complain to each other. The mirror might reveal mud on our face, but we blame the mirror and accuse it of being muddy and making us look bad. This is why couples will have the same argument for decades: they don't see their own patterns and thus are unable to change them. Just as suffering is a signpost for where we are stuck, the conflict that arises in a relationship is a mirror for our own stuff.

Ideally, our relationships are a positive feedback loop of joy and happiness, but more often, we are stuck in negative feedback loops of increasing hurt. One person gets angry when the other withdraws, which makes the first person get even angrier and the second person withdraws even more. We have to know our core issues in order to short-circuit the negative cycles that perpetuate suffering and create disconnection.

Not as Loving as We Think

Stephen and Ondrea Levine write, "the distance from your pain, your grief, your unattended wounds, is the distance from your partner" (Levine & Levine, 2010). The fact is, the reactive triggered part of us is simply unable to connect to another person. This is confirmed by psychology and neuroscience. We have higher cortical functions that are able to empathize, understand, and see another point of view. We also have a reactive, emotional limbic system. When we get triggered by our partner, our limbic system takes over and shuts down our capacity to be mindful and empathetic. We literally "flip our lid." Only after we have cultivated that capacity to notice our reactions without getting so caught up in them, will we finally have peace in our relationships.

The lesson from spiritual gurus and couples' therapists is the same: we must break free of our habitual reactions. Love can heal us and has the power to transform us, but only if we show up for it and are willing to do the work.

We all marry our unfinished business, so if you want your love life to survive, you have to finish your business! The next time you are angry at your partner, perhaps even furious, try this out, "Thank you darling, for doing the job I unconsciously hired you for. Thank you for pointing out exactly where I need to go and highlighting the wounds I desperately need to heal."

In previous chapters, we discussed how genuine spiritual practice deepens our ability to meet this world with an open heart. Yet there are countless anecdotes in spiritual communities from participants who have overwhelming experiences of love, understanding, and compassion in the moment, only to return to their home or family life to fall into the exact same patterns of reactivity.

There is a famous story of a Zen master named Su Dongpo, who wrote a poem expressing just how enlightened he had become:

I bow my head to the heaven within heaven,
Hairline rays illuminating the universe,
The eight winds cannot move me,
Sitting still upon the purple golden lotus.

Impressed by himself, Su Dongpo sent a servant to hand-carry this poem to his friend across the lake to another Zen master, Fo Yin. He was sure that his friend would be equally impressed. When the manuscript was returned, Su Dongpo found that the word "fart" was written in large letters across it. He was shocked. He burst into anger: "How dare he insult me like this? That lousy old monk! He's got a lot of explaining to do!"

Full of indignation, he rushed out of his house and ordered a boat to ferry him to the other shore as quickly as possible. He wanted to find Fo Yin and demand an apology. However, Fo Yin's door was closed. On the door was a piece of paper, for Su Dongpo. The paper had the following two lines:

The eight winds cannot move me,
One fart blows me across the river.

The most important part of this lesson is that Su Dongpo used it as an opportunity to learn and be humble. He still had very far to go.

Spiritual retreats are designed to push every button so that you have no buttons. Loving relationships will do the same. A relationship is where our attempts to keep a separate self, collide with our desire for connection. They will bring to the surface every unhealed wound, unrecognized trauma, and entrenched emotional patterns. Our partners get on our nerves so we can look at why the nerves are there in the first place. In relationships, we want to be loving and see ourselves as loving, until our egos are hurt or an old wound resurfaces. We then become reactive, defensive, and often critical. We might even go to a couples' workshop or read a self-help book and have some really useful tools to use, but if we are caught up in layers of triggers and reactivity, we aren't in a place to use them.

More Grist

There is another more sinister aspect of how our upbringing affects our adult romantic relationship. Obviously, what happens *to* us has a great effect on our development. But what happens *around* us is also just as important. Kids learn by modeling, by picking up on how people in their environment behave. Kids learn best by example and if a bad example is set, that's going to be bad news for their future. Alcoholism, abuse, obesity, a propensity to cheat, all these things are passed down from generation to generation. This is why in restorative justice we say, *hurt people hurt people*: those that have been hurt at an early age often go on to hurt others. Anyone that causes suffering is suffering. Those we label as "bad" are really just wounded.

Our unhealed wounds continue to bleed and will eventually stain our entire life. Another reason to finish your business is so you don't pass it on to your children. James Baldwin observed, "Children have never been very good at listening to their elders, but they have never failed to imitate them" (Baldwin, 1993). Psychologists have found that the strongest predictor of a child's well-being is the parent's self-understanding and awareness. If you want to fix your child, fix yourself.

The reality of interdependence teaches that everything, including you, is a result of causes and conditions. Bad behavior is the result of causes and conditions. The conflict we experience in relationships is there to show us what patterns we absorbed in the past that don't serve us in the present. We can then honor our parents by continuing the good parts of their lives and letting go of the bad parts. It is possible to end a pattern that was passed down across many generations if the person is willing to face it and resolve not to repeat it.

Ending intergenerational trauma is a lot easier said than done. The fact is, we all have shadows, and they are called shadows for a reason. We would prefer not to face them or address them. It takes courage to face our own stuff. As we learned in chapter two, when we finally see the darkness that must be integrated with our light, we often shy away. This is why most couples quit therapy after the fourth or fifth session—when the actual necessary work comes up, couples cut and run. This is also why many people don't call back after a wonderful third or fourth date. They are afraid of what might come up with deeper intimacy.

Unwilling to face the necessary pain and suffering of growth, partners close off. Instead of seeing critiques or complaints as guides to our own blind spots, biases, opinions, and assumptions that the ego loves to hold onto, we get defensive. Therapists know they can't just point out a client's shadow; the hard truth is almost always met with blatant denial. If you tell someone they have a temper, they will probably throw a chair across the room while yelling about how wrong you are. Nobody wants to feel pushed or pressured into change. Therapists have to invite their clients to discover the truth for themselves; there's no other way. This takes time and dedication, two things that make an intimate relationship perfectly suited for our own healing and integration.

Dr. John and Julie Gottman run the infamous "Love Lab" that observes couples interacting in an attempt to separate the "masters" from the "disasters." Their research has found that successful couples have a sweet spot ratio of positive experiences to negative ones. That magic number is five positive experiences for every one negative one. This finding is intuitive: the good times together should outweigh the bad times. Maybe you get into an argument on Wednesday, but that's ok because the other days of the week you shared some loving and supportive moments.

But why isn't the ratio of positive experiences negative 20 to 1, or 100 to 1, or more? Simple. If there is no negativity at all, it means you're not growing. You're not experiencing the stress or suffering that occurs with healing and growth. Couples that have a preponderance of only positive things usually have something going on underneath the surface. Perhaps they are avoiding addressing problems and simply sweeping them under the rug. There's often little vulnerability and little learning.

Conflict isn't something to avoid in relationships, it simply indicates the real friction that occurs when two totally separate worlds collide. There's a saying that if you are constantly sweeping problems under the rug, the rug will bunch, and sooner or later, you'll find yourself tripping over it and falling on your face. Having no negativity at all might sound good, but it usually is the result of avoidance and denial. Trying to stuff and hide your problems only makes them stronger in the long run. You're not taking risks, approaching mystery, or practicing vulnerability. Love is organic, if it's not growing, it's dying.

Fortunately, being able to repair conflict in a relationship will make it better in the long run. It is like working out to make a muscle stronger. When we lift something heavy, a microscopic tear happens in our muscle fibers, and in repairing that tear, our muscles get thicker and stronger. When we are able to bring up conflict in a relationship, be vulnerable and held, and come to an amicable conclusion, the relationship gets stronger too. We realize we can weather any storm, solve problems together, and move with greater ease. Even with such an extreme betrayal as infidelity, a relationship can move through it and end up stronger on the other side if, and that's a big IF, the situation is processed and understood thoroughly. In facing our shadows, in making the darkness conscious, we become more healed and whole. Some say every cloud has a silver lining, I say every shadow is surrounded by gold.

The reality of love and suffering teaches us that the only way to heal is to meet our wounds with tenderness and compassion. It can be our therapist, our partner, a group like AA, or even ourselves. For many of us, that inner child is still there, and the only way to move on in our adulthood is by holding that child within us with understanding and compassion.

Another Reality

If love is the realization that something in the universe is real, a loving relationship is one where we come face to face with the knowledge that our own ideas and beliefs aren't the only real ones either. Relationships require us to face a reality beyond our own; to move from thinking that our own perspective is the only real one, to acknowledging another separate reality that is just as real and true. This leads couples' therapists to offer simple advice like "accept the reality that your partner is not you" and "be an advocate for your partner's separate reality and potential."

In earlier chapters, we learned an important part of nonattachment is recognizing that what we think and believe is really not that important. Our mind is just an organ that regurgitates conditioning, and other people are often the trigger for those reactions. The comedian, George Carlin, quipped, "Have you noticed that everyone driving slower than you is an idiot, and everyone driving faster than you is a maniac?" Our reality is filtered through the lens of I, and our intimate relationships force us to let go of the illusion that we are the centers of the universe. That "I" is no longer *numero uno*.

Is our partner messy, or do they just prefer to clean once a month while we prefer to clean once a week? Are they careless about the children, or think it's more important to accommodate with love rather than discipline with anger? Arguments happen in relationships when both partners are trying to force their own reality on the other, believing that there is one objective reality that they both need to agree on. Successful relationships recognize that there isn't one objective reality, there are two subjective realities, and both are valid.

Every person in a relationship needs to ask themselves at some point, Do I want to be right, or do I want to be happy? Do I want to be correct, or connected? This choice is always present in every argument and conflict. Unfortunately, the more we feel our views challenged, the more we dig our heels into the ground and resist. Hence the funny line, "I'm sorry, I can't hear you over the sound of how right I am."

True listening is one of the hardest and most difficult tasks to ask of us human beings. Mostly because it requires us to step outside of our own heads and turn down the static and noise of our own internal thinking. Most of us try to listen to another person while there's a radio going full blast in our own heads, "They really think that? The nerve ... I have such a better and funnier story than this one, I can't wait until they finish speaking ... oh I better look interested, I better start nodding my head, oh, I think they just told a joke, I should smile..." and on and on. Most dialogue is just two interrupted monologues, as each person waits for their turn to express their own perspective. Real listening requires us to quiet our own minds and actually hear what the other person is saying, to see another reality that is just as valid as our own. This is why self-regulation is one of the biggest and most important skills to have in relationships. If you're constantly interrupting your partner, unable to listen and getting increasingly angry, you're not regulated, and unable to truly connect.

I See You, I Hear You

Therapists call the process of accepting your partner's reality, "letting your partner influence you." The poet, Mark Nepo, calls it a willingness to listen and actually "be changed by what we hear." The point is if we want to love we have to be open to change. Unfortunately, the ego hates change and will try to avoid it at all costs. While both partners in a relationship can work on letting their partner influence them, in heterosexual partnerships, the man tends to be the person who needs to learn to accept influence from his female partner, especially if he grew up in a patriarchal culture.

Sometimes we love based on how we were loved; other times we love the way we want to be loved now. Hoping our partners get the message, we do the things for them that we want done for ourselves. We offer kisses on the neck because we want kisses on our neck, we clean the house because want things done for us. But this fails to acknowledge that two different people want two different things, and neither are mind readers. Partners in a relationship often get mad when they don't get the things they never asked for. So rather than clean the house because you want your partner to clean the house or get mad that your partner doesn't clean the house, you do two things. First, express your wants clearly without judgment or criticism. Second, ask your partner what you can do for them, what their love language is, what they feel to be missing in the relationship, and what you can do to make it better.

There's even a term for this relationship strength: *perceived partner responsiveness*, "the extent to which individuals believe that their romantic partners care about, understand, and validate their thoughts and feelings" (Stanton *et al.*, 2019). This is why we say that intimacy is *into-me-see*—can you see the innermost core of this being in front of you? Love takes us deep into the essence of another, the innermost good, and in our loving, it allows that innermost good to blossom and come forward. We love our partners when we see the best in them and reflect the best of them back. The absolute best thing we can say to our partners is, "I see you, and I am here for you."

Therapists have found the need to be seen to be relevant across all relationships, even the ones the therapists have with their clients! As Lori Gottlieb wrote in her book on the therapeutic process, the most important factor in the success of a psychological treatment is the patient's experience of "feeling felt" (Gottlieb, 2020). Research has found that the therapist's ability to attune to and respond to their patient with loving acceptance was a greater predictor of outcomes than using any particular psychological method. Even medical doctors are less likely to get sued for malpractice if their patient feels seen and listened to, and employees are less likely to quit if they feel their boss validates their experience.

This is why it is so important to step out of our own subjectivity: it's often wrong. Or at the very least, distorted and limited. We don't see the world as it is, we see the world as we are. If you're constantly looking for problems, you'll find them. Like the pickpocket that sees only pockets, it's easy to look at our partners and only see what is wrong with them. But when you look at couples that are happy and couples that are unhappy, they usually do the same number of nice things for each other. The happy people are more likely to see, recognize, and express appreciation for nice acts. The unhappy couples don't see the loving acts of their partner and instead see only deficiencies.

Relationships are mirrors in how they show us our own stuff. But we can also be mirrors to each other to reflect back the goodness that we are. We can interrupt our own partner's negative thinking. When they are looking at themselves with a frown in the mirror in the bathroom, that's when we get to walk in and say they are the most beautiful thing we have ever laid our eyes upon. We love each other into being; we walk each other home. Meditation is often described as planting the seeds of positive intention in the heart and watering them with our loving presence. In partnership, *we can water each other's seeds*, shine the light of our own attention on the seeds of love, acceptance, and compassion in our partner's heart and nurture them to grow.

Expectations Minus Reality

There is another big reason our loving relationships are so hard: our expectations are sky-high. From a young age, we have been pummeled with the idea that once we find "the one" we will live "happily ever after." Psychologists call these *destiny beliefs*, which unfortunately do not make for a good, long-term relationship. Research shows partners that hold destiny beliefs actually tend to break up more quickly and more often, particularly when things start to become challenging. When partners in a relationship with destiny beliefs encounter a problem in their relationship, they conclude they must be with the wrong person, rather than work together to solve the problem.

Rather than destiny beliefs, people in more traditional cultures where marriages are arranged have *growth-oriented beliefs*. They know they are starting from just a seed and set the intention to grow the relationship as much as possible. While "self-selected" marriages based on love and sexual attraction tend to feel less love over time, those in arranged marriages tend to feel more in love as time grows. People who believe in romantic destiny tend to become unhappy quickly when relationships go through challenging times. People with strong growth beliefs, in contrast, think that partners can cultivate a high-quality relationship by working and growing together. People with destiny beings are focused on *finding* the one, while those with growth-oriented mindsets are focused on *being* the one.

What most people think of love is really just the beginning of love. It's easy to fall into the trap of destiny beliefs because the first stage of a relationship is so intoxicating. Psychologists call it *limerence*, polyamorists call it *new relationship energy*, most people call it the *honeymoon phase*, those first 6–18 months of falling in love with all the butterflies, obsessive thoughts, and ecstasy that results. It's easy to think you finally found the one, your soulmate, the most perfect person ever and that these feelings will last forever. Unfortunately, they rarely do, and when our idealistic love fades away to a more realistic love, we suffer as a result. But it's a good thing to finally realize our "perfect person" is just as imperfect as we are, and the new challenges that arise are there for us to grow and learn what love truly means.

In other words, love tricks us. We "fall in love," getting pulled into a new relationship with great sex, chemistry, and the most perfect, beautiful person. At the beginning, the ecstasy of love motivates us to spend hours getting ready, showing up all polished and shiny at the front door with flowers and a box of chocolates. When we are on our best behavior, what's not to love? Then, once we have made all sorts of promises for the future, discussed the best names for our children, and moved into the same apartment, in a lovely plot twist, love puts us face to face with our own stuff. At this point, it's too late, we have already committed, already fallen for the other.

Since there is no turning back time, we might as well work through the conflict and grow as a person. Love "knows" our ego tries to avoid pain, and the necessary change that comes with it. So it "traps" us first. Many of us would never jump so quickly into love if we knew all that it was going to ask of us. Hence the line that one partner in couples' therapy says, "but I love you!" and the other replies, "Don't you threaten me!" No one wants their safe little snow globe world turned upside down. But if we want intimacy, true intimacy, it's a risk we all have to take.

A humorous quip goes, "Sometimes we meet someone and try to cure their suffering. When we realize we can't, we marry them." We often enter into relationships with wounds we hope to heal, often in ourselves, but sometimes in the other. Not only do we think they are the perfect person for us, but that *we* are the perfect person for *them*. That is until we realize that we cannot love someone and try to change them at the same time. In true loving relationships, there is nothing to change. The mystics, philosophers, and scientists all agree—loving presence means having no agenda and no judgment.

Many people have the experience where the aspects that originally attracted them to a person end up being the exact things that end up annoying them the most. We like how they are mysterious until later on they become emotionally unavailable and withdrawn. We like how they are clean until they start criticizing our own mess. Whether their taste of adventure turned into never being around, their confidence ended up as stubbornness, or their eccentricity turned into a lack of self-control, relationships put us face to face with the reality that any strength has a weakness, anything light hits will cast a shadow. So we are put with the challenge to love this person, all of them, with every ounce of compassion and understanding we can muster, with no judgment, but a respect for their wholeness and how they came to be the person that they are.

Enormous Pressure

Our expectations are high because we have an incomplete vision of love, and also because there is more pressure on the intimate loving relationship than ever before. The relationship therapist and expert, Esther Perel, notes that the modern romantic relationship is expected to fulfill the needs that an entire village used to be responsible for. With the dissolving of extended family communities in our increasingly separated and isolated world, we now expect one person to be our sexual partner, intimate partner, life partner, emotional confidant, therapist, best friend, bank account, caregiver of our children, house cleaner, and chef.

We no longer marry out of duty or because our family's farm is next to our spouse's family farm. We marry someone because they make us happy, they serve a multitude of needs, and if a relationship isn't serving our happiness, it is now socially acceptable to leave it for a better one. Today, the survival of the family depends on the happiness of the parents, leading to a profession that never existed before in human history: the couples' therapist. Just a few hundred years ago, the idea of forming a lifelong bond based on such a fleeting and amorphous feeling of love was unheard of. Now, couples' therapists are faced with the monumental task of keeping two people perennially happy and in love, in a world where "til death do us part" lasts a lot longer than it ever did before.

Our expectations of loving relationships are enormous; there is more pressure on the intimate relationship than ever before, and beyond that, we expect our relationships to fulfill the role that God and religion used to fulfill. In previous chapters, we talked of the ecstatic joy that is found in mystical awakening, as well as the cultivation of the heart that spiritual practice offers. In our increasingly secularized and scientific world, we now often expect our relationship to fulfill the needs that the Church used to. We expect meaning, transcendence, ecstasy, awe, and wonder from our romantic partnerships. We expect our partners to revere and worship us. We don't just want an orgasm, we want a great, toe-curling cosmic explosion that dissolves the sense of separation to experience the Ultimate Unity.

The language of love has permeated the writings of the mystics, and the language of the mystics has permeated our love. Many enter into an intimate relationship seeking the Ultimate Union. We want to hear from our partners the words of Matthew 28:20, "Surely I am with you always, to the very end of the age." Defining trust as being a "confident relationship with the unknown" sounds a lot like faith. And for many of us, "falling in love" is a leap of faith, a trust and a surrender into another person and situation that is impossible to predict.

When I interviewed couples' therapist, Dr. Bruce Chalmer, about successful relationships, he said every relationship must have faith. Not just the kind of faith that two can work together and deepen their partnership, but a type of faith that reality is right to be as it is. The same way we put our faith in God's plan, we put our trust in the Universe that things are right to be where they are, even if it's painful.

Just as free will is the ultimate gift from God, we now have more freedom in our intimate relationships than ever before. No longer does one person work and one person stay at home, one parent is in charge of the money and the other takes care of the kids. Everything is up for grabs, everything is negotiated. What used to be defined by culture, society, or family of origin is now whatever two people decide it to be, including money, space, time, when and how to eat, sleep, talk, have sex, fight, work, and relax. With such a wide-open landscape, no wonder there are a few bumps when we try to traverse it.

Answering the Call

So what are we to do about this tremendous pressure? We answer the call. We let our personal love become divine and our divine love become personal love. We seek to become the most loving, kind, generous, and supportive people we can possibly be. Our destiny is to become love.

That means doing the necessary work and keeping our hearts open to the hell of our own reactions and conditionings. The absolute best thing we can do for our partners is work on ourselves. The best thing our partner can do for us is work on themselves. I remember one lecture by a monk who said, somewhat humorously, "My desire to cultivate a peace within myself grew out of a compassion for everyone who has to put up with me." A huge reason to work on oneself is simply the recognition that sometimes we are a difficult person to be with.

It's All Connected

Remember, everything is connected. When one thing changes, so does everything else. If you want to change your partner, change yourself. If you want your partner to open their heart, open your own. Accept responsibility for something that went wrong and watch your partner do the same. The quality of your relationship will change when you change what you bring to it. If you expand your love, your partner will fill in that space. You're in it together.

Earlier we talked about the principle that hurt people hurt people. Well, the opposite is true too: *healed people heal people*. Once you have integrated your own shadow and grown fully into love, and created a solid partnership, then you are ready for the next big step: extending that love to more and more beings, shifting from "me" to "us" to "all of us."

Which brings us to another reason why we all struggle in relationships: our society is not set up in any way that serves love. We don't live in a society that prioritizes love and cherishes relationships. You can go through 16 years of education without someone ever teaching you how to forgive, how to communicate your feelings, how to resolve conflict, the foundations for a successful partnership, or how to adjust your relationship when kids enter the equation. Sex education in the United States is lamentable; love education is nonexistent. We teach biology, physics, history, and chemistry, but we don't teach the skills to benefit our intimate relationships. We don't learn about attachment theory, soft start-ups, bids, heart rate variability, forgiveness, or how to say goodbye to someone we love who is dying.

For love to truly flourish, we must realize it doesn't exist in an isolated vacuum but is intimately connected to the world around it. And for that love to flourish, the environment must be conducive to its growth. The love in our romantic partnerships is like a flower, it needs space, light, and nutrients. It won't grow in a barren wasteland. For that, we must restructure our society and our very world to support and cherish love for the gift that it is. We must see that one intimate relationship is just the beginning, as we learn to love more and more people and widen our circle of compassion to encompass all beings.

Chapter 7

The Love of Humanity

What if the mightiest word is love? Love beyond marital, filial, national, love that casts a widening pool of light.
Elizabeth Alexander

Love is the reason we are here on Earth. Nothing is more meaningful or powerful than the expression of love. Every problem in the human condition is the result of a lack of love, and every solution is more expansive and inclusive love. Every human being has an extraordinary potential for love, but like any potential, there are things we must do for it to become realized. This means cultivating three components of love: attention, understanding, and action.

Attention Is the Food of Love

Attention is the food of love. Our attention nourishes and sustains our love. As Simone Weil put it, "Attention is the rarest and purest form of generosity" (Popova, 2015). Just as sound needs to travel through the medium of air, our love needs to travel through the media of our attention. The basic idea that "our love begins with our attention" is lesson three of *The Seven Lessons of Love*. I wrote those lessons many years ago and the more I learn and discover about the nature of love, the more truth I find in them.

To truly be there for someone, you have to actually be there—body, mind, and heart. Since we all need to be heard, love means showing up fully to listen. The best gift we can offer another human being is our presence. This applies not just to romantic relationships with another person, and not just to our family and friends, but also to ourselves and to the world.

Attention on Ourselves

To begin our discussion on attention being the food of love, let us first look at ourselves from when we first came into this life.

Needing love in the form of our attention, begins as soon as we come into this world. Young infants need attention, they demand attention, and if they feel they are not getting the attention they need, it triggers the most basic survival concerns of, "Will I survive?" As infants we not only need someone to pay attention to us to get our physical sustenance and keep us safe and sheltered, but we also need the attention of love and affection in order to develop our mental and emotional capacities. We need someone to gaze at us so we learn facial expressions, talk to us so we learn language, and comfort us with touch so we understand the importance of physical closeness and intimacy. We need someone to soothe us when we are emotionally agitated, and to offer an emotional scaffolding for us to build off.

If we did not experience loving attention as a developing infant and instead were often neglected, we would grow up to be wary and avoid emotionally connecting with others. If we received sporadic attention, overly imposing attention, or full-on abandonment, we would develop a more anxious attachment that wants connection but is afraid it will leave. This results in us often being wary and overly diligent of our partner's behavior.

Since our more challenging attachment patterns resulted from a lack of attuned loving attention, they can only be repaired by that same loving attention, which we can offer to ourselves, right here and now. Meditation is often described as a kind of "spiritual reparenting" in which we can give ourselves the loving attention we did not receive from our parents. This is one of the most fundamental lessons I have learned from the many compassion cultivation trainings that I have taken and guided: *we have the capacity to heal ourselves with our innate loving nature.*

When I interviewed Dr. Heather Bartos on what self-love looks like, she explained that most people's idea of "self-love" is usually a form of indulgence that manifests as escapism. The magazines tell us to go to the spa, get a massage, pour a glass of wine, have some dark chocolate, or make ourselves a bubble bath. Although self-care can be an important part of self-love, if it means avoiding our own emotional issues, those issues will come back with a vengeance. True self-love means accepting our imperfections and being present with our emotions. Paradoxically, to become a "perfect" person, we must accept all our imperfections. If we cannot be with imperfections, if we cannot access the suffering of life, we cannot love.

The couples' therapist, Terry Real, defines healthy self-esteem as the capacity to hold yourself warmly and tenderly in the face of your screw-ups and imperfections as a human being (Real, 2023). When I first heard that definition, I thought that it sounded a lot like keeping your heart open in hell. Self-love is not cliche affirmations like "you are perfect and beautiful," to put on the bathroom mirror. Self-love recognizes that we are imperfect, we will make mistakes, we might lose our temper or wake up on the wrong side of the bed, and we are still deserving of love. No matter what mistakes we make, at the end of the day we are worthy of love, warts and all. Self-love involves bringing compassion and acceptance to all parts of ourselves, even the parts of ourselves that have a hard time loving those other parts.

Self-love knows it is our destiny to love and be loved. Self-compassion means meeting whatever is going on inside of us with kind-hearted attention. "Can you keep your heart open in hell?" seen through the mirror of self-compassion looks like the two-fold question, "What is happening inside of me?" and "Can I meet it with kindness?" The beginning of healing is relating to our inner life with acceptance and compassion. There's a reason the Buddha taught mindfulness of the breath and mindfulness of the body as the gateway to freedom: our healing happens right here, right now, inside of us, and we already have what we need. No PhD or external knowledge necessary. We can trust in our inherent goodness, stop being so hard on ourselves, and embrace the mess.

Good News

One of the best things we can do for ourselves is love ourselves. One of the hardest things for us to do is love ourselves. We hold ourselves the same way we were held. We love based on how we were loved.

Fortunately, most of the obstacles to more self-love are misconceptions about what self-love is. Most misgivings about practicing self-love, kindness, and compassion are simply not true. Many people think that if they practice more self-acceptance, that will undermine their motivation, particularly on the path of self-improvement. If we accept ourselves for being overweight, will that undermine our motivation for attaining a healthy weight?

The comedian, Jim Gaffigan, quipped, "I don't stop eating when I'm full, I stop eating when I hate myself." Many people think that inner aggression, self-hatred, and self-criticism are effective motivating forces for good. If we hate ourselves for eating junk food, that will in turn motivate us to eat better; if we dislike our bodies, it will motivate us to go to the gym.

However, the research shows that this is simply not the case. First off, our tendency for self-criticism undermines our self-confidence and leads to a fear of failure. If we know we will be hard on ourselves for failing or missing the mark, we are less likely to try new things out of fear of punishment. If we know we will be criticized, even by ourselves, we will be a lot less likely to do it. The research actually shows that those who love themselves more are no less likely to have high personal standards. In scientific speak, self-compassionate people are "less vulnerable to the affective consequences of thwarted goal progress" (Hope *et al.*, 2014). Perfectionism is its own kind of suffering.

Another obstacle on the path to more self-love is when people conflate it with selfishness or narcissism. People often associate self-love with self-indulgence and feel a sense of guilt over taking care of themselves. But self-compassionate people have more compassion for others too; it is not a matter of selfishness but a matter of understanding that love that comes from a place of wholeness and fullness is more effective and longer lasting than love that comes from a place of emptiness. Self-love, as a practice to better love others, is rooted in the same principle of putting on one's own oxygen mask first. Can you expect to fill up someone's teacup if your teapot is empty? How many teacups can you fill if there is a hole in your pot? Self-love is giving oneself the energy and health that lets one be of better service to others.

The research confirms that self-love is not associated with being indulgent or selfish. Nor is it associated with narcissistic behaviors like stealing or abusing others for one's personal sake. Rather, true self-love means wanting long-term health over short-term pleasure. Self-compassionate people engage in healthier behaviors like exercise, eating well, drinking less, and going to the doctor more regularly. When we love ourselves, we become the best version of ourselves. When we love another, we invite them to become the best person they can be.

Have you ever noticed how hard it is to connect with someone who is disconnected from themselves? Well, it works the other way around too. People who are more connected to themselves are more caring and supportive in their interpersonal relationships. By connecting to our own experience, we are able to feel more empathy and understanding for others who are going through or have gone through a similar experience. We can then offer kind and understanding attention to others, which coincidentally, is the best thing we can offer to another human being. True acceptance of another human being is the most beautiful invitation there is. Unfortunately, if we have little interest in our own emotional world, we will have little interest in our partner's inner world. So too, we often reject in others what we have rejected in ourselves. Only by accepting ourselves in all our mistakes and imperfections will we learn to love others through theirs.

Attention To Others

There is a reason why therapy is so effective and why talking to a friend is so healing: attention is the food of love. The lessons from contemplative practitioners and the scientific findings on neuroplasticity are the same: what we pay attention to matters. We all need to be seen, recognized, and understood, not treated like problems to be solved. Most problems can't be solved, but they can be shared. In hard times, we don't need a cure, we need a witness. The first step to being there for another person is to actually be there—body, mind, and heart—communicating, "You matter and you are loved." We can't be everything to each other at all times, but we can offer a shoulder to cry on, an ear that listens, and a hand to hold. All parts of us need to be heard and held. If we aren't free to cry, those tears stay inside, form into a pool, and we drown in it. This is called depression.

People talk a lot about the five love languages: service, giving, words, time, and touch. Whenever I see those five actions, I think about how kind-hearted attention covers all five of them. Quality time is when two partners in a relationship remove any distractions in order to connect emotionally. Our time and attention are also gifts that we can offer in each and every moment. If we want to offer words of affirmation, we do that with eye contact and by giving our undivided attention. Physical touch, of course, involves our loving attention too. The act of lovemaking is one of the few times in a person's life when they are present the most, which is one of the biggest reasons why it is such a pleasurable experience.

You will never fully or completely know your partner or what goes on in their internal world. You will never understand the full depth of their magnificence. You can only remain curious, open, and committed to deepening your understanding of them and continuously growing in intimacy. This reflects one of the biggest crises today: the crises of our time. We spend way more time gazing into our phones than our partner's eyes, stroking our screen instead of our partner's cheeks. If attention is the food of love, then our love is starving because our phones, apps, media, ads, and more vie for our limited and increasingly thinning attention. Our challenge then, and the challenge of our times, is to learn to slow down again and learn to be fully present with each other and ourselves.

Attention is a healer. Offering it is an act of service, which is not just limited to our partners. Giving loving attention to those who need it is a wonderful form of healing one can offer the world. When I work with men in prison, one of the biggest challenges for the "men on the inside" is feeling that they have largely been forgotten by society. Life sentences have a feeling of "lock them up and throw away the key." The sense of isolation from the world is its own special kind of torture. Many prisoners simply want their stories to be heard by a world that doesn't seem to care.

Love Is Understanding

If you want to truly love someone, you have to get close to them. If you want to love another person, you have to listen to their story. This would solve so many problems in the world, because when we actually listen to another person's story, we realize our own similarities and common humanity. We learn the truth of the old adage, "Be kind to everyone you meet, because each person is fighting a hard battle." Everybody is suffering in some way, and if we are able to listen to their suffering, it would not only alleviate some of their troubles, but our own issues won't seem so isolating either. We will realize that whatever we are going through in our own lives, others are also going through their own trials and tribulations.

You cannot have love without understanding. Imagine coming home after a rough day of work and telling your partner about your day. At the end of sharing your unique struggles, your partner replies, "I'm sorry I wasn't listening, but I wanted to say I love you and you're perfect." Such an empty platitude completely fails to meet you in that moment and falls flat. We need to understand our partner, their plights, struggles, hopes, and dreams, in order to truly love them.

Love without understanding can create a lot of suffering. Imagine gifting your spouse flowers that they are allergic to or consoling an alcoholic friend by offering them a drink. The monkey will think it's saving the fish from drowning by putting it up in a tree. The same act that creates happiness in one person can create suffering in another, and it is wise understanding that knows the difference.

If you do not know *why* someone is suffering, you won't know how to alleviate them from it, and your method will probably exacerbate it. In partnership, we jump to what therapists call *premature problem solving*, when we try to fix someone's problem before taking the time to listen and give space for those challenging emotions.

A lot of family therapy is not focused on solving specific problems. Instead, research has found that *understanding* is the vehicle for the cure. Once we know how past and current patterns contribute to the problem and commit to changing those negative reactions, the problems will dissolve naturally. Once the father understands how his overworking and travel away is contributing to his son's diminishing school attendance, his understanding will change his behavior to better take care of the family. No doubt about it: understanding leads to healing.

Understanding Is Love's Other Name

We must bring understanding to our love in progressive circles as well. In the United States, it may be easy for a white person to say, "I love people of all races" and it might feel true from the perspective of the speaker. Perhaps they do not have an ounce of prejudice or implicit bias in any cell of their being. But how genuine is that love, if they do not understand the plights of marginalized Americans? If a person does not see and seek to understand the injustice and violence that is happening, then their love is empty and their words are empty.

Perhaps a follower of a certain religion says that they love *all* of God's children, and that their God loves everyone too; but they also believe homosexuality is a sin and gay people are going to hell. Is it truly love if they perpetuate the prejudice, hatred, and violence against gay and lesbian people? Is it love if they don't understand this person's queer love is the same as their straight love, that this is who this person is, nothing will change that, and they must understand a perspective outside of their own and share in such common humanity? If you do not see the suffering of marginalized people, you can't love them.

As the mud nourishes the lotus, being with suffering nourishes the flowers of compassion and understanding. We again can learn from the Buddhists, who do not talk of good and evil, but that we can be more or less mindful and more or less skillful in our relationships. Less understanding creates more suffering, more understanding lessens suffering.

Understanding is love's other name. The deeper the understanding, the deeper the love. Listening to another person's story is a gateway to peace in this world. There is an inscription at the Murambi Genocide Memorial in Rwanda that reads, "If you knew me, and if you really knew yourself, you would not have killed me." Violence stems from a sense of *othering*, and evildoers in the world will intentionally create a sense of separation to get people to do evil acts. Sometimes *othering* involves complete dehumanization, like when the Hutus called the Tutsis cockroaches during the Rwandan Genocide, or the Nazis referred to the Jews as rats during the holocaust.

The solution to shifting away from "us versus them" to "us versus the problem" is to listen to the "other side," hear their stories, and embrace our common humanity. Henry Wadsworth Longfellow put it the same when he wrote, "If we could read the secret history of our enemies, we should find in each man's life sorrow and suffering enough to disarm all hostility" (Longfellow, 1857). True understanding always begets compassion. Suffering wants to be understood; suffering wants to be loved.

This is another fundamental lesson of attention. To find the courage to be present in this moment, we have to find the courage to be present in all moments. Whether we are bringing our attention to the flower blooming before us, or the injustices all around us, it is the same. In this way, our attention can bring positive change to the world, but it will only do so if we practice the third step: action.

Love Is a Practice

At the end of every Learn to Love podcast episode, I ask my guests, "What do you wish everyone knew about love?" It is one of my absolute favorite questions to ask. Each answer is both an inspirational and profound reminder that few things are as beautiful or transformational as love. It's heartwarming to hear things like, love is so much more expansive than people realize. Love is our birthright. Love is the most real thing on this planet. Love can always be given freely. Keep in mind, these are professionals, not idealists, so it is encouraging to hear from so many psychologists, therapists, scientists, and educators that love is the greatest source of meaning and happiness.

There is one answer that keeps coming up in almost every episode. It is a message that is crucial in not only understanding love, but also realizing why love can completely change our lives. The message that keeps coming up again and again is that love is not a thing that you have; rather, it is a verb you can express. Love is an action, and you can choose to bring it into your life every day, and in fact, in every moment.

In short, love is a practice. Love is not an agreement to be in a relationship, but a commitment to continuously care and value this other person for exactly who they are in the moment. Love is not something you receive but something you give, not something you feel but something you express, and not something that happens to you, but something you choose to bring into your life. Recognizing that love is a verb is one of the most transformational shifts of perspective we can have. It will change not only our relationships, but our very world.

Seeing love as a verb means recognizing that you are not in a relationship, but that you are in a continuous process of relating. It is not something that you can accumulate, it is only something you can do. And you can "do" love a million and one ways. As a result, love is walking a path of discovery; not only of the vast landscapes that is another person's world, but also in all the ways we can offer our love to others, all the big and small gestures of kindness that make life worth living for ourselves and others. The path of love is one of the most rewarding acts that there is, one that encourages us to become the best version of ourselves. "There is a nobility in compassion, a beauty in empathy, and a grace in forgiveness," wrote novelist, John Connolly. Nobility, beauty, and grace, these are all benefits of the practice of love. Like any practice, we must consciously choose to do it to reach our fullest potential.

Love Is a Call to Action

Love as a verb asks more of us: it asks us to do something. Love with just words is often empty; it matters how you show up and embody that love. Love is a call to action, not just to sit on our butts and wish love for others, but to actively be of service to others and to use one's privilege to remove the obstacles in other's way. Seeing love as a verb means recognizing the privileges one has and actively helping others with less. Seeing love as a verb means combining our love with activism, integrating our love with who we vote for, what we march for, and how we spend our money. Rather than talk about love we are asked to fully live it, not just on a personal level, but on professional and political ones too. Living from love means nonviolence but does not mean nonaction. It means working in the world with compassion for all beings, giving special attention to the most affected by injustice.

Many people are starting to recognize the narcissism so endemic in spiritual communities and the spiritual bypassing that enables it. Certain lineages have long known about the "spiritual ego" and how the ego can so easily hijack spirituality for its own benefit. As practitioners experience growth through meditation and spiritual practice, they can easily unintentionally adopt a "holier than thou" ascetic, thinking they are better than others. On the way to becoming "awake", they begin to decry how everyone else is so "asleep," a kind of narcissism that becomes so easily parodied. In thinking they are holier than others, spiritual bypassers end up being the least holy of all. Spiritual work, which should recognize we are all in this together, becomes limited to self-help. It's okay to work on ourselves in order to then serve others, but many people never get to that second step.

The way out of an inflated sense of self, then, is a path of selflessness. A path of giving and generosity. A path of service, karma, and *seva*. The path of justice. It is a path of seeing love as a verb, not just a subject to be worshiped in a temple or church, but to be actively brought into the world through concrete action. As Krishna tells Arjuna in verse 6.3 of the Bhagavad Gita, "Action is the means for a sage who seeks to mature in discipline." Once we have calmed the mind and opened the heart, our true work in the world begins.

Fortunately, in pockets, people are beginning to recognize the need for concrete and courageous loving action. There is an entire movement known as "engaged Buddhism" that seeks to apply insights from meditation practice and dharma teachings to situations of social, political, environmental, and economic suffering and injustice. Meditation communities have faced criticism of naïve navel-gazing while the world around them crumbles. It should come as no surprise that Thich Nhat Hahn became a huge proponent of engaged Buddhism when he was meditating in Vietnam during the war, so the monks could attend to the sick and help the needy.

Now, in Zen communities, you will find "Awakening to Whiteness" workshops. The Buddhist leader Joan Halifax teaches just as much about economic, racial, and climate justice as she does about finding peace and discovering the reality of impermanence. Great leaders like Tara Brach are speaking out about racism and white privilege. One of my favorite meditation centers, East Bay Meditation Center in Oakland, has social justice written into its core and you will find sessions on subjects like "Embodying the Timeless Wisdom of Reverend Martin Luther King Jr. for Black, Indigenous and People of Color."

Love Is Justice

It seems fitting to remember the quote by Cornel West that, "justice is what love looks like in public." When our love becomes a verb and when we bring it to the streets and our capitals, it looks a lot like fighting for equality for all peoples. When we widen our circle of compassion to more and more people, we have no choice but to include fighting for the rights of those most marginalized by society. We expand the us in "us versus them" so much it eventually just becomes *us*. Seeing love as a verb means seeing how we are all connected, how our actions, past, present, and future connect each other, and if we are to love everybody, that means helping everyone too.

The more I think about keeping our hearts open in hell the more situations I find relevant. Keeping our hearts open means staying fully human in our relationships, not shutting down our emotions or closing the source of kindness, compassion, and understanding within us. For some, an open heart in hell means talking to their estranged parents, for others, holding their child having a tantrum. Maybe it's speaking in front of a group, talking to a therapist about the pain of grief, or sitting down with someone with the opposite political beliefs. For some it is working in a hospice, for others, it is becoming a caregiver for their helpless partner going through cancer treatment.

When I interviewed the human connection coach, Emily Gough, she said we must find the courage to have difficult conversations. She emphasized that the conversations we are avoiding the most are the ones we most need to have. An open heart in hell is compassion, but it's also forgiveness. It's listening, but also acting for the good of others. In public, it is bearing witness to truth, like the South African Truth and Reconciliation Commission or the Rwandan Gacaca courts. An entire country facing hard truths in order to move on and heal is perhaps one of the largest mass actions of keeping hearts open in hell. If an entire country can keep its heart open through Apartheid (in the case of South Africa) or genocide (in the case of Rwanda), we can keep our hearts open in our own hells too.

Components of Compassion

Attention, understanding, action. We see all these elements work together with the unification of love and suffering: compassion.

By recognizing that compassion too is a verb, we begin a lifetime journey of opening the heart. To help better understand just how compassion can be a verb, it will help to understand what are known as the four components of compassion. Sometimes called the four dimensions, core aspects, or levels of compassion, understanding each component will help us bring more love and compassion into our daily lives.

Compassion is our heart's natural response to suffering, whether in ourselves or in others. Perhaps the easiest definition of compassion is our capacity to be with suffering with an open heart. Both contemplative practitioners and researchers have found there to be four components to compassion:

- *Cognitive awareness* of suffering
- *An emotional response* to that suffering
- *A wish* for that suffering to be relieved
- *A readiness* to act

Those are the four layers: think, feel, intend, act. Put differently, awareness, empathy, intention, action, uniting together mind, heart, soul, and body. As a psychologist would put it: cognitive, emotional, intentional, motivational.

Cognitive Awareness and Sympathetic Concern

Our first level of compassion is simply recognizing that somebody else is suffering in some way. If you are sitting at a bus stop and you see someone fall off their bicycle, it doesn't take a genius to realize that person is probably in some pain from the fall. Similarly, if someone is hungry, in the hospital, or their business just went broke, we can understand they probably did not want these things to happen and are suffering too.

A cognitive awareness of suffering is important to compassion because we can apply it to people and experiences very different from our own, including things we have never experienced before. Reading books and memoirs can grow our ability to see things from another person's point of view. This first component of compassion is what you might call the cognitive, intellectual, or mental level.

The next step to compassion is empathy. This level is not a cognitive empathy of seeing someone's point of view, but a deeply emotional one where we actually feel and sense someone else's suffering in our own body. This is sometimes called the "affective" or "emotional" component of compassion. Remember that the root of the word compassion comes from the Latin word *compati*, which means "to suffer with." Our emotional component to suffering involves a shared feeling. This emotional affect allows us to say with honesty, *I know what you're feeling, because I feel it too.*

Our sympathetic concern should not be confused with pity, which is looking down on someone from above. Rather, we enter the same emotional space that they are in. When somebody is telling you that they are sad because they got fired from their job, you would use active listening to not only understand what they are going through but feel and empathize with their sadness.

A Wish and Responsiveness

Compassion has mental and emotional components, but it does not stop there. Compassion is not just something you think and feel, it is also something that you do. Our next step is to bring our compassion more into the world by setting the intention for that suffering to end. The third component of compassion involves a wish or desire for the suffering of another to end. This is a natural capacity that all human beings have. Even babies show comforting behavior to another baby who is crying.

This intentional level is important. Even though it is layer number three, that does not mean we have to wait for the mental and emotional responses to occur. First thing in the morning we can set an intention to be more compassionate that day. Before we make a challenging phone call, we can set the intention to make our communication as compassionate as possible.

Once we set our intention for others to experience less suffering in their lives, we are ready for the final component: action. The fourth component of compassion involves a motivational level, where we are ready to act. This step involves letting our desire to help manifest as concrete action. Compassion is not simply an inner movement of thought and emotion but an outer movement of intention and action. Compassion involves doing things to make the world a better place.

All four levels of compassion represent different skills that can be improved and developed. If any layer is lacking, your compassion will be lopsided and incomplete. There are many times when someone acts on their compassion without empathizing with the person they are helping, and as a result, their help is the entirely wrong method for the situation. There are other times when we might recognize suffering but not actually do anything about it. Sometimes our empathy is so strong we can't think straight. We must find balance.

Other People's Problems

When I went to graduate school to study all things related to love, I decided to major in East-West Psychology, so I could deepen my understanding of Western Mystical Traditions, Eastern cosmology, and modern psychology. At the time, many other students had decided to become therapists. This path didn't resonate with me, and I remember when one student asked me, "Why don't you want to become a therapist?" I replied, "Well, to be honest, I don't want to sit in a room and listen to other people's problems."

Looking back at that statement, I cringe, but also see that I was on the beginning of my path and it's natural to have an aversion to the suffering of others. The spiritual journey often starts *selfish* but always ends *selfless*. We might come to yoga or meditation to gain flexibility or reduce stress, or we major in psychology to better understand our own trauma. Eventually, the practice of internal work shifts more external and becomes like the Bodhisattva committed to alleviating the suffering of all beings. At the time, I still had much work to do on myself before I could even think of doing work for others. I was too consumed with my own problems to be of any service. I wasn't in touch with my own emotions and couldn't imagine the overwhelm of listening to those of others. My heart was closed.

It took many years of personal development and intentionally cultivating compassion to get to where I am today. Now, I *love* listening to other people's problems! I absolutely love it. I want to listen to other people's problems all day every day. I can't think of more important or impactful work. It is such a divine and intimate experience for someone to open up their emotional world to you, and in doing so, a heart-to-heart connection is made.

Before with a closed heart, I was only at step one of the four components of compassion, the mental recognition that somebody else was in pain. Just knowing about suffering isn't very fun. After several compassion cultivation trainings, I didn't just *know* about suffering, but *felt* it in my body. I realized the mind *thinks*, but the heart *feels*. Such empathic resonance creates a real connection, and there is powerful healing with deep compassionate listening. By linking the shared feeling of compassion with an intention and motivation to alleviate it, suffering then becomes a source of aliveness and meaning.

The Beauty of a Compassionate Response

I now see that compassion is a wonderful emotion, and being with someone who is suffering gives you a way to experience it. Being present with suffering is a gift. Once I came to this understanding, I applied to my second master's degree to become a full-fledged therapist, to experience the gift of compassion with my clients every day. In psychopathology class, my professor explained what therapy is about. *Psyche* means soul, *pathos* comes from Greek and means suffering, and *ology* is study, thus psychopathology is the study of human suffering. The therapy office is like a suffering laboratory, two souls come together to share in this essential human experience and try to figure a way out.

People don't just share their problems in the therapy office, they share their deepest thoughts, emotions, and fears. Clients share things with their therapists that they don't share with anybody else, even their spouses of decades. Such deep vulnerability and sharing are a precious gift. It also points to a major problem in today's world. While everyone is suffering in some way, most people suffer in secret. Many are afraid to tell their family, spouse, or employer of their suffering out of fear of retribution, or that it will make matters worse. This bottling up of our pain isn't healthy, which is why having a safe and welcoming space to share is so healing.

One of the most interesting things about the therapeutic container is that the most important factor for a beneficial therapeutic relationship is love. However, the psychology world is very aversive to the *L*-word, so instead they dance around it with terms like *unconditional positive regard* and *therapeutic bond*. Therapists are taught the importance of active listening without judgment, emotional attunement, warmth, curiosity, empathy, acceptance, normalization, and validation. Instead of words like *union* or *intimacy*, one textbook on essential skills for therapy said a therapist must successfully *join* with their clients, which is the "sense of connectedness" that arises when the client feels the therapist understands, respects, and cares about them (Patterson et al., 2018). At first, I thought *join* was a funny word that conveniently avoids the word *love*, but then I remembered: *If we want to love another person, we have to join them.*

The best thing a therapist can do is accept their client in their totality, all the good and bad, light and dark, successes and failures. This is extraordinarily healing. The most impactful exchange I ever had with my therapist went like this: "I have these terrible thoughts, does that make me a terrible person?" To which she replied, "No, not at all. You're not a terrible person." In that simple reply, I stopped resisting the thoughts, and they were able to go away on their own in due time. Being told we are not terrible makes us less terrible, being told we're not broken makes us less broken. Love is seeing the light in another and reflecting it back.

Be There

We all have a need to be known and are simultaneously terrified of being known. The therapist acts as unconditional love, in turn giving the client permission to accept their darkness too and be put on the path to healing. The evidence shows that we all want to hear from our healthcare professionals the exact same thing we want from our partners, "I hear you, and I'm here for you." Or Thich Nhat Hanh's mantra, "Darling, I know that you are suffering. That is why I am here for you." Attention is the purest form of love; loving presence is our most precious gift to offer another, both personally and professionally. If you want to heal a human being, listen to them and understand them. Say with your body, heart, and mind, "You are not alone."

Another reason therapy is so effective is the *consistency*. Adults that experienced abandonment, neglect, and instability during childhood finally receive the message that there are people who will stick around and care for them, and people whom they can trust. The strength of the relationship between therapist and client is more important for healing than any theory or technique the therapist uses. The most healing thing anyone can communicate to another is that the world is safe, kind, and trustworthy.

Just like we put a bandage over a cut, or our mother kissed our skinned knee, compassion covers our wounds, soothing our suffering and allowing true healing to happen. Our need for someone to be there for us begins at birth and never stops. Compassion communicates safety. All our lives we carry a wish for reassurance that says, "It's going to be ok, I am here for you." You can be that reassuring voice. You don't need to have all the answers or the ability to fix the situation right away, but you can offer safety and security by wrapping the other in a warm blanket of your own heart. Safety is a prerequisite to vulnerability, not a precursor. Like a dog trusting someone enough to show its belly, compassion communicates safety enough for us to reveal the more tender parts of ourselves.

Compassion is the key factor in preventing empathy burnout, because it includes the mindfulness aspect that allows us to notice our empathic response without getting caught up in it. Empathy tends to be linked with shared pain and emotion, while compassion is deeply connected to the parts of the brain associated with care, learning, decision making, and reward. But compassion doesn't stop at emotional connection, we have to tune in to our intention too. The Buddha said, "Our entire life arises from the tip of our intention" and without it, we are just stuck in the weeds. Intention holds promise, it is something we can cultivate right now. This is the beginning of love and the opening of the heart. We must also have the motivation to help, to get off of our butts and do something about it.

Compassion Arises from Commonness

Another key component of compassion is connecting our suffering to the suffering of all of life. Rather than suffer and wallow in a "why me?" state of mind, we use the power of mindfulness to *dis-identify* from the suffering and use the power of an open heart that sees it in the context of all the suffering of life. This is the practice of seeing our *common humanity*. This is the final step in our process of embracing emotions with a wide-open heart. In Chapter 1, we discussed shifting from "I am angry" to "I am feeling anger." Then we can encompass that painful emotion even more to "this is pain arising in an open field of loving awareness." Then we widen the circle even further and say, "this is the pain of life that we all share in." As Stephen Levine writes, "My pain is a tragedy; *the* pain is a further teaching in compassion" (Levine, 2013).

This is perhaps the quickest way to alleviate one's suffering: *to let go of the one that suffers*. By moving from "my pain" to "the pain" to "our pain," we let go of the idea of a false self and instead see ourselves as sharing this one life with everyone else. The French author and political activist, Jacques Lusseyran, put it marvelously when he wrote, "Unhappiness… comes to each of us because we think ourselves at the center of the world, because we have the miserable conviction that we alone suffer to the point of unbearable intensity. Unhappiness is always to feel oneself imprisoned in one's own skin, in one's own brain." Remember, anywhere we don't want to be is a prison. A lot of the time, we are the ones that put up the bars, creating an illusion that we are alone in our suffering and the only person to have ever suffered this much in the history of mankind. That is until we realize millions of people have gone through, are currently going through, and will go through, exactly what we are going through.

Compassion is best understood experientially, beginning with ourselves. Take a few minutes to reflect. How are you feeling right now in this moment? Are you tired, excited, bored, or anxious? Where are you struggling in your life? Are you having challenges around work, physical or mental health, your family, a friend, or your love life? Are you suffering in any way? Do you have any achy joints or sadness concerning the loss of something important? Do you want to be happy? Right now, do you find yourself wanting more peace, calm, or joy in your life?

Final question: *Do you think anybody else feels, or has felt, exactly the same way?*

The Movie of Us

That is the mental shift that brings us back to compassion. We get out of what Krishna Das calls the *Movie of Me* and into the *Movie of Us*. We drop out of our limited sense of self that puts us at the center of our own completely right, justified world, and instead widen our circle of love to include others; even those with distinctly separate belief systems than we have.

One of the most powerful exercises I like to do in workshops is what is called the "Just like me mantra." In the exercise, participants partner up and look into each other's eyes. I will narrate the experience with such statements as, "Just like me, this person wants to be happy. Just like me, this person does not want to be in pain. Just like me, they have hopes, dreams, and aspirations, and just like me, they have had failures and setbacks." The experience is powerful because we often feel alone in our own experience. Our internal world of challenging thoughts and emotions can seem so far removed from the external world that also happens to contain "other" people.

As soon as we truly pay attention to the people around us, we realize that they have the same emotional world we do. They have the same sad and happy moments, the same joy and the same tears. We have the same hopes, needs, dreams, and aspirations. When people reflect after the exercise, one of the most common experiences is an overwhelming feeling of love for the other person, even if it was a stranger they just met. As Zen master, Dōgen put it, "A fool sees himself as another, but a wise man sees others as himself" (Dōgen *et al.*, 2005). Comparing ourselves to others creates jealousy, envy, and competition, but seeing others as ourselves cultivates connection.

In practicing compassion, I no longer think of helping others and a relationship of *helper* and person being helped. This is simply two souls recognizing each other, sharing in their common humanity, being *there*—which is nowhere else but *here*—for each other. "True compassion does not come from wanting to help out those less fortunate than ourselves but from realizing our kinship with all beings," writes Pema Chödrön (Chödrön, 2018).

When we say *life is suffering* we mean "Suffering is an experience we can all share in. Connecting to each other's suffering is one of the most glorious expressions of love that there is." We can keep our hearts open in each other's hells and share in our deep human vulnerability. Rather than always having to run away from suffering, compassion liberates us.

Expanding Our Love

Quite fantastically, the path of compassion is also the path to happiness. When I interviewed self-compassion teacher, Victoria Brattini, she mentioned that highly self-compassionate people tend to be more resilient, more productive, less afraid of failure (because they know it's fundamental to the human condition), spend more time savoring the positive, and are able to express gratitude more easily. Modern scientific research has confirmed this, so has 2000 years of contemplative traditions. If we meet ourselves with love, we will meet others with love too.

It's natural to approach life from a self-centered way, to spend most of your day focused on your own needs: eating, going to the bathroom, buying something that brings you pleasure. But only thinking about yourself invariably leads to insecurity and loneliness. If, instead, we can meet this life focusing on love and compassion for others, happiness will follow us like the sun appearing behind the clouds. If you want people to love you, commit to loving others. If you want out of your own suffering, commit to alleviating the suffering of others. While our society tells us to be selfish consumers, the true path toward happiness is that of kindness and generosity. Now more than ever, we need compassion. We need compassion for those who are sick, those who have died, and those who have lost someone who has died. In this time of separation, compassion is our connection. In the politics of division, compassion is our bridge. When caught up in the prison of a lonely and isolated world, compassion is the secret passageway to intimacy and joy.

It's not easy to shift from "me" to "we," because our society runs in the exact opposite direction. We live in what many refer to as "the cult of individualism" that sets us up as a separate individual, and tells us we must differentiate ourselves from others, to prove ourselves, to divide up those individuals into better and worse. Individualism breeds a search for *betterism*, which often manifests as even worse *isms*: racism, sexism, nationalism, classism. One way to elevate your sense of "I" is to lower everyone else's. Another way individualism manifests is patriarchy, which embraces stereotypically masculine qualities as better than feminine ones. A person who is competitive, stubborn, and easily angered is seen as good, while someone who is caring, tender, and compassionate is seen as weak.

Because we are all connected, anything that hurts, targets, or puts those on the bottom also hurts those at the top. I work with a lot of men and they are all suffering under patriarchy too, although many don't realize it. They are unable to get in touch with or communicate their feelings, unable to cultivate true intimacy with a gender that has been labeled as "opposite" and in many countries, second class. Individualism thrives on separateness, while compassion creates connection.

All of Us

There is a Zen saying that enlightenment means to become of "no rank," meaning an awakened being realizes they are neither worse than any king nor better than the poorest of the poor. This idea is mirrored in Galatians 3:28, which says there is no distinction between Jew or Greek, slave or free, male or female, for all are one with the divine. Spirituality doesn't make us above others, but *among* them. To be holy is to be humble. We wash another's feet and serve food to the hungry. As we shift from "I" to us, we can also apply "us" to greater and greater circles, as we examine our relationship with the world.

For the world to live, the cult of the individual must die. We must move from an individual worldview to see a greater relational biosphere that connects us all together, and then finally, a larger ecological web. Once we extend our love to all human beings, we must continue to expand our hearts to include nonhuman beings too.

Chapter 8

The Love and Suffering of the World

> *When the animals come to us*
> *asking for our help,*
> *will we know what they are saying?*
> *When the plants speak to us*
> *in their delicate, beautiful language,*
> *will we be able to answer them?*
> *When the planet herself*
> *sings to us in our dreams,*
> *will we be able to wake ourselves, and act?*
> Gary Lawless

I have been on this planet for almost four decades now, and a lot has surprised me about the human condition—like the unpredictability of the future and how we are all just winging it, trying our best while making a litany of mistakes along the way. From what a miracle life can be to how fragile it is. One day, someone is here, laughing in the doorway; the next day, they are gone.

I have also been surprised at the excruciatingly slow pace of social progress and the stubbornness of powerful institutions to make any sort of meaningful change. This complacency has become particularly salient when I look at large corporations and governments, who seem to do nothing to stop the casual and wanton destruction of the natural world. It has astounded me to know that smart, honest, kind, hard-working people—executives, engineers, lawyers, scientists—will kiss their families and kids before heading to work for oil corporations that will pay them millions of dollars to lie to government officials at the expense of the planet.

I first learned about climate change as a kid and have since seen very little done to stop it. I have seen a lot of false pledges, empty posturing, and greenwashing. While I try to be a more conscious consumer, like practicing vegetarianism, using reusable items, recycling, biking instead of driving, taking public transport, and all of those other things we are told to do to save the planet, I then get to see tens of thousands of my tax dollars go to the US military, a bigger polluter than more than 100 countries combined, along with my own money in the bank going towards those same deceitful fossil fuel companies.

The short-sightedness and selfishness of our prevailing way of life breaks my heart daily. Every day, we hear more about the lack of progress in slowing the extinction of species, the poisoning of our waters, and the pollution of our air. The world has lost two-thirds of its wildlife in the past 50 years, WHO data shows that almost the entire global population (99%) breathes air that exceeds WHO limits for levels of pollutants in the air, and over half of US waters are too polluted to swim or fish in. Humans are the sole cause of the current Sixth Extinction, which we get to see daily as the Great Barrier Reef collapses and fish populations plummet.

Living in the state of California, we now have three seasons: wet season, dry season, and fire season. It's enough to make anyone go crazy, and indeed people are, as psychologists have noted the rise of "climate anxiety."

One of the biggest questions I keep asking is "Why?" It's a question I love to engage with in my own classes and workshops, where I have people get in groups and ask themselves a very simple question: *Why is the modern world so extremely casual about wanton environmental destruction?*

Why Do We Allow Such Destruction

If we are to come to a solution about saving the world from human destruction, we have to look deeply at why we have been so complacent for so long. We have to get to the true root of the issue.

Often, people cite answers from philosophy, science, or religion that put human beings above all else. Ever since the book of Genesis declared "Let us make mankind in our image, in our likeness, so that they may rule over the fish in the sea and the birds in the sky, over the livestock and all the wild animals, and over all the creatures that move along the ground," many peoples throughout time have put humans above all other creatures in the world, seeing human domination as divine destiny.

But the myth of man's specialness is not just expressed in religion. Ever since Descartes wrote "I think, therefore I am," humans have believed that our superior brain power makes us a superior species. Science tends to confirm humans to be the top of the food chain due to our brains being more complex than any other animals on the planet, sometimes going as far to say we are the only truly sentient beings.

But if we really want to get to the root of it all—into why this view is so harmful and why it has persisted for so long—we must examine how our love and suffering relates to the world we live in. Are we loving the world the best we can? Are we able to see the suffering we ourselves are creating? If not, why not?

More Disconnected Than Ever

Love and suffering are a question of relationship and connection. Last chapter we talked about how all violence and destruction stem from an attack on *other* and a defense of *self*. The same applies to violence in the natural world; we don't see the trees, clouds, rivers, and oceans as ourselves, let alone the salamanders and sea slugs. While the average person feels like a stranger in a strange land, a visitor to this planet, a separate "thing" caught up in an alien and hostile environment, this is an illusion. We may think we are a bird landing on a branch trying to figure out how the tree functions, but in reality, we are the branch itself, part of the same life. We must *re-learn* to *re-love* the world.

If we let it, the heart can dissolve this illusion of separation. The mind is what creates the duality that "we" and "I" are somehow separate from "the world" and "other,"leading us to think violence and destruction waged against a mountain or a forest is not the same as violence to ourselves. Albert Einstein called this "a kind of optical delusion" of our consciousness, which acts as a prison that we must break free of to widen "our circle of compassion to embrace all living creatures and the whole nature in its beauty." This illusion of separation is deeply embedded in our very language, as we refer to ourselves as a subject ("I") and the world as an object ("it"); this subject/object duality is the root of much of the violence and social ills in the world.

This illusion creates a kind of hubris that leads us to believe we are somehow above the land and, therefore, are not affected by its destruction. This illusion manifests in other fundamental dualities, that of mind versus matter, spiritual versus material, or the idea that "human" and "nature" are not part of one whole. Thinking we are distinctly separate from the living and breathing natural world gives us an illusion of safety; that somehow our destruction of the waters and air will not affect us.

The average human today is incredibly disconnected—more than ever before—from the natural world that sustains us. As we move from our home to the car, to the road, to the parking garage to the elevator to the air-conditioned office with fluorescent lighting, we spend every minute of our days surrounded by artificial, man-made environments. We take subways through tunnels into cities. Some people go their entire lives without ever sleeping outside underneath the stars, without ever touching the earth below all the concrete. When we're outside, we bring our screens with us, plugging our headphones in to listen to other people talking. We listen to the news more than the rivers. We sit in front of our TVs much more than sunrises and sunsets. We rarely feel the grass brush up against our skin or touch rock polished by rain.

This Exquisite Planet

We have traded the magical for the material, the sacred for the scientific, the spiritual for the secular. Science and modern advancement have increased the width of our life but not the depth, giving us an abundance of materials but a lack of meaning. Those we call "magicians" use simple trickery, pretending to disappear birds and rabbits into thin air. Meanwhile, caterpillars are disappearing into butterflies, flashes of lightning appear and disappear from nothing, apple trees transform the earth into sugar. Bees are making tiny hotels full of candy made from flowers. The wonders of life are all around us. Every moment in this life is already enchanting, already infused with awe.

In her incredible book *Braiding Sweetgrass*, Professor of Environmental and Forest Biology, Robin Wall Kimmerer, wrote about this stark contrast that she observed in her students over the years. Robin noted that 20 years ago, students would come to her classes on forestry with memories of being children and playing in the creeks and forests behind their houses. They would want to learn more about the frogs they used to catch and the fireflies they used to see at night. But in more recent times her students come to her not with memories of playing in the living world, but of seeing these things on TV shows like *Planet Earth* (Kimmerer, 2013).

This is one of the deepest sufferings we experience in this world: the pain of separation. As children, we have a fear of abandonment. As adults we feel distant from our own lives, caught up in a trance of unworthiness in our minds, lonely even in crowds of people. This suffering is fertile ground to wake up to the interconnectedness of the world, to return to a sense of belonging and at-homeness with our bodies and this breathing, living Earth.

John Seed, founder and director of the Rainforest Information Centre in Australia, wrote, "May we turn inwards and stumble upon our true roots in the intertwining biology of this exquisite planet. May nourishment and power pulse through these roots, and fierce determination to continue the billion-year dance" (Macy & Gahbler, n.d.). The division between humans and nature is starker than ever before. If we are to save the world, we must recognize our own connection and kinship to all living beings.

Come to a Sense of Belonging

Since the root cause of our casual disregard is separation, the solution is to see our inherent connection to all that is — to understand that this "environment" we are always talking about saving is the same living and breathing apparatus as us. We must see the truth of who we are: a loving awareness connected to all that is. As Llewellyn Vaughan-Lee put it, "The world is not a problem to be solved; it is a living being to which we belong. The world is part of our own self, and we are a part of its suffering wholeness. Until we go to the root of our image of separateness, there can be no healing" (Vaughan-Lee, 2016). We must see the world as ourselves and discover what the philosopher, Arne Næss, termed the "ecological self."

In Chapter Two, we talked about the importance of recognizing our interdependence. Interbeing is similar to the Nguni Bantu term *ubuntu* (I am because we are); the Lakota phrase *mitákuye oyás'iŋ* (all are related); the Penobscot word *N'dilnabamuk* (to all of my relations); and the Maori value of *whanaungatanga* (kinship and connection). These concepts exemplify the importance of recognizing our relationships with each other and the world and of seeking to live in harmonious relationship with the past, present, and future.

The first step to becoming caretakers of the world is to see our mutual causality, the interconnected, interdependent, interrelated nature of reality that says humans and nature are one and that we must take care of our counterpart if we are to survive. If we realize the truth of *this is* because *that is* and *this is not* because *that is not*, we will soon discover that we humans exist because the natural world exists, and we will no longer exist if the plants, trees, and animals do not. If we are to save ourselves, we must save the world. In saving the world, we save ourselves. Evolution has already confirmed that we are all related, all part of one tree of life; why don't we finally act like it? *Native* and *natural* share the same root, we are all natives to this natural earth. It is time to create a peaceful coexistence with all things.

The illusion of separation fuels the greed that is destroying the world. As a seemingly separate, small self, we seek to possess more and more, to claim as much as we can of "me" and "mine." There is a story of an accomplished Anthropologist from a prestigious university in New York who went down to the Amazon to learn from the tribes there. At one moment, he steps into a gentleman's hut and sees a small bed, axe, and stool. He asks the man living there, "How does it feel being poor? All you have is a few belongings. Meanwhile, I have a large flat in a nice building, great furniture and appliances, a couple of nice cars, and a large retirement account." Hearing this, the man invites the Anthropologist outside and gestures broadly to the land in front of them. "You have some things. But I have this land, these rivers and waterfalls, mountains and valleys, beautiful birds come to visit me every day. I have a million places to rest and find my heart at home. I also have the pleasure of knowing my great-great-grandchildren will have what I have. What do you have, a small box in a building?"

The moral of the story: when we seek to possess things for ourselves, to claim a small portion of the world as *mine*, we fail to see the abundance that is all around us and fail to feel the joy in giving to others. As the Lakota man, Lame Deer, taught, the only reason to own something is to give it away. That way, everyone is taken care of, and everything belongs (Lame Deer et al., 2009).

Paying Attention

Being present isn't just about noticing the sun, flowers, and birds around us. It also means remaining present through the challenges as well, turning our attention to the issues that matter and not running from the individual and collective work that needs to be done. The same loving attention we can offer ourselves is the same loving attention we can offer each other, which is the same loving attention we can offer the world.

This is the final lesson on loving the world and cultivating our loving presence—taking it all in with a wide-open heart and keeping it open even in the midst of climate crises, mass extinctions, and radioactive waste. The noted environmental activist, Joanna Macy, confirms "the most radical thing any of us can do at this time is to be fully present to what is happening in the world" (Jamail, 2017). We have to open to our own pain, anxiety, despair, and fear at the death of our Earth. We must walk head-on into the pain to get to the other side.

Paying attention means seeing the horrors of the world while still keeping hope and love in your heart. It means observing bad actions without judgment for the people taking those actions and trusting that the good nature of all things allows for the chance to win people over to the cause with love. Chögyam Trungpa encouraged, "Hold the sadness and pain of samsara in your heart and at the same time the power and vision of the Great Eastern Sun. Then the warrior can make a proper cup of tea" (Chödrön, 2018). First, we get in touch with our tender heart, then we open to the courageous heart, then we can start to do the important work that we have to do in the world. Your proper cup of tea might be writing to your congressman or attending a protest. It might be going vegetarian, even though it's hard, out of a compassion for all living things.

Activists throughout history have repeated the lesson that the real impediments to progress are not those who work against it, but those who sit on the sidelines. While it might be easy to avoid the news and turn a blind eye to the suffering of the world, problems do not disappear simply because we ignore them. A stance of neutrality always helps the oppressor.

Many people in life are focused on one relationship: the romantic one with another person. They forget that we are in constant relationship with the world around us. The Gottman Institute says it just takes 20 minutes a day to further one's intimate partnerships. What does 20 minutes a day look like to deepen our relationship with the Earth?

Starting the Conversation

I started this chapter by saying I couldn't understand why so many people are so casual about wanton environmental destruction. That was until I got into the work of the activist, Joanna Macy, also mentioned earlier. She does one particularly transformative exercise that involves bringing in multiple voices to the conversation. First you pick any environmental issue, like plastic pollution or the burning of fossil fuels. Then you have four role-players talking about the issue: a proponent, an opponent, a child seven generations from now, and a nonhuman entity.

For example, the first person is an environmentalist who wants to ban fossil fuels. The second person is the oil worker who wants to earn a living for their family and believes that they are serving society by drilling the oil that families use to drive to soccer practice and fly home for Christmas. The third person is a child seven generations from now who wishes to live in a hospitable world. Finally, the fourth entity could be any living entity—a clam that relies on the ocean's temperature and acidity staying constant, or a polar bear that lives on a shrinking ice in Antarctica.

By bringing all these voices together, true understanding happens. We realize that even those who "destroy" the environment, like a logger or miner, believe they are doing good. Perhaps they are earning a living for their family or providing wood for other people's houses. The seventh-generation human brings into the conversation the Seventh Generation Principle which is based on the Haudenosaunee (Iroquois) philosophy that decisions we make today should consider seven generations into the future. One huge obstacle to environmental change is humanity's incredible shortsightedness, which the seventh-generation principle can help to manage.

Finally, the nonhuman gets a voice too. It is that final entity's voice that is so important and so transformative to the conversation. After all, who speaks for the trees and meadow voles? This voice is the one most missing, and most crucial. The final piece to the love and suffering puzzle is to deepen our understanding of all sentient beings who are suffering and to listen to what they are trying to say. In our endlessly polluting, poisoning, and radioactive world, most sentient beings are screaming for help, if their voices haven't already gone silent altogether. If we actually listened to the Earth, we would hear her crying too.

Now is the time to give Mother Earth a seat at the policy table. Just as we have included huge swaths of the population under the protection of justice and equal rights, it is time to extend that to the natural world. The whole world is our teacher, love is the lesson, and suffering is a reminder we have more to learn. Our final lesson is to love the Earth, and to do that, we have to shift our entire worldview.

Shifting Our Worldview

When I teach the philosophy of spirituality, one of the hardest tasks is to get students to shift their frame of reference, to think about the world in a different way. Our thinking is so conditioned by our society and culture, we are like fish not knowing the water that shapes our world. I like to start by pointing out that humanity has come up with four fundamental models of the universe. The first one, primarily coming from the West, is that life is a machine. It says life is a mechanical process. It is *created*, the result of actions and reactions. We believe that if we can reduce life down to its parts and figure out how those parts work together, we can understand the world we live in. Jesus was a carpenter, God was the creator, and children ask their parents, "How are babies *made*?" This frame seeks to create order through domination and interprets action through the law of cause and effect.

The second model is that life is an organic process. This is the model from the East, primarily China and Japan, that life is less of a machine and much more of a river, or a flow. While the West seeks to establish order on a chaotic universe and to conquer nature, the East is more focused on being in harmony. Life is already perfect and our task is to align ourselves with it. There is the Tao, the way, the attuning to *chi* energy, and the balance of *yin* and *yang*. While the West would say the universe is *wei*, or manifested through action, in the East they say life moves according to *wu wei*, nonaction.

The first model sees a mechanical universe, the second an organic process, and the third model views life as a drama. This is the Indian perspective that our bodies are just costumes. We are all wearing masks, playing a part of a divine drama together as manifestations of God, which is the ultimate reality, Brahman. Life is *lila*, a play, or dance of the divine. That ultimate divine reality got bored and decided to split into a trillion pieces to experience the world in trillion ways simply for the fun of it. All the world's a stage, we are merely players, and we are caught up in this drama like a good movie, not realizing it is all *maya*, or illusion. These first three models tend to be the ones most familiar to my students, although they are most entrenched in the mechanistic, materialistic worldview.

But there is a fourth model that is just as important and one that requires a complete shift in the way we perceive reality. This model has existed long before the other ones, and has been ignored, suppressed, and experienced failed attempts at being completely eradicated. This model does not say life is a machine, an organic process, or a drama. It says that *life is spirit*. It says that life is swimming with spirit, absolutely infused with divinity, and that this physical world directly overlaps with and is integrated with a spiritual nonmaterial reality.

Everything we see, touch, smell, taste, and hear is a manifestation of this Great Spirit, and our task is to connect deeply to it with reverence and love. There is a spirit of the Earth, the spirit of the stars, the spirit of the sky, the spirit of the cosmos and the wind, the spirit of the coyote, jaguar, hummingbird, beaver, deer, bear, mouse, and elk, the spirit of the stones, and the spirit of the plants. This universe is a presence to be communed with, learned from, and instructed by. We are all flowers of the Great Spirit's garden, sharing a common root. The Lakota term is *Wakan Tanka*, in Kiowa it is *Daw-Kee*, meaning Great Spirit or Great Mystery, and this worldview is shared amongst many indigenous cultures.

You might call it *Shamanism, animism,* or deep ecology, or you might call it a personal and spiritual relationship with every creature and thing in this sacred life. You might call it the world's oldest religion when the divine was still part of the physical world and not some outside entity. You might not call it anything other than a recognition of the way things already are, a precious moment infused with interrelated sacredness.

After all, many Native American languages do even have a word for religion, since their entire existence is permeated with spirit. It is a valid, necessary, and needed worldview that has much to teach us about how to meet the suffering of the world with a love that can hold it all.

Life Is Spirit

We have to move away from seeing the world as a material resource, or merely a stage for the real drama of humanity to take place, and instead see the world as sentient as we are. Self-proclaimed geologian, Thomas Berry, wrote that we must recognize this universe not as a collection of *objects* but a communion of *subjects* (Berry, 2006). To see the world as a communion of subjects is the model found across a wide variety of indigenous cultures, and I believe the perspective most missing in today's world. While we might give some subjectivity to our pets and some mammals, in the Western mind the world is full of objects and materials to be used or disregarded. This is easy to see in our language: just look at what you call a "someone" and what you call a "something." When referring to a tree we say, "*it* grows," when stepping on an ant we say, "I killed *it*." Meanwhile the Chickasaw word for animal is *Nan okcha*, which means *all alive,* explicitly embracing the sentience of all living creatures.

We must re-integrate and value the wisdom from indigenous and nature-based cultures, the peoples that have been living in right relationship with the Earth for millennia. These many perspectives don't look at the Earth as an inanimate object, but a living divine spirit, often a feminine one. What you might call Pacha Mama, Madre Tierra, Mother Earth, Etenoha, or Gaia. A breathing animated spirit that connects us all. The Earth is a living being with natural intelligence, who can communicate and guide us on our way. When we describe the world as a mechanical process, it loses its soul.

As Sherri Mitchell of the Penobscot nation wrote, our umbilical cord was cut when we were born, but our umbilical connection with the Great Mother nurtures and sustains us for the remainder of our lives. What we call birth is just moving from one womb to another (Mitchell, 2018). You could say the same about death too.

We have lost the soul of the world; we have denied the living essence of this world. Most humans think they are the only ones with intelligence; we also think we are the only ones with souls. In Latino folk medicine, this soul loss is known as *susto*, and much of our cultural sickness of today is because we have cut off that spiritual connection. To heal ourselves, we must connect to the Motherland and learn the original mother tongue, which includes the languages of the birds, rivers, and trees.

Earlier in this book we talked about the difference between relative and absolute truth. Science teaches the relative, but spirituality teaches the absolute. Relatively, we are all sons and daughters of our mothers. But absolutely, Mother Earth has given birth to all of us: you, me, your mother, her mother, the bluebird and the bison, the vulture and the vole, wood and woodpecker. In our discussion of the mystical experience, we considered that few things would seem as blasphemous as a feminine God giving birth to the world in an action of ecstatic, sensual love. But that is exactly what many indigenous cultures believe, and the missing link in our cosmological understanding of our role in the universe. To see heaven not as something to find in the afterlife, but that heaven is right here, and we are its caretakers. We are not here to have dominion over life's creatures, but to cultivate a deep kinship and connection to all the manifestations of spirit.

Seeing Everything as the Mother

Gaia is the Ultimate Bodhisattva, an awakened being of love and light committed to the peace, joy, and happiness of us all.

We can see everything as the Mother; not only the creative force that gives birth to the world around us, but also all mothers throughout history who have given birth to every person that ever lived. The poet, Joy Harjo, a member of the Mvskoke Nation, and the first Native American Nobel Laureate of the United States, encourages us to remember this truth, "Remember your birth, how your mother struggled, to give you form and breath. You are evidence of / her life, and her mother's, and hers" (Harjo, 2008).

In earlier chapters we learned that every human being needs love, from birth until death. Well, the same need applies to the world. The trees, mountains, fish, deer, and insects need our love too. For a long time now, I have been exploring the basic idea that for us to save the world, we must first love it. The reason humanity continues to condone such egregious environmental destruction is because we do not feel a sense of kinship and belonging with nonhuman life.

Part of cultivating a loving relationship with the Earth is to see that this relationship is reciprocal, and we can only dream of giving the Earth the same amount of love that She gives us. The love of Madre Tierra is unconditional; the flowers, trees, rivers, and mountains are given to us freely and openly. There is the Native American prayer, "Bless me to love what comes from Mother Earth and teach me how to love your gifts." Rather than put our faith in a separate God in some otherworldly realm, we can put our faith in the essence of the Earth, the trees, and the wide-open sky.

Being in Relationship

I remember first learning of *The Three Sisters*: corn, bean, and squash. At first, I thought it was a quaint metaphor that the Iroquois and Cherokee used to express how well these plants grow when they are planted together, in that they nurture each other like family as they mature. Then I learned it's not a metaphor at all, but an invitation to a deeper understanding of living in right relationship. These plants *are* our sisters, and we are in relationship with them just as they are in relationship with themselves. Leigh Joseph, of Squamish heritage, writes in her book *Held by the Land* that all plants are considered relatives, each with their own "spirits, names, interconnections, needs, and power" (Joseph, 2023). And just like any relationship, it comes with responsibilities. We have a responsibility to the Earth, our mother, and to all of her children.

The Asháninka people of the Amazon jungle also consider all living entities as relatives. Plants are sisters, birds are brothers, armadillos are brothers-in-law. Many animistic cultures don't have a word for *nature* the way that we in the West use it to mean everything that is not human. Humanity is part of nature, nature is part of humanity. The world is our body, in our body there is the world.

Our materialistic modern world might view a tree as inert matter to be turned into an Ikea coffee table, but seeing the tree as a relative considers the needs of that tree, and thinking how we might give back the gifts it offers us in the form of oxygen, nourishment, shade, and inspiration. We are asked to nurture and give back anything that we receive and make the relationship reciprocal. For example, if we pick one flower, we might consciously plant five new seeds in return. If we convert an acre of grassland into farmland, we can purchase five acres elsewhere for conservation.

In Chapter 5, we learned that humans evolved to co-regulate each other. Intimate relationships soothe our nervous system. The same applies to our relationship with the Earth. Walking in nature, whether it's beautiful woods or a peaceful mountain, is incredibly regulating to our nervous system. As soon as we step out of the office and step into the forest, our body relaxes. Few things are as grounding as having our bare feet on bare earth, in soft grass, or co-mingling with warm sand. Ecopsychologists have shown that being in nature lowers blood pressure and stress hormone levels, enhances the immune system, increases self-esteem, reduces anxiety, and improves mood. Even patients in hospitals in a room with a tree in the window heal faster than those with a view of the parking lot.

We know that safe, stable, and nurturing relationships are healing. Well, few things are as stable as a redwood tree or rivers that have been flowing for millions of years. We have a fundamental need to belong and can see that we belong to the land. We can pray to the Earth, lay our blessings at the feet of flowers. Perhaps the current increase of many mental disorders is due to us being out of relationship with the Great Mother.

Some archaeologists say the worst invention for the female half of humanity was the plow. While hunter-gatherer societies tended to be strongly egalitarian and often matriarchal, when communities settled on land, *brawn* became the most important factor for farming and survival. It takes a lot of strength to handle a plow, and the more strong hands you have in the field, the more you can grow. So men went to the farms and women went into the home to focus on making more men to work on the farms. What a painfully ironic coincidence that the subjugation of women coincided with the creation of an instrument to more effectively and disastrously extract resources from the Great Mother. It should come as no surprise that 10,000 years of male domination has brought us incredibly out of balance with the Earth Goddess. The Mohawks, and other Iroquois nations, were matriarchies for thousands of years before any European settler uttered the word "feminism." Saving women will, no doubt, save the world.

Many indigenous activists are now using the word *rematriation* to describe the important work of coming back to right relationship not just with all women, but with the Great Mother too. Rematriation is the feminine side to the patriarchal idea of repatriation and involves Indigenous people reclaiming their ancestral remains, culture, and resources. Rowen White, a Seed Keeper and farmer from the Mohawk community of Akwesasne, calls rematriation a returning "back to Mother Earth, a return to our origins, to life and co-creation, rather than Patriarchal destruction and colonization, a reclamation of germination, of the life-giving force of the Divine Female" (White, 2018).

Ayni: Reciprocity

Unfortunately, because of our disconnection to the natural world, "nature" becomes an abstract concept. We are told there is an "environment" somewhere that we need to "save," rather than told to cherish the land exactly where we are now, and to offer the Great Mother our admiration and respect. Mother Earth is always loving us, and it is up to us to love her back.

In my own practice, I have found that the more I love the world, the more I see it as loving. The more I see the world as loving, the more I love the world. The more kindness I offer to the plants and animals, the more kindness I receive. This is one of the great lessons of love—that the more we give away, the more we have. One translation of the term *metta* is *gentle rain*, because when it rains, the droplets touch everything. The rain doesn't discriminate where it lands. This is a lesson of the Great Mother's unconditional love—it touches everything. She holds, supports, and nourishes us all. Our human shame for destroying the Earth and all its wonders won't help the Earth, only love will.

I have gone down to the Peruvian Andes many times to study with the incredible healers there. You might call them shamans, medicine people, keepers of the Earth, day keepers, *curanderos,* or *chasquis*. I call them Jose, Leti, Wilma, Selva, Walter. For many, the path of the shaman is a long and arduous apprenticeship, and suffering is practically a prerequisite.

In contrast to many charlatans who call themselves shamans to make a quick buck, true shamans have gone through an intense *shamanhood* or *shamanship*. Shamanhood is the path of the wounded healer, one that often requires more than just one rite of passage. Whether it's days of fasting alone in a cave or atop a cold mountain, it takes tremendous effort to "break on through to the other side," and sometimes near death experiences to get there. One shaman I've worked with had to work up to fasting for 10, then 20, then 30 and 40 days. Another healer I worked with said that when she was in her mother's womb, her mother was struck by lightning, leading her to be born slightly disfigured. This was the mark of Father Sky, and the beginning of her energetic work.

Each time I go down to the Andes I deepen my understanding of the Quechua word *ayni*, which means reciprocity, or "today for you, tomorrow for me." You might also call it "right relationship." As one elder told me, "You in the North are concerned with being right. We in the South are concerned with being in *right relationship*." *Ayni* was one of the commandments of the Incan religion that is still alive and well today. It reflects how everything is mutually connected and interrelated, and if we are to "take" from the great Pacha Mama, we must also give back. In this culture, there is no concept of *individual* well-being, because it is so intertwined with the wellness of the community and the world. All of creation is in relationship, all of life is meeting, and we are here to make our connection as loving as possible.

Back to the Earth

The connection people have there with the land is inspiring. It is also difficult to explain what it really means to be connected to the earth or be part of a culture that has tended to the same area for thousands of years. The land is in their very DNA, the rivers course through their blood, as they pray to the water, the wind, and the mountains. The Incan civilization had no writing or money, and yet, no hunger either. They were incredible farmers, able to overcome malnutrition in a topographically challenging place by being deeply in touch with the land, plants, and changing seasons. They have over 4000 varieties of potatoes, 400 types of corn and 3000 types of grains. They are as familiar with their land and its life as they are the faces of their brothers and sisters.

But what's even more interesting is how they talk to plants and refer to them as living sentient beings, singing to them as they harvest. I remember the first time I was told that we can talk to plants, and thought it was a bunch of hogwash. To think that plants are intelligent beings capable of communication seemed absurd, and most definitely contrary to modern science. It would take many years, many walks, energetic practices, and listening to great wisdom teachers for me to realize that the nature on this planet doesn't just have something to *show* us, it has something to *tell* us. If you want to learn something about the world, let the world do the teaching.

The ethnobotanist, Mark Plotkin, once said, "The rainforest holds answers to questions we have yet to ask" (Plotkin, 2015). It is easy to interpret this statement in a purely scientific sense, but to me, it means we can see every sentient being as an innate subject with its own things to say, if we take the time to ask and listen.

When we see the gifts Mother gives to us, any responsible child would give gifts of reverence and thanks back. One particularly moving ceremony is the Peruvian *Despacho* Ceremony from the Q'ero people. *Despacho* means "offering" and the ceremony involves wrapping a gift to be offered to Pachamama. After thanking the seven directions, opening the sacred space, and offering prayers to the ancestors, the guide of the ceremony will create a bundle of items with spiritual and special significance, like cookies for sweetness and rice for abundance. Participants are asked to create *k'intus,* bundles of sacred coca leaves, that represent prayers to their own families, land, and dreams to the future. All the materials are then wrapped with blessings and individual prayers of all the participants, before being "offered" to the Great Mother by tossing it into a great fire.

At my first *Despacho* ceremony, I remember thinking it was silly to create such a beautiful offering just to destroy it. Then our leader reminded us that in nature nothing is ever lost, everything is transformed. The ashes of the offering return to the earth to nourish the land, the air becomes full of divine grace, community is formed in the ceremony itself, and our hearts will never forget the love that was cultivated. It is now one of my favorite things to do.

This Sentient Earth

Nowadays, many people are concerned with discovering life on other planets. Few are focused on getting in touch with life on *this* planet. When the ethnobotanist, Wade Davis, went into the Amazon to study plants, he asked one tribe how they were able to differentiate different species of varieties of plants that to the naked eye appear the same. Quite simply, they replied, they take the leaves of the plants out into the light of the full moon to hear them singing in 13 different keys (TED, 2020). How different is that perspective from taking a slice of a petal and putting it underneath a microscope?

In the Peruvian Andes, I was told by a medicine man that the mountains were *Apus,* or grandfather spirits, that help direct our destinies. Like talking to plants, at the time I thought it was a quaint idea, not a description of the way things are. Growing up in an *I-It* culture, rather than in *I-Thou* consciousness, I saw the material world as lifeless and barren, a resource to be developed. There is a stark difference between seeing the "red rocks" in the desert areas of the United States and being told about the mineral content and tectonic plates that formed them, rather than the creation myth of the Ute people, who says a great flood once went through the land and the mud mixed with the blood of their ancestors. This mixture of red blood and brown clay formed the layers of rock we see today.

After much unlearning and learning, I now see even the most barren mountains as guiding spirits, the most desolate landscapes as exploding with sentience. Every living thing has its own language, speaks wonderful words, and sings beautiful songs. The Lakota say the stars are the breath of the Great Spirit, and our own breath connects us to the entire cosmos.

In a famous speech, Chief Seattle explains the stark contrast between the "White Man" and the "Red Man" (Suquamish Tribe, n.d.):

> There is little in common between us. To us the ashes of our ancestors are sacred and their resting place is hallowed ground. You wander far from the graves of your ancestors and seemingly without regret. Your religion was written upon tablets of stone by the iron finger of your God so that you could not forget. The Red Man could never comprehend or remember it. Our religion is the traditions of our ancestors—the dreams of our old men, given them in solemn hours of the night by the Great Spirit; and the visions of our chiefs, and is written in the hearts of our people.

After learning what it means to be connected to the land, in our trainings we changed how we ask where students are from. We don't ask for the home city, state, and country, which are arbitrary boundaries drawn by governments. We ask what mountains, plains, rivers, valleys, and coasts they grew out from and remain connected to. We don't ask about their likes and dislikes, we ask about whose shoulders they are standing on, and who are the ancestors that helped them become the person they are today.

We don't just talk to the plants, we sing to them. We walk in the forest singing *Now I walk in beauty* and watch how the trees light up. We sing *Todo es Mi Familia,* with lyrics that express how the animals, plants, mountains, and sea are sacred and our family. We sing to Sister Moon, Father Sky, Mother Earth, and Grandmother Ocean. We walk mindfully, letting our feet kiss the earth as Pachamama kisses us back. If we wish to pick a flower, pick up a leaf, or move a pebble, we ask permission. Sometimes the plant says no, sometimes the Mother says yes.

At first, I simply enjoyed singing the songs that speak of the condor, rivers, and Great Mother. When I got more into it, I realized these songs were part of an oral tradition and conveyed wisdom and understanding of the world. Upon deeper reflection, I realized we aren't singing *about* these entities, we are singing *to* them, a way of giving thanks and energy to all of our relations. Prayer, reverence, chanting, dancing, ritual, ceremony, and song, these are all ways to practice *ayni,* giving back.

N. Scott Momaday, of Kiowa heritage, says it clearly, "Those who deny the spirit of the earth, who do not see that the earth is alive and sacred, who poison the earth and inflict wounds upon it have no shame and are without the basic virtues of humanity." By reclaiming the Earth, we reclaim ourselves.

Building a sacred relationship with the Earth takes time. In today's modern society, no one has time to do anything, let alone slow down and give reverence to the Earth. Earlier in the book we mentioned the spiritual journey of 18 inches from the head to the heart, which can take many lifetimes. But for most of us, this difficult and humbling spiritual journey involves traveling just one inch, where we finally arrive at the ground beneath our feet.

Much of our current economic development is just stealing from future generations. Chief Oren Lyons of the Onondaga Nation says that when their people place their feet on the earth, they imagine the faces of their grandchildren looking up at them from the soil. Every step and every decision considers the needs of these future generations. All life arose from the earth, and all future life will arise from the earth. Layer by layer, each new generation will come. While a geologist looks at layers of the land and sees the past, the earth carries all life for the future. We think we were given this world by our parents; in truth it is a loan from our children.

There is a story where a despondent nun goes to their teacher. The nun complains she hasn't found God anywhere. She searched all over the cathedral, looked up at the windows, climbed up the bell tower, and still couldn't find God. To which their teacher replies, "You have looked up, forward, back, left and right, but you forgot to look down." We have forgotten what is most essential, always here, and already present—the earth and ground beneath our feet.

Saving the Earth

Remember: compassion is a relationship amongst equals. For us to save the whales or the rainforest, we must see ourselves as equal entities in this shared web of life. We no longer condone sexism and racism. Generations from now, the same will be said of our current *species-ism*, putting the human race above all other creatures on the planet.

If we see everything as the Mother, we will see ourselves as children of the Earth, every human being as our brother and sister, all being taken care of by the world around us. The Great Mother supports us on every level, from the food, water, and air that nourishes us, to the need for peace and tranquility that a walk in the woods provides. The poet and environmental activist, Gary Snyder, observed that we won't save the world out of guilt, but only because we love it.

Seeing ourselves as children of the Earth also points to our own naivete while recognizing the wisdom of this loving Earth. In just a few hundred years since the Industrial Revolution, we have made an awfully big mess of things. It would be silly to think that the solution to our problems is simply technological advancements in the form of solar panels and recyclable materials. We need a spiritual solution, not a scientific one. There is a Zen haiku, "The wise person enters the forest without disturbing a blade of grass, the water without even a ripple." We can become wise by living in this world without negatively affecting it.

We must feel our bare feet walk on the earthen ground and touch the same places that our ancestors did thousands of years ago, while letting ourselves be touched by the same wonder and beauty.

The Earth is on its own timescale. There's a funny scene in the book *Catch-22* where one soldier is explaining how important it is to fight for and believe in one's country. To which another man replies, "The frog is almost five hundred million years old. Could you really say with much certainty that America ... will last as long as the frog?" How absurd our mental attachments are to concepts and countries when we should be resting our hearts in the timescale of the land. Many countries have laws around burning their flag, but few protections against burning the ground upon which it stands.

The solution to humans living in harmony with the Earth is to see that the Earth has been living in harmony with itself for millions of years. Life already has it all figured out. Day turns to night, stars circle the sky, the seasons change, and the geese fly north. Life is already sustainable, it is human behavior that is not. The animals were here before us; we are one of the youngest species on the planet and we still have much to learn from our elders.

We are mere babies in the grand scheme of the cosmos, and all that we hold dear is just a blink of an eye on the time scale of the universe. Unfortunately, the world might disappear in that same blink of an eye, if we do not learn to live in the right relationship with The Great Mother. When we touch the Earth with humility, we will either discover either a fertile ground for a bright future, or a wasteland. We must cherish *all* the mothers: our own, others, and the Earth. We are not separate. When we poison the earth, we poison ourselves.

Scientists have found our bodies and blood are full of microplastics, which shouldn't come as any surprise to those who see how everything is connected. During retreats, we sit in a circle around the fire singing *"Earth, my body, Water, my blood,"* which is not some metaphor but a way of describing the way things are. Violence to the earth is violence to ourselves; saving the earth is saving ourselves. We're all in this together. As one aboriginal activist group put it, "If you have come here to help me, you are wasting your time. But if you have come because your liberation is bound up with mine, then let us work together."

In Chapter 3, we explored the idea that because the Spanish didn't listen to the local Mayan population, they weren't prepared for the natural disasters that destroyed their churches. Well, the Earth is experiencing an unprecedented level of natural disasters, from fish kills to forest fires to coral bleaching, because we too have failed to listen to the indigenous people who know what it means to live in harmony with all beings. There's no scientific discovery needed to save ourselves and the world, the wisdom and knowledge is already here, if we can listen to, put forth, and center the people, cultures, and elders that hold it.

Old knowledge must be learned anew. As Sherri Mitchell writes in *Sacred Instructions,* indigenous peoples have been waiting for such a shift, "My people have been dreaming of the time when our way of life would be embraced, rather than attacked; when our wisdom would be sought, rather than shunned; when we could stand united once again with all our relatives within creation."

It's time to shift the human race from the path of domination and destruction to a new one of cooperation and conscious co-creation. In a world based on private property and private gain, no new law or technology will save the Earth, only an elevation of human consciousness will do it. We need a shift of the human heart that cherishes the sacredness of all of life.

In Closing

Suffering makes us feel limited, stuck in our own pain, thinking "Why me?" But love connects us and opens us. Love puts us in right relationship with each other, ourselves, and the world. Black Elk, of the Oglala Lakota people, put it this way, "The first peace, which is the most important, is that which comes within the souls of people when they realize their relationship, their oneness with the universe and all its powers, and when they realize at the center of the universe dwells the Great Spirit, and that its center is really everywhere, it is within each of us."

This brings us to a wonderful definition of Spirit: *that which infuses all things and transcends all things.* The divine is utterly beyond us yet totally within us. We learn these fundamental truths from the ultimate gurus of life: love and suffering. Love and suffering have so much to teach us, including that no one wants to suffer, and love is the path to peace. They teach us that life is sacred and that all living beings are sacred.

Love is not an emotion to feel, it is an infinite energy to experience, never anywhere else than right here. Seeking love will only take you in the wrong direction. Suffering is a call to action, and we must be willing to face the suffering of the world if we are to save it. We feel lost and disconnected because we have forgotten who we are and our kinship with all beings. Humanity is suffering because of a grand amnesia; we long for connection because we have forgotten our connection to all things.

We must remember. The word *remember* is the opposite of *dismember*, which means to take apart. By *re-membering*, we put ourselves back together, we *re-collect* the disparate parts of ourselves to become one with the unified whole. We then become fully in the present moment, the most beautiful moment of our life, and the joy that lies therein. The wonders of life are here, heaven is here, the kingdom of God is here, Nirvana is right now. We are already walking in the Pure Land of the Buddha and are held in the womb of the Great Mother. This is the ultimate *re-mindfulness* practice: remembering why we are here, where we came from, the goodness in others, and the preciousness of every moment. I hope you remember your perfection throughout the rest of your days.

I'd like to close with a letter.

My beloved reader, beloved child, beloved mirror, I know that you are suffering. I am suffering too. That is why I am here for you; thank you for being here for me. Suffering is a part of life, it's here to serve your awakening to the beauty that you are. I'm so proud of you for making it this far. Not just in this book, but in your life, in the face of incredible challenges and immense pain, here you are. A smile that lights up a room, eyes deeper than the ocean, a heart beating lakes of blood, trillion of cells ecstatically dancing together for that cup of coffee to reach your luscious lips in the morning. Infinity and eternity are too small of words for you.

Take a breath. Did you notice you just took in a molecule from The Buddha, Jesus, and Gandhi? Do you feel this loving exchange with the trees? Although you might feel lonely, you are connected to all things. These words, the sun, the stars, the child playing in the sandbox like you used to. Although you might feel weak, you are strong beyond measure. Although there might be times when all you want to do is close down, that beautiful beating heart of yours wishes to open even more. You can do it. You can keep your heart open in hell, no matter how big or small the hell you are going through right now. You are loved. You are lovable, loving, and loved.

There is no need to change who you are. Be who you are. Just be. Trust in your heart, trust in the unknown, trust that you got this and fake it if you have to. I don't care about the mistakes you've made, the lies you have told, the depression that looms, or the trauma that wets your heart with tears. Some scars we see, most we can't, many never heal. But that doesn't change the truth: you deserve all the love your heart can hold. And then some. And then some more.

All that matters is that you picked yourself off the ground, dusted yourself off, and set an intention to love again. And again, and again. Little by little, you can learn to love your life. I believe in you and hope one day you believe in you too as much as you believe that birds can fly. No need to worry, all is well, all is perfect, especially you. We are walking together, hand in hand, on this journey back home to see the love in ourselves as the same love in all.

Afterword

One of the great myths we are taught is that life is logical. We're told humanity has most of life figured out and it's up to future scientific endeavors to fill in the gaps. With enough measurements, variables, and theorems, we will know what reality is and be able to understand the movements of atoms as well as the stars. But this is hardly the case. If the universe is anything, it's paradoxical. Jung said only paradox comes anywhere near to comprehending the fullness of life and it's one of our most valuable spiritual possessions. How are we in God, and God is also in us? Zen and Taoist teachings are full of paradoxes, including Shunryū Suzuki's saying, "If it's not paradoxical, it's not true."

Suffering is a paradox too. Suffering stinks, and it is grace. Suffering is perfect and asks us to alleviate its burden. It teaches us to help others and to improve our situation, but also that everything is exactly as it is supposed to be. In accepting it, we become free of it. We can look to the divine and see total perfection, and look to the Earth and see total suffering, and see our incarnation as meant to alleviate suffering without forgetting the beauty of it all. This uniting of duality makes us a conscious being and puts us on the path of the heart.

In seeing the perfection of it all, we love it all and become it all. Love is like the mushroom that grows in ashes, the lotus flower that blooms from the mud, the tree reaching up towards the sun laughing at gravity along the way. Despite the endless suffering of our insignificant existence in a lonely, cold, and isolated universe, love makes it all worth it. We are here for the big and small moments of shared joy that turn into a shared love, to awaken to the true nature of a loving interconnectedness amongst us all.

Background

My religion is love and I worship at the altar of the heart. I have devoted my life to the cause of love, traveling the world and speaking with everyone that I could find who could tell me about their own perspective on love. We are in an information age and have the extraordinary opportunity to learn from every great teacher who has ever lived. I have a master's degree in a Global Psychology program that taught many of the subjects in this book. I have perennially been on the lookout for programs, trainings, retreats, and immersions that help to grow the heart and open up to the love inside and all around us. I'm grateful for all the teachers I have met along the way.

As I continued this path, I realized that my spiritual life is like a tree with five limbs. The center trunk is love, and the five limbs are five traditions that I keep returning to: Mahayana Buddhism, Western Mysticism, Indigenous Wisdom, Yogic Practice, and Scientific Empiricism. I appreciate all the approaches I have been exposed to, but these five approaches have been the most inspiring and will be my focus for the rest of my life.

The Mahayana Buddhists have the Bodhisattva path that encourages a love and compassion for all beings, and a path of action that seeks to be of service to others. The Western Mystics from Judaism, Christianity, and Islam are the ones most likely to transcend the religious dogma that keeps these institutions in conflict, and instead teach an all-encompassing love that unites us all, practices compassion for all beings, and encourages peace through nonviolence. Indigenous Wisdom is what this world so desperately needs if it is to survive, learning from those who have learned how to live in harmony with the Earth and to reify the nonhuman world as just as spiritually endowed as we are. The practice of yoga gives me something to do every day to link the intelligence of mind with the wisdom of the body, to open the heart, and be in touch with suffering without getting so caught up in it.

Finally, any spiritual path needs a healthy dose of skepticism and empiricism, as this world is rife with frauds, charlatans, abusers, fake gurus, plastic shamans, and all sorts of nonsensical flim-flam. We can welcome in the mystery of the great unknowable unknown, while also teasing out fact from fiction, using scientific progress to boost our spiritual development, rather than hinder it. In my experience, psychology is about healing, spirituality is about transformation, and they can work together like two wings of a bird.

I know these belief systems have different, and often conflicted, cosmologies. I do not personally believe that all religions point to the same one Universal truth (the Perennial philosophy), but that we can celebrate the multitudes of different perspectives without needing to lump them together or reconcile their disparities. I also know that my individual experience is limited, and do not claim to be an expert on any of these subjects. I don't claim to speak for any of these traditions nor am I representing these lineages. I hope my writings point to the millennia of wisdom contained therein. There are a lot of people out there who know a lot more about these practices than I do. Any mistakes and misunderstandings are completely my own.

Of course, this is my path, and your path is just as unique as you are. I don't expect anyone to walk in my footsteps and instead hope everyone stands up for love and removes anything standing in the way of love. May these words inspire you to be like the sun that spreads the light of its unconditional love across this sacred blue planet.

About the Author

Zacharias of the Beach lives at the intersection of here and now, in the heart of the Great Mother, in the state of Ananda.

His form did a lot of learning at California State University East Bay, California Institute of Integral Studies, and Northwestern University. His formlessness did the unlearning at The School Yoga Institute in Guatemala, Himalayan Yoga Association in India, Sunshine Network in Thailand, and meditation centers in Thailand, Nepal, and Malaysia.

His *somebody-ness* made a name for himself by getting words published in many poetry magazines and online journals, and his form works daily as a yoga teacher, relationship coach, therapist, podcast host, and Director of The Heart Center love school. His *nobody-ness* prefers walking in the California Redwoods, breathing in the air of the Apus, and being a mirror to reflect back the light of the beloved in everybody.

You can dispel the illusion of separation by connecting with Zach on social media @zachbeachlove and learn more at www.zachbeach.com.

References

Chapter 1

Castaneda, C. (2016). *The Teachings of Don Juan: a Yaqui Way of Knowledge*. University Of California Press.

Chah, Achaan (2013). *A Still Forest Pool: The Insight Meditation of Achaan Chah*. Quest Books.

Doyle, G. (2020). *Untamed*. The Dial Press.

Epstein, Mark (2019). *Advice Not Given*. Penguin USA.

Frankl, V. E. (1946). *Man's Search for Meaning*. Beacon Press.

Gibran, Kahlil, (Knopf, Alfred A, trans.) (2018). *The Prophet*. (Original work published 1923.)

Hass, Robert, et al. *The Essential Haiku: Versions of Bashō, Buson, and Issa*. Hopewell, New Jersey: Ecco Press, 1994.

Hirshfield, Jane (16 December 2021). *The Fullness of Things* (K. Tippett, Interviewer). https://onbeing.org/programs/jane-hirshfield-the-fullness-of-things/.

Hirshfield, Jane (n.d.). *Seeing Through Words — Matsuo Basho*. The Haiku Foundation Digital Library. https://thehaikufoundation.org/omeka/items/show/605.

Isha Foundation (25 December 2016). *Suffer No More*. https://isha.sadhguru.org/en/wisdom/article/suffer-no-more.

Mitchell, S. (1993). *The Enlightened Heart: an Anthology of Sacred Poetry*. Harper Perennial.

Muller, F. Max (2014). *The Dhammapada*. Literary Licensing, LLC.

Oliver, M. (2006). *Thirst*. Beacon Press.

Shantideva (2008). *The way of the Bodhisattva: a translation of the Bodhicharyavatara*. Shambhala.

Shunryū Suzuki and Dixon, T. (2020). *Zen Mind, Beginner's Mind*. Shambhala.

Simpkins, C. A. and Simpkins, A. M. (2020). *Buddhism for Beginners: a Guide to Enlightened Living*. Tuttle Publishing.

Chapter 2

Academy of American Poets (1995). *Kindness by Naomi Shihab*. https://poets.org/poem/kindness.

Carl Gustav Jung (1993). *Psychology and Alchemy*. Princeton University Press.

Halifax, J. (2005). *Meditation: Tonglen or Giving and Receiving: A Practice of Great Mercy*. https://www.upaya.org/dox/Tonglen.pdf.

Laozi and Mitchell, S. (2006). *Tao Te Ching: a New English Version*. HarperCollins.

Major, Brett C. *et al.* (2018). "Well-being Correlates of Perceived Positivity Resonance: Evidence from Trait and Episode-Level Assessments" in *Personality & Social Psychology Bulletin*, 44(12), pp.1631–1647. https://doi.org/10.1177/0146167218771324.

Isha Foundation (October 16 2019). *Sadhguru Quotes*. https://isha.sadhguru.org/en/wisdom/quotes/date/october-16-2019.

Thich Nhat Hanh (1991). *Peace Is Every Step*. Toronto Bantam Books.

Chapter 3

Brown, B. (27 March 2018). *Defining Spirituality*. https://brenebrown.com/articles/2018/03/27/defining-spirituality/.

Brown, B. (4 November 2020). *Brené on Strong Backs, Soft Fronts, and Wild Hearts*. https://brenebrown.com/podcast/brene-on-strong-backs-soft-fronts-and-wild-hearts/.

Dostoevsky, F. (2008). *The Idiot*. Oxford Paperbacks.

Kaur, V. (2020). *See No Stranger: a Memoir and Manifesto of Revolutionary Love*. One World.

Keating, T. (2011). *Divine Therapy and Addiction: Centering Prayer and the Twelve Steps*. Lantern Books.

Keating, T. (2014). *The Human Condition*. Paulist Press.

King, M. L. (1967). *Where Do We Go from Here: Chaos or Community?* Boston Beacon Press, p.81.

Kornfield, J. (23 October 2011). *The Ancient Heart of Forgiveness*. Greater Good. https://greatergood.berkeley.edu/article/item/the_ancient_heart_of_forgiveness.

Kushner, H. S. (1983). *When Bad Things Happen to Good People*. Avon Books.

Levine, P. A. (1997). *Waking The Tiger: Healing Trauma: The Innate Capacity to Transform Overwhelming Experiences*. North Atlantic Books.

Mahfouz, N. (2016). *Palace of Desire*. Anchor.

Merton, T. (2007). *New Seeds of Contemplation*. New Directions Book.

Moore, T. (2016). *Care of the Soul: A Guide for Cultivating Depth and Sacredness in Everyday Life*. Harper Perennial.

Ó Tuama, P. (17 September 2020). *The Facts of Life*. The on Being Project. https://onbeing.org/poetry/the-facts-of-life/.

Rohr, R. (2009). *The Naked Now: Learning to See as the Mystics See*. Crossroad Pub. Co.

Chapter 4

Buber, M. (Smith, R. G., trans.) (2000). *I and Thou*. Scribner Classics.

Easwaran, E. (2007). *The Bhagavad Gita*. Nilgiri Press.

Jensen, D. H. (2013). *God, Desire, and a Theology of Human Sexuality*. Westminster John Knox Press, p.59.

Julian Of Norwich (Hudleston, R., ed.) (2006). *Revelations of Divine Love*. Dover Publications.

Keating, T. (2002). *Open Mind, Open Heart*. A&C Black, p.136.

Mckenna, M. (2007). *Mary: Shadow of Grace*. New City Press.

Merton, T. (1968). *Conjectures of a Guilty Bystander*. Image Books.

Murdoch, I. (1959). "The Sublime and the Good" in *Chicago Review* Vol. 13, No. 3, pp.42–55.

Nepo, M. (2013). *The Little Book of Awakening: Selections from the #1 New York Times Bestselling The Book of Awakening*. Conari Press.

Rumi, J. al-Din (Barks, C. and Moyne, J., trans.) (2004). *The Essential Rumi*. Harper One.

Shah, I. (2002). *Neglected Aspects of Sufi Study*. Octagon Press Ltd.

Starr, M. (2013). *The Showings of Julian of Norwich*. Hampton Roads Publishing.

Butcher, C. A. (trans.) (2018). *The Cloud of Unknowing*. Shambhala.

Thomas Merton (Naomi Burton Stone and Brother Patrick Hart, eds.) (1979). "Rebirth and the New Man in Christianity" in *Love and Living*. Harcourt Books, p.199. https://cac.org/daily-meditations/remain-in-me-2016-04-04/.

William, J. (2020). *Varieties of Religious Experience: a Study in Human Nature*. Editorium.

Chapter 5

Academy of American Poets (n.d.). *Horses at Midnight Without a Moon by Jack Gilbert*. https://poets.org/poem/horses-midnight-without-moon.

Baldwin, J. (1985). *The Price of the Ticket: Collected Nonfiction, 1948–1985*. St. Martin's/Marek.

Brach, T. (1 July 2011). *Awakening From the Trance of Unworthiness*. Tara Brach. https://www.tarabrach.com/inquiring-trance/.

Buddhist Society of Western Australia (31 March 2023). *Finding the Truth*. Ajahn Brahm. YouTube. https://www.youtube.com/watch?v=npixvAjZ5to&t=2736s.

Farhi, D. (2005). *Bringing Yoga to Life*. HarperCollins.

Gunaratana, H. (2009). *Beyond Mindfulness in Plain English: An Introductory Guide to Deeper States of Meditation*. Wisdom Publications.

Hendry, E. R. (20 November 2013). *7 Epic Fails Brought to You by the Genius Mind of Thomas Edison*. Smithsonian. https://www.smithsonianmag.com/innovation/7-epic-fails-brought-to-you-by-the-genius-mind-of-thomas-edison-180947786/.

References

Hirshfield, J. (10 April 2015). "Jane Hirshfield: Felt in Its Fullness" in *Tricycle: The Buddhist Review*. https://tricycle.org/article/felt-its-fullness/.

Horan, D. P. (2014). *The Franciscan Heart of Thomas Merton*. Ave Maria Press, p.15.

Iyengar, B. K. S. (2006). *Light on Life*. Rodale.

Kaur, R. (2020). *Home Body*. Simon & Schuster, Canada.

Keller, H. (1903). *Optimism: An Essay*. New York, T. P. Crowell and Company; Boston, The Merrymount Press.

Libreria Editrice Vaticana (3 January 2008). *General Audience of 30 January 2008: Saint Augustine of Hippo (3)*. https://www.vatican.va/content/benedict-xvi/en/audiences/2008/documents/hf_ben-xvi_aud_20080130.html.

Menakem, R. (2017). *My Grandmother's Hands: Racialized Trauma and the Pathway to Mending our Hearts and Bodies*. Las Vegas, NV Central Recovery Press.

Morin, J. (2012). *The Erotic Mind*. Harper Collins.

Paoletti, G. (15 November 2017). *The Excruciating Bullet Ant Glove Test of The Mawé People*. All That's Interesting. https://allthatsinteresting.com/bullet-ant-glove.

Rohr, R. (2013). *Immortal Diamond: the Search for Our True Self*. Jossey-Bass.

Schopenhauer, A. (2004). *On the Suffering of the World*. Penguin Books.

Simpson, D. (2021). *The Truth of Yoga: A Comprehensive Guide to Yoga's History, Texts, Philosophy, and Practices*. North Point Press, A Division of Farrar, Straus And Giroux.

Wachowski, A., and Wachowski, L. (Directors) (1999). *THE MATRIX*. Warner Bros.

Wagner, D. (5 October 2014). *An Apache Dance into Womanhood*. Azcentral. https://www.azcentral.com/story/news/local/arizona/2014/10/05/apache-dance-sunrise-ceremony-womanhood/16616029/.

Chapter 6

Baldwin, J. (1993). *Nobody Knows My Name: More Notes of a Native Son.* Vintage Books.

Baldwin, J. (1993). *The Fire Next Time.* Vintage International. (Original work published 1963.)

Botsman, R. (5 August 2018). *Trust-Thinkers.* Medium. https://medium.com/@rachelbotsman/trust-thinkers-72ec78ec3b59.

Cortese, C. (2016). *Wasp Queen.* Black Lawrence Press.

De Mello, A. (2011). *The Way to Love: The Last Meditations of Anthony de Mello.* Doubleday.

Gabor Maté (2010). *In the Realm of Hungry Ghosts: Close Encounters With Addiction.* North Atlantic Books, Lyons, Colorado.

Gottlieb, L. (2020). *Maybe You Should Talk to Someone: A Therapist, Her Therapist, and Our Lives Revealed.* Mariner Books.

Hendrix, H., and Hunt, H. (2019). *Getting the Love You Want: A Guide for Couples.* St. Martins Griffin.

Herman, J. (1992). *Trauma and Recovery.* Pandora.

Levine, S., and Levine, O. (2010). *Embracing the Beloved.* Anchor.

Stanton, S. C. E., Selcuk, E., Farrell, A. K., Slatcher, R. B., and Ong, A. D. (2019). "Perceived Partner Responsiveness, Daily Negative Affect Reactivity, and All-Cause Mortality: A 20-Year Longitudinal Study" in *Psychosomatic Medicine*, 81(1), pp.7–15. https://doi.org/10.1097/PSY.0000000000000618.

TEDx Talks (2 September 2016). *Relationships Are Hard, But Why?* Stan Tatkin. YouTube. https://youtu.be/2xKXLPuju8U?si=Ajj2gjYAhBIOVZrZ.

Chapter 7

Chödrön, P. (2018). *Start Where You Are: A Guide to Compassionate Living.* Shambhala.

Levine, S. (2013). *Becoming Kuan Yin: The Evolution of Compassion.* Weister Books.

Dōgen (Wright, T. and Uchiyama, K., trans.) (2005). *How to Cook Your Life: From the Zen Kitchen to Enlightenment.* Shambhala.

Hope, N., Koestner, R., and Milyavskaya, M. (2014). "The role of self-compassion in goal pursuit and well-being among university freshmen" in *Self and Identity, 13*(5), pp.579–593. https://doi.org/10.1080/15298868.2014.889032.

Longfellow, H. W. (1857). *Prose Works of Henry Wadsworth Longfellow, Volume 1 of 2*. Boston, Massachusetts: Ticknor and Fields, p.452.

Patterson, J., Williams, L., Edwards, T. M., Chamow, L., and Grauf-Grounds, C. (2018). *Essential Skills in Family Therapy, Third Edition: From the First Interview to Termination*. Guilford Publications.

Popova, M. (19 August 2015). *Simone Weil on Attention and Grace*. The Marginalian. https://www.themarginalian.org/2015/08/19/simone-weil-attention-gravity-and-grace/.

Real, T. (15 March 2023). *Learning to Live a Non-Violent Life*. Terry Real Homepage. https://terryreal.com/articles/live-a-non-violent-life/.

Chapter 8

Berry, T. (2006). *Evening Thoughts: Reflecting On Earth As a Sacred Community*. San Francisco: Sierra Club Books.

Chödrön, P. (2018). *The Wisdom of No Escape: And the Path of Loving-Kindness*. Shambhala.

Harjo, J. (2008). *She Had Some Horses*. W.W. Norton & Co.

Jamail, D. (13 February 2017). *Learning to See in the Dark Amid Catastrophe: An Interview with Deep Ecologist Joanna Macy*. Truthout. https://truthout.org/articles/learning-to-see-in-the-dark-amid-catastrophe-an-interview-with-deep-ecologist-joanna-macy/.

Kimmerer, R. W. (2013). "Braiding Sweetgrass" in *Braiding Sweetgrass: Indigenous Wisdom, Scientific Knowledge and the Teachings of Plants*. Milkweed Editions.

Lame Deer, Erdoes, R., and Rosenberg, R. (2009). *Lame Deer, Seeker of Visions*. Simon & Schuster.

Macy, J., and Gahbler, N. (n.d.). *Pass It On*. Spirituality & Practice. https://www.spiritualityandpractice.com/book-reviews/excerpts/view/20826.

Mitchell, S. L. (2018). *Sacred Instructions: Indigenous Wisdom for Living Spirit-Based Change*. North Atlantic Books.

Momaday, N. S. (2020). *Earth Keeper: Reflections on the American Land*. Harper, An Imprint of HarperCollins Publishers.

Plotkin, M. (17 July 2015). *What's Disappearing from the Amazon — Even Faster Than Wildlife?* G. Raz, Interviewer; TED Radio Hour, https://www.npr.org/transcripts/421468062.

Suquamish Tribe. (n.d.). *Chief Seattle Speech — The Suquamish Tribe*. Suquamish Tribe. https://suquamish.nsn.us/home/about-us/chief-seattle-speech/.

TED. (2020). Wade Davis: Cultures at the Far Edge of the World. https://www.youtube.com/watch?v=bL7vK0pOvKI.

Vaughan-Lee, L. (2016). *Spiritual Ecology: The Cry of the Earth*. The Golden Sufi Center.

Joseph, L. (2023). *Held by the Land: A Guide to Indigenous Plants for Wellness*. Wellfleet Press.

White, R. (19 March 2018). *Seed Rematriation*. Sierra Seeds. https://sierraseeds.org/seed-rematriation/.

O-BOOKS

SPIRITUALITY

O is a symbol of the world, of oneness and unity; this eye represents knowledge and insight. We publish titles on general spirituality and living a spiritual life. We aim to inform and help you on your own journey in this life.
If you have enjoyed this book, why not tell other readers by posting a review on your preferred book site?

Recent bestsellers from O-Books are:

Heart of Tantric Sex
Diana Richardson
Revealing Eastern secrets of deep love and intimacy to Western couples.
Paperback: 978-1-90381-637-0 ebook: 978-1-84694-637-0

Crystal Prescriptions
The A-Z guide to over 1,200 symptoms and their healing crystals
Judy Hall
The first in the popular series of eight books, this handy little guide is packed as tight as a pill bottle with crystal remedies for ailments.
Paperback: 978-1-90504-740-6 ebook: 978-1-84694-629-5

Shine On
David Ditchfield and J S Jones
What if the after effects of a near-death experience were undeniable? What if a person could suddenly produce high-quality paintings of the afterlife, or if they acquired the ability to compose classical symphonies? Meet: David Ditchfield.
Paperback: 978-1-78904-365-5 ebook: 978-1-78904-366-2

The Way of Reiki
The Inner Teachings of Mikao Usui
Frans Stiene
The roadmap for deepening your understanding of the system of Reiki and rediscovering your True Self.
Paperback: 978-1-78535-665-0 ebook: 978-1-78535-744-2

You Are Not Your Thoughts
Frances Trussell
The journey to a mindful way of being, for those who want to truly know the power of mindfulness.
Paperback: 978-1-78535-816-6 ebook: 978-1-78535-817-3

The Mysteries of the Twelfth Astrological House
Fallen Angels
Carmen Turner-Schott, MSW, LISW
Everyone wants to know more about the most misunderstood house in astrology — the twelfth astrological house.
Paperback: 978-1-78099-343-0 ebook: 978-1-78099-344-7

WhatsApps from Heaven
Louise Hamlin
An account of a bereavement and the extraordinary signs — including WhatsApps — that a retired law lecturer received from her deceased husband.
Paperback: 978-1-78904-947-3 ebook: 978-1-78904-948-0

The Holistic Guide to Your Health & Wellbeing Today
Oliver Rolfe
A holistic guide to improving your complete health, both inside and out.
Paperback: 978-1-78535-392-5 ebook: 978-1-78535-393-2

Cool Sex
Diana Richardson and Wendy Doeleman
For deeply satisfying sex, the real secret is to reduce the heat, to cool down. Discover the empowerment and fulfilment of sex with loving mindfulness.
Paperback: 978-1-78904-351-8 ebook: 978-1-78904-352-5

Creating Real Happiness A to Z
Stephani Grace
Creating Real Happiness A to Z will help you understand the truth that you are not your ego (conditioned self).
Paperback: 978-1-78904-951-0 ebook: 978-1-78904-952-7

A Colourful Dose of Optimism
Jules Standish
It's time for us to look on the bright side, by boosting
our mood and lifting our spirit, both in
our interiors, as well as in our closet.
Paperback: 978-1-78904-927-5 ebook: 978-1-78904-928-2

Readers of ebooks can buy or view any of these bestsellers by clicking on the live link in the title. Most titles are published in paperback and as an ebook. Paperbacks are available in traditional bookshops. Both print and ebook formats are available online.

Find more titles and sign up to our readers' newsletter at
www.o-books.com

Follow O-Books on Facebook at **O-Books**

For video content, author interviews and more, please subscribe to our YouTube channel:

O-BOOKS Presents

Follow us on social media for book news, promotions and more:

Facebook: O-Books

Instagram: @o_books_mbs

X: @obooks

Tik Tok: @ObooksMBS

www.o-books.com